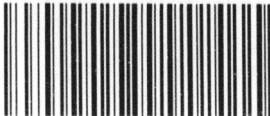

GW01458893

Brick Agent

BRICK AGENT

Inside the Mafia for the FBI

•

Anthony Villano
with Gerald Astor

Quadrangle/The New York Times Book Co.

This edition published by arrangement with Ballantine Books,
a division of Random House, Inc.

Library of Congress Cataloging in Publication Data

Villano, Anthony.
  Brick agent.

  1. Villano, Anthony. 2. United States. Federal
Bureau of Investigation—Officials and employees—
Biography. 3. Organized crime—New York (City)
4. Mafia. I. Astor, Gerald, 1926–   joint author.
II. Title.
HV7911.V54A33   364.12′092′4 [B]   76–52818
ISBN 0–8129–0687–X

Contents

Brick Agent

1

Another Triumph at the Bureau

Since the story I am about to relate contains charges made to me by others, and I have not been able to prove the truth of these charges beyond a reasonable doubt, I have decided not to use the Agent's real name. The point of my story is not to prove that he was guilty but to show how the Bureau completely bungled an investigation involving serious corruption charges against one of its agents.

Throughout the book pseudonymous names are introduced with the use of an asterisk.

ONE NIGHT EARLY IN 1973, I got a telephone call from Fred Juliano.* Nineteen years as an FBI agent had accustomed me to late-evening talks on the phone. In fact, I looked forward to them, because out of these informal after-hours conversations came the most valuable element in my business: information.

Fred Juliano worked as a special agent in another part of the New York City office of the Bureau. Our paths crossed frequently, and we had occasionally worked together on cases. On this evening, Juliano bullshitted for a while; then he fed me a teaser.

"If I told you I heard there was an agent on the take in the New York office, who would you suspect?"

"I haven't any idea," I answered. I was willing to humor Juliano until he got around to the real purpose of the call.

But he persisted with the game. "Would the taker be in your division, Organized Crime?"

"Sure, it would have to be. You wouldn't expect an agent on Selective Service Violations or some naive guy on the pussy posse to accept a payoff." It struck me now that Juliano had not called to talk about anything else—he really did have information concerning allegations of a bribe of an FBI agent.

"You think about this and then we'll talk more about it in person," urged Fred. The easy, gossipy tone with which he had begun our conversation was gone. I thought a moment and then told him that since we'd have to meet on another matter in the near future anyway, we could talk more then about his suspicion. We arranged an appointment for a couple of days later.

It was logical of Juliano to assume that if anyone in the organized crime division would have an idea about who was an agent on the take, it would be me. He knew I'd developed more members of organized crime as sources of information than anyone else in the FBI and that I had sometimes gone undercover.

When Fred and I met at a downtown Manhattan coffee shop in early February, he got to the point right away.

"Give me some names of guys you would suspect."

"I don't think I could guess in a million years."

"It would have to be a savvy guy, right? Like maybe a former city cop?"

I admitted that seemed reasonable, since agents assumed most cops were takers in one way or another.

"Wouldn't it probably be a guy who handled organized crime, say gambling cases?"

"Sure," was all I could answer. But there were nine hundred plus agents in New York City, maybe two hundred of them on OC. And we had a lot of ex-cops in the Bureau. I was still way behind his leads.

"Shit, I don't have any idea who it might be."

"What do you think about Tommy Miglio*?"

Juliano had dropped a name I knew well, one that opened up all sorts of possibilities and also had personal meaning for me.

In 1958 the Bureau began to pay serious attention to the problem of organized crime. Squads of about twenty-five agents each were set up to monitor La Cosa Nostra families in the larger cities. The number of squads varied, depending on the strength of LCN in a particular area. Chicago had two squads; Philadelphia, St. Louis, Los Angeles, Miami, and Detroit, one apiece. A town like Cleveland, where the Bureau knew of only about six LCN members, did not even require one full-size squad. On the other hand, in New York City, where there were five functioning LCN families, the office detailed a squad for each.

I first met Tommy Miglio in 1966, when I was reassigned from Utica to a New York City organized crime squad. We hit it off quite well at first. He was a charming guy, quick-witted and a marvelous raconteur. For a number of years before joining the Bureau he had been a New York City cop, so he had plenty of material from which to draw for his stories.

For a while we were friendly associates on the organized crime squads. Our duties consisted mostly of checking out addresses through tax records, verifying auto registrations, learning who was related to whom, and trying to keep everybody's whereabouts up to date; at that time we did a minimum of tapping and bugging. Although it was by then eight years since the Bureau had accepted the existence of La Cosa Nostra, the campaign still consisted of gathering background information on the known Mafiosi, an approach similar to that used by the Bureau on Communists and left-wingers. We were thus in an excellent position to arrest immediately and intern all known members of organized crime and their sympathizers in the event that the Mafia declared war on the United States—but we weren't doing much about controlling its everyday activities.

Time passed, and the layer of congeniality between Miglio and myself thinned, finally eroding altogether. Some of our differences were trivial, but there were serious run-ins, too, most of them generated by my impatience with his inability, or disinclination, to develop sources inside La Cosa Nostra. In one of our first conversations, I told him that I had decided to work in my own way on organized crime, using the same system in New York that I had used in Utica. Miglio agreed with me that developing sources of information inside LCN was the best way to attack the problem. We started out as friendly rivals to see who could "turn" the most LCN members. Within two years or so I had three; he still had none. The next member-source candidate I discovered struck me as being fairly easy to turn, and I suggested to Miglio that he could do it.

The candidate was Eddie Valente,* and there was a story about him that showed he was a very weak guy. While in Dannemora Prison he'd had a run-in with Joey Gallo, the troublesome rebel in Joe Colombo's group. In the course of the dispute, Gallo called

Valente a rat. Instead of hitting Gallo over the head with a lead pipe, Valente tried to hang himself—a poor way to preserve his honor.

When he came out of Dannemora on parole, Valente, who had been under a Colombo caporegime named Charlie "the Sidge" Lo Cicero, was placed under another captain in Colombo's organization, Carmine "the Snake" Persico. The basic table of organization for a crime family sets a boss at the top, an underboss and consigliore (counselor) immediately below. Next in rank come the caporegimes, the captains who each have a number of soldiers or button men under their command. The Snake was aptly named, a completely ruthless hood who would kill anybody in his group whom he suspected of being an informer.

Colombo was very sharp—the youngest member of organized crime's national commission for settling jurisdictional disputes and head of a major LCN family big in loansharking, hijacking, and gambling. There was also a small narcotics trade handled exclusively by Carmine Persico, whom Colombo judged as more than capable of keeping Eddie Valente in line.

Now, a timid guy like Valente is a good prospect as a source. I had found out from a close friend of mine in the New York State Parole Office the date and time Valente would next report in, and told Miglio that all he had to do was be there when Valente left the office.

Miglio told me about it a week later. "I waited for Valente outside the parole office. We approached him, but he didn't want to talk to us."

"We approached him . . ." That meant Miglio had another agent with him. I had discovered, as Miglio should have, that you can only develop a confidential informant on a one-to-one basis. I came down hard on Miglio for something he should have realized, and also for simply letting Valente walk away. He just said: "I don't want any part of the guy."

That incident wiped out much of my confidence in Miglio as an effective agent in the Organized Crime area. Nevertheless, I brought him in on a second attempt to turn a source. I was working on a target named Johnny Torre,* a knockaround guy, never "made" (never officially inducted into LCN). He had done lots of time already on a drug rap, so he had plenty more hanging over his head if he was caught misbehaving again. That made him an ideal type of subject.

I spotted him spending some time in East Harlem, open territory frequented by members of both the Gambino and Genovese families. Late one night I invited Johnny into my car for a chat. I explained who I was and what I wanted. He answered me very politely: "I'm not a member of Cosa Nostra, and I don't think I could be an informant. Please don't embarrass me by asking me." Made guys, as well as individuals like Torre who worked for official members of organized crime and enjoyed their respect, often used the word "embarrass" to describe their reactions to being seen in the company of agents—and having to explain it to their associates.

I reminded Johnny Torre of all that hard time he might be forced to spend in Atlanta. "I'd rather go back and serve it than become an informer," he said.

I figured that if I couldn't frighten him with the prospect of unserved time, maybe I could get something else to hang over his head. I knew the clubs and saloons where Johnny hung out and decided that Tommy Miglio and I should tail him. We had a "smooth" car (a rental rather than some obvious-looking government issue) and we followed Torre to the Bronx. He parked in front of an apartment. Miglio went to find out where Torre was in the building, while I stashed the car. When I got to the lobby, Miglio told me, "I lost him."

Now we had to do it the hard way: start on the sixth floor, the top story of the building, and work our way down, putting our ears to the doors, hoping to hear the sounds of a card game or something. We got lucky. We heard Torre's voice in a conversation with a woman, so at least we had located one of his hangouts. But nothing ever came of all of my attempts to turn Torre, even though I talked to him several more times.

Tommy Miglio's superiors may have had the same thought—that he was not a terribly effective agent in the penetration of organized crime. In any event, Miglio was transferred to the gambling squad. Thus he would be potentially useful to the division, yet not involved in the more sensitive operations.

The gambling squad was one of two specialty squads (the other was Hijacking) set up to combat what were considered primary activities of the Mafia. Together with the five squads concentrating on the Mafia families, they made up the organized crime division in New York City. There were four other divisions, each with a Special Agent in Charge (SAC): Internal Security chased radicals, who, in J. Edgar Hoover's view, would qualify as elements of the Red Menace; Espionage pursued foreigners plotting sabotage or spying in the United States; General Criminal worked on kidnappings, auto thefts, bank robberies, and the like (in smaller cities the men assigned to Organized Crime were part of this division); Administrative took care of the Bureau paperwork and technology. Each SAC had an assistant, and then a supervisor was the last in the chain of command over the agents. A large city such as New York had an assistant director, John Malone, in charge, with a number of SAC's reporting to him. A small office like Utica might only have a single SAC.

My disaffection for Miglio did not slacken after his transfer. For instance, I could not get over the fact that he was sympathetic to the Italian Anti-Defamation League (later known as the Italian American Civil Rights League), invented in 1970 by Joe Colombo to direct his anti-FBI campaign. Miglio would often casually observe to agents like myself and even to one of the U.S. attorneys in charge of prosecution of organized crime in Brooklyn, that in his opinion the Bureau harassed people just because they were of Italian background. He seemed to think that Joe Colombo had a good point. It struck me as extraordinarily naive of Miglio to overlook such an obvious ploy by a man who headed an LCN family and was up to his eyeballs in everything from loansharking to heroin imports.

Juliano now told me the following story about Miglio, one that Miglio subsequently denied. As we will see, the Bureau investigated this story but ultimately closed its investigation, claiming there was no evidence to prove Miglio had been bribed.

On an early spring morning in 1971, a New York City detective friend of Fred's was moonlighting as a bartender on South Street. The neighborhood includes the Fulton Street Fish Market and is alive and buzzing when the rest of New York is still tucked away in bed. Bars down there are already open and doing business when the sun rises.

Around six A.M. on this particular day, Al Salamone* entered the place. Salamone was a very well thought-of soldier in the Vito Genovese Family. He had a country home as well as an apartment in town. He was of medium build, about five seven.

According to Juliano, Salamone now approached the moonlighting detective and asked him to call Peter Lombardo,* a sergeant in one of the city precincts and a friend of the detective's. The detective advised Salamone that Lombardo would not be on duty until eight A.M. Salamone left the bar but returned promptly at eight, at which time the detective reached Pete Lombardo on the phone and told him that Salamone wanted to meet him there.

Some time later, Juliano continued, Sergeant Lombardo arrived. In search of privacy, he and Salamone adjourned to a back room. Salamone left the premises first. Then Lombardo strolled out to the front and took the detective to one side. "Here's something for you," he said, handing the detective two hundred dollars. "We just got fifteen thousand dollars to fix a case for Salamone." When the detective looked a bit pained at the amount given him, Lombardo apologized. "I only get part of it. The FBI agent on the case, Miglio, gets the major piece. He's going to make the fix."

Juliano's detective friend was still unhappy over his share. A day or so later he ran into Sergeant Lombardo, who confided, "This was bullshit. There was no real case. It was really a shakedown." The detective was still pissed off. He brooded about it for nearly two years before he shot off his mouth to Fred Juliano.

Juliano at first was uncertain as to how to proceed with the fragmentary information. The detective, a lifelong friend, had sworn him to secrecy and vowed that he would deny everything if Juliano attempted to make a case out of the matter. Juliano was troubled. He was friendly with Miglio and knew Tommy was close to the cop Lombardo, who had a bad reputation.

A short time later, Juliano said he had heard that a number of cops had been suspended pending an investigation into a shakedown racket run by what was called the "sergeants' club." Among those to be charged was Sergeant Peter Lombardo. Juliano thought this might open everything up. He sought out Miglio in the New York offices, mentioned Lombardo's new problems, and then bluntly added: "I hear you made a big score."

"What are you talking about?" demanded Miglio.

"I hear fifteen big ones went down," persisted Fred.

Miglio continued to play the innocent. "I don't understand."

Juliano dropped his bomb. "You thought there were only two people involved, but there were three."

"Who else knows about this thing?"

"Just my friend," replied Fred.

"Did he get anything?" Juliano held up two fingers. "That motherfucker Lombardo," growled Miglio. "He held out on me."

Juliano said he assumed then that Miglio thought the two fingers meant two *thousand* dollars instead of the two hundred his detective friend had told him he'd been given. Juliano corrected Miglio on the real sum.

Miglio then volunteered that he had "scored ten thousand dollars," and asked Juliano if his friend was okay. "Will he tell anyone else?"

"No, but he's damn sore and disappointed."

"I'm going to the old man," said Miglio, "and see that nobody else finds out."

Miglio did not elaborate on the identity of the "old man," but to Juliano it could only have been Al Salamone. Some time later, when Juliano bumped into Miglio again, Tommy cheerfully announced: "Don't worry, everybody's lips are sealed. I'm okay."

It is possible Miglio was joking or that Juliano misunderstood him, but Fred told me he felt that Miglio was admitting to having taken a bribe.

Fred was an easygoing guy who liked to joke around. Whenever you met him he'd start telling you about good times, funny incidents. It was a taste he shared with Miglio, who enjoyed partying, and talking about it later. So it was not unusual that on this second meeting Miglio drew Juliano deeper into his confidence. "There's a fortune to be made out there," Fred remembered Miglio's telling him. "Like a hundred grand in no time at all —it's better than being assigned to Las Vegas." It seemed that the "wiseguys" (official LCN members) were willing to pay big money just to find out what kind of bullets people used, who the cops or the feds were after, what phones were bugged.

The conversation frightened Juliano, and for good reason. Fixing a case was the least of the services a crooked agent could render. Suppose he started to sell out informants, particularly member sources in organized crime? None of them would live twenty-four hours. And Miglio knew the names of even the most confidential ones. In the office, agents often held long discussions about informants, dropping names that could be heard by many employees. Even though they had been checked by Security before being hired, there was still a big risk. People caught up in personal crises could change, could turn. The criminal informants were supposed to be known by codes, with only a few top people aware of their real identities. But office loudmouths talked about CIs without any regard for security. I had often complained about it, but to no avail. Not only would there be a lot of blood spilled if an agent gave those CIs up, all the years spent on penetrating organized crime would be wasted. In fact, Juliano said he had heard rumors that there was a contract out on a member informant.

Fred finished his account of corruption with a plea. "Look, Tony, you're the guy who has to get Miglio out of the Bureau. He's dangerous to everyone." But, anxious as Juliano was, he still refused to come forward himself and he was adamant that he could not back me up if I tried to use him as my source of information because that would force him to breach the confidence of his lifelong friend, the New York cop. I guess Fred told me about the affair because he felt that I was highly regarded in the Bureau and I had the most experience in dealing with organized crime.

Juliano thought the case that had produced the alleged bribe had to do with hijacking. Actually, Al Salamone figured in a large bag of people swallowed up as part of a gambling ring run by Joe Colombo. Although we'd had very little evidence against Salamone, his was a name we knew; we threw it into the pot, hoping that the more ingredients we added to the stew the tastier the grand jury would find it.

In April 1971, when we pulled in Salamone as part of Colombo and company's operation, Miglio had raised a big stink. He insisted that as part of his work on the gambling squad he had been developing Salamone as an informant, and that when the organized crime squads made their arrests they hadn't bothered to tell him that Salamone was named in one of the warrants. The Colombo thing went down right after the ring discovered that we had their Brooklyn meeting place bugged. We had only started to watch Salamone's operation, which was connected to Colombo's business in Brooklyn.

Usually, if you had a thing on a man who was assigned to another agent, you would consult that agent. If he said, "Aw, to hell with him, he's not giving me any good stuff, go ahead and pinch him," you'd make the bust. At the very least the case agent would have a new club over his target: cooperate or get sent up. On the other hand, if a case agent really had something going, there were ways to arrange an out for his client. Salamone was Miglio's case, and it was just through a failure of internal communications that Miglio was kept ignorant.

But that didn't count for much as far as he was concerned. Miglio bitched loud and clear. "Fine friends you guys are, busting this guy and making me look like a horse's ass. I had to find out about it when I called him up on the telephone."

John McGinley, one of the supervisors, pulled the file that Miglio kept on Salamone and found that it showed nothing at all in the way of information drawn from Salamone. Miglio told McGinley that nothing was on paper because he had obtained information that was so sensitive and so confidential that he had decided not to write it down.

McGinley had the perfect solution. "Tommy, look at it this way. We haven't got any case at all against Salamone. You've got a great opportunity. Tell Salamone that we really do have him but that you can use your influence to get the charges dismissed." The indictment that named Salamone was indeed dropped about three weeks after his arrest. And by early 1973, when twenty months had passed during which Miglio was supposedly cultivating Salamone after the charges had been dropped, we still had none of that supersensitive information Miglio claimed to have coaxed out of Al Salamone.

After twenty-four years with the Bureau, I was considerably less naive about special agents. I knew now that agents were not quite what J. Edgar Hoover had claimed them to be. We classified guys in ways that the founding father of the modern FBI never dreamed. One category was the boozers, the guys who could not get through the day without sneaking drinks. For them the perfect day ended around lunchtime when a winebuyer, usually some corporate executive with a fat expense account, invited them out for a classy meal and free liquor. The Bureau never discouraged contacts with representatives of industry, and in some cases the winebuyer was a former agent. The relationship was mutually beneficial: The establishment supported Hoover at appropriations time, and we gave them special attention when they had troubles.

The supervisors at the Bureau shut their eyes to the boozers unless forced to look. One of our agents in the New York office criminal division was a big, backslapping Irishman, a heavy hitter who had problems at home. Most of the guys in the office knew about his long hours in the bar and ignored it. But I heard that we had a very good, high-level informant in one of the Soviet bloc embassies who occasionally fed us stuff about operations there. He advised our agents that this embassy was trying to turn an FBI man. Apparently reasoning that a drinker would be easiest to turn (even though his job in the criminal division meant that he knew next to nothing about the activities of agents in espionage and spy divisions), they had selected our heavy hitter as a target. Bureau internal security put the agent under surveillance. They never saw anyone from the embassy approach him, but the surveillance reports inevitably spelled out all of the time he spent in saloons. The result was that he was retired with a forty-percent disability pension, a neat way of removing a problem without sullying the reputation of the Bureau.

A second group of agents was known as the shoppers—guys out in the street who spent much of their time searching for bargains. They knew the difference between the prices of a Schick 601 at Macy's and Korvette's.

Then there were the jocks, the regular visitors to the New York Athletic Club or the Y. Some of them combined their pleasure with ambition by inviting Bureau inspectors to lunch at a place like the New York Athletic Club. There the guest could stuff away a fancy meal, complete with stiff drinks, and be introduced to some of the political and business heavyweights of New York.

The students attended classes at night and studied during whatever time they could squeeze out of their duty hours. The Bureau did not wholeheartedly approve of this, particularly if the aim was to develop an income-producing interest, like real estate. On the other hand, the bosses felt that it added to the prestige of the organization if an agent passed the bar or earned a Ph.D. in Russian.

Another very active unofficial subdivision was the investors. They read the *Wall Street Journal* and *Barron's Weekly*—and not just to keep abreast of where organized crime might be tempted to launder its funds. The investors watched the daily stock ticker, popping into the branch offices of brokerage firms scattered throughout New York City. And if in the course of official business they met insiders in Wall Street, they kept up their contacts long after the Bureau's work had been completed. There were a number of sub rosa investors' clubs within the Bureau; they were particularly busy during the active stockmarket days of the 1960s. Generally, a wife, child, or close relative served as a beard to hide from the Bureau the securities or business investments of agents.

And there were the lovers. Thanks to Mr. Hoover and friendlies in the media, the job of agent carried a certain amount of glamour—and it was not difficult for agents to capitalize on the image when forming romantic liaisons. The Bureau's attitude about sex was not wholly negative; it simply could not tolerate any public notice of bedroom activities that fell outside the narrow limits determined by a wetfoot bachelor Baptist like J. Edgar Hoover. An agent careless in covering his tracks would suddenly find himself transferred a few hundred miles away from the scene of his indiscretions.

I knew of a high-ranking administrative supervisor in the Washington, D.C., office who was having an affair with a female employee of the Bureau. Her mother wrote a letter to the Bureau about it, and as a result the woman was forced to resign and the supervisor was demoted to a brick agent and transferred to a field office hundreds of miles from Washington. However, he continued to drive to the city every weekend to spend a couple of days with the woman. Upon learning of this, her mother fired off a second letter to the Bureau. Hoover's hatchet men could no longer touch the woman, but the Bureau shifted the man to an office fifteen hundred miles away.

"To hell with them," he told me. "I'll fly in every weekend." I asked if he weren't worried that he might be canned and lose his pension—he was only months away from eligibility for retirement. "They know better than that. There are dozens of guys working at Bureau headquarters who have situations like mine. They wouldn't dare dismiss me."

One interest that was wholly absent from agents' lives was politics. I never voted, and I doubt that very many other guys did, either. Who was President and who was in Congress didn't matter, to Hoover or to us. I think this attitude is one more indication of the isolation of the Bureau from the rest of the United States. Usually, local police are quite active—within the limits of the law, presumably—in municipal elections. Policies and salaries are set by mayors and city councils, so the cops tend to look out for their own interests. We didn't have to worry about such matters, thanks to the power of Hoover and the institution itself, the Bureau.

The fact that agents can be categorized as jocks, students, and so on does not mean that the Bureau was a worthless collection of drunks, money grubbers, and sexist pigs. There were simply a great many hard-working, conscientious agents who on occasion had other interests than their job. Still, they were at least as dedicated to their trade as most people. The only point to make about the preoccupations of agents is that the interests and behavior of the Feebies is much the same as it is for the rest of Americans.

There was one classification that was never discussed. Unlike most other law-enforcement bodies, we had no list of takers. Bribes to agents were so unheard of that the possibility never crossed our minds, any more than a public health official in New York worries about an outbreak of yellow fever.

Only once in my career did anybody ever hint at a payoff to me. In the mid-1960s, I was seeking sources of information inside organized crime, and was given the name of Joseph Asaro, an old captain in the crime family of Joe Bonnano, who had recently done a disappearing act. Asaro was just one of hundreds of names the Bureau had agents check out to determine whether they were active and what kinds of cases might be made. Asaro was the personification of a Mustache Pete, a small, gnarled man in his seventies, tough, loyal. One son, Joseph junior, was an 88 fugitive—unlawful flight—and there was a warrant out for him. The son had served about eight years on an armed robbery rap and then jumped parole.

Another agent named Joe Stabile and I went to see the old man at his home in East New York, near the border between Brooklyn and Queens. His wife opened the door. We did not identify ourselves, saying only that we wanted to talk with her husband. We weren't wearing the usual uniform—white shirt, tie, and hat; we could have been a couple of wiseguys. The wife spoke little English, so my partner talked to her in Sicilian. Asaro's daughter came to the door, too. She was an exotic beauty—fair complexion, dark hair, almond eyes. She got the same kind of wiseguy impression.

The two women ushered us in to see Asaro, who was in bed, looking like the model wisdom-dispensing patriarch. As soon as we entered, I flipped out my FBI credentials. Asaro started hollering at his wife and daughter for letting us in. They screamed at us, the usual "You have no right to be here" stuff.

My partner shrewdly asked old Asaro, "Whose house is this, theirs or yours?" That did it. He had to show he was the big man, insulted that the women had taken over. He ordered them to get the hell out of the room.

I came on as the nice, easy, sympathetic agent. "Mr. Asaro, we're not out to harass a sick old man. We just need a little information. Do you know where your son Joe is?" (We knew he was in Montreal, but it was a way to start.) I was wasting my breath. This was a guy from the old school. I could have put a gun to his head and blown an ear away and he wouldn't have told me a thing. Asaro was a marvelous actor, even shedding a couple of real tears. "I wish I did know where my boy is. I know he is dead. If you could do me one favor, please find out where my son is buried. I would like to visit his grave before I die. If you can arrange that, perhaps we can talk again."

It was a performance worthy of an Academy Award, particularly in that a couple of months later the Royal Canadian Mounted Police and the Quebec provincial police broke down the door to an apartment and surprised a small gathering that included Vic Cutrone, a big drug wholesaler in Canada, young Joe Asaro—and poor sick old Joe senior. No charges were filed against the two older men, but young Joe was deported to the U.S. and packed off to the pen to serve the rest of his time.

So far I had gotten nowhere with the Asaros. I tried another son, Jerry, who had a kid up on a bank robbery rap. He too had tunnel vision: would rather see his son do hard time than give me anything.

Next I decided to try Mickey Zaffarano, Asaro's son-in-law and the husband of the beautiful woman I saw at the old man's home. Zaffarano himself had shortly before come out of jail on parole. With another agent I visited Zaffarano's place of business, a loft building in lower Manhattan. When the two of us came off the elevator, we flashed our credentials at a man lounging near the front of the place. From another area, a second fellow pushing a hand truck heaped with cartons saw us identify ourselves. He instantly reversed direction and hurried to the other end of a storeroom with the hand truck. Meanwhile, from photographs, I recognized Zaffarano in one of the small offices. I walked in, introduced myself, and said, "I know the man with the hand truck had some swag. Tell him not to have a heart attack. We're not here to search or make a case, just to talk."

Zaffarano laughed; he was a big handsome guy, a little given to paunch. Things became even more congenial when he ordered in lunch for us, roast-pork-with-plum-sauce sandwiches. But when I mentioned that I would like some help from him, his laugh was a little less friendly. "I'm not that kind of person." I said that I had met his wife and she was great-looking; he laughed again and told me he lived with another broad. We parted company amiably and I gave up on the Asaro clan.

A year later, I happened to be in our office when Mickey Zaffarano was brought in to be processed for parole violation. It seems Mickey, who was later to earn the dubious title of "Porn King of New York," had somehow gotten caught while still on the threshold. The agents handling him were apparently giving him a hard time and I heard Zaffarano growl at one of them, "I'm going to get you on film someday." I walked into the interview room and greeted Mickey. He remembered our pleasant chat. After I commiserated with him for a while, he asked if he could speak to me privately.

When we were alone, Zaffarano asked if there was anything I could do to keep him from going back to prison. He had more than a year to serve on an old charge. I answered that maybe I could work it out, with his help.

"Bullshit," he said. "I couldn't do anything like that. I don't use an electric razor—I got to look at myself when I shave. What I mean is, is there any other way?"

It wasn't hard to figure out that he was talking about money. "You're going to have to come up with a number, Mickey," I answered. "And if the number is right, okay. Otherwise, I'll take you for attempted bribery."

"Go fuck yourself" was his retort and he laughed.

When they finished processing him, he was taken out to the elevators in cuffs. By coincidence I happened along while they were waiting there. "Just for the hell of it, Tony, what would have been the right figure?"

"I might have considered a million."

"You're crazy," he said.

That was the closest I ever came to having anything offered to me. And I had never heard rumors or gossip about any other agents taking a payoff until I received that call from Fred Juliano. While I no longer thought all agents automatically qualified for the community of saints, I was among the faithful who believed we were uniquely incorruptible. Furthermore, one informant inside the Bureau could cause the deaths of people who trusted me and could destroy everything I had worked for.

Altogether I had given twenty-three years to the Bureau. All things considered it had been a satisfying career. However, I was now in my mid-40's; at an age when a severe jolt, a death, a divorce, or the collapse of a long held ideal, forces one to stop and think about where one's been, where one's going.

During all of my enthusiastic pursuit of the underworld and its connections and corruptions in respectable society, and in spite of my frustrations with the bureaucratic bumblers, it had never occurred to me that organized crime might have penetrated the FBI—that the one citadel of purity might have been breached. It seemed so foreign to the character of the Bureau. But then, as I thought about it, my life and career as an agent wasn't typical either.

2
Beginning in Brooklyn

WHEN I WAS A KID, Vaughn Monroe's orchestra recorded "Sam, You Made the Pants Too Long." On the flip, and less popular, side was something called "Gee, How I'd Like to Be a G-Man." But the only thing I knew about the FBI was what James Cagney showed me in the movies and Lava soap presented on its radio show *The FBI in Peace and War.*

My father was born in Italy. After he emigrated, he quickly earned U.S. citizenship through service in the Army during World War I. He worked hard at his trades, carpentry and caulking, and he taught me how to work with my hands and use tools. Much later, I traded on this knowledge as an agent. I became adept at picking locks and, most important, at discovering drops, the concealed caches of money and weapons. I found them behind electrical outlets, in windowsills, under shower floors, and inside closet poles.

My mother was a native-born American who grew up in Pittston, Pennsylvania, which some people say is the cradle of the U.S. branch of the Mafia. The town had its share of bad guys. My mother said her father would not allow the children in his family to walk on East Railroad Street because that was the stronghold of the Black Hand.

The Brooklyn neighborhood where I spent my childhood was predominantly Jewish, with a sprinkling of Poles, Lithuanians, and Irish. There was one other Italian family on the block. Supposedly, two of the sons belonged to the Mafia and after one of them tried to quit the organization, both brothers were found in gunny sacks, the bodies pockmarked with ice-pick wounds. I remember the wailing of the women at the funeral.

At fifteen I and a group of friends found jobs in Manhattan's theater district. We checked coats and sold orange drinks, cigarettes, and candy. We augmented our incomes by selling people better seats after the house lights went off and by watering the orange drink. The concessionaire monitored our intake by keeping track of the number of cups we took from the stand. But by reusing half-empty cups—filling them up again with water—we could sell nine bucks' worth of drinks for the boss and another nine for ourselves.

Some of us pinched items from the pockets of the coats that were checked. Once I carried home a set of brass knuckles from an overcoat. Loafing around my neighborhood one day, I flashed the brass knuckles. A cop in the area saw them and collared me. He wanted to know how I had obtained them. When I explained to him that I had "found" them in the theater, he released me after extracting a promise that I bring him some cigarettes from the theater, since they were in short supply. It was my first experience with payoffs to the police, except that I never delivered the butts.

My mother forced me to church every Sunday; she even followed me to see that I entered the place. But then I would duck out the side door and exercise my religiosity at a nearby poolroom, where some very tough kids hung out. But I stayed away from their increasingly felonious activities.

I managed to keep afloat at Boys High in Brooklyn, but school bored me and my attendance was irregular. I usually cut classes on Wednesdays to work the matinees. The bright-lighted fun of Broadway, even though it was dimmed out during the war years, made the worth of academic studies seem secondary. I had discovered sex also, and I was a frequent visitor to Central Park; it was a time when the place was still for lovers rather than muggers.

At this stage in life I believed in God the Father, my country, and that success meant a white shirt and tie. I was already unwilling to accept or to follow rules that I considered arbitrary. And I had become skeptical of the abilities and common sense of those immediately above me, although I kept my faith in leadership that was many levels higher. The theater concessionaires might have been jerks, but I was sure the guy who owned the theater was something else. The cop who rousted me for the brass knuckles was dishonest, but surely the captains and inspectors would never have tolerated such cheap corruption. If the local priest seemed unpleasantly human, the cardinal, I was sure, was one step from sainthood.

A few months after my seventeenth birthday, having persuaded my father to sign his permission, I enlisted in the Navy. It was August 1945, and the war was over. I was assigned to a small aircraft carrier. My naval career was uneventful; I went my way, staying out of trouble but usually ignoring restrictions I considered capricious.

Everything nearly came to an end one night in Philadelphia. At a bar in a rough section called Kensington, I caught on with a married chick. She told me to wait while she checked to make sure there wasn't anybody home at her apartment. So I sat with my beer bottle at the bar until a big black laborer came into the place. I made a really stupid remark to him—I had a lot to unlearn in my racial attitudes—and he invited me to discuss the matter outside.

In the Police Athletic League and in the Navy I had done some boxing, but I decided I wasn't going to waste my pugilistic talents on this dude. So when I went outside I carried my beer bottle with me. Reaching the pavement, I swung the bottle as hard as I could and smashed it on top of his head. Blood, beer, and glass splashed us both, but the blow didn't make any lasting impression on my opponent. He didn't even blink—just closed in on me, grabbed me by my kerchief, and held me while he beat me to a pulp.

Suddenly he stopped. "Be quiet," he said. We listened. A siren told us a police car was approaching. "You better get your ass out of here or you'll be in trouble," he warned me. He actually shoved me, bloody and in a semistupor from beer and punches, onto a trolley car, and I escaped.

It was such a humane and generous gesture and I had been such a bastard. If I had been picked up by the cops that night, the Bureau when it investigated my application would have found the record and rejected me. Years later, after I had become an agent and was working in Philadelphia, I went looking in the Kensington area for my benefactor to thank him, but I never found him.

When I left the Navy in 1947, I had no trade, only an equivalency high school diploma from correspondence courses in the service. I couldn't find a job immediately; there was a minor recession at the time. I discovered literature, and for three months I lay around the house reading poetry and novels, all the stuff I had ignored in high school.

But I had to get a skill for a job, so I studied stenotype for three or four months with the aim of becoming a court reporter. When I had almost completed the course, a friend mentioned that the FBI had openings for stenotypists. I put in an application just for the hell of it. And then I realized that this was a potential employer who would thoroughly look into a candidate's history. All my sins passed before my anxious eyes. At that, I didn't suffer as much as a shirttail uncle whom I had listed as a reference. He had been selling Irish Sweepstake tickets, which were technically illegal, and when an agent came to see him he almost had a coronary. But the agent calmed him down; they weren't interested in his offense, only in me.

The Bureau accepted me. At a salary of $2,600 a year I plunged into the steno pool, one of two males in a group with about fifty girls. It was a little embarrassing, but the agents were delighted to have some male employees. They could come to us with the details on obscenity cases, files on white slavery and interstate prostitution. There was then, as there still is, a certain prissiness. I remember one agent asked me if I would correct a mistake in the transcription of something he had dictated. I saw the initials of the girl who had done the transcription and for the moment couldn't understand why the agent didn't simply hand the document back to her. It was a loyalty study and in the course of the report the applicant was described as being a conscientious person who had "a good appearance"—except that the woman who took the dictation (and who was about to be married) had transcribed "a good penis."

Male stenotypists also proved very useful to agents when they needed someone to take down a statement away from the office. The agents felt protective of the women, feared that they might become hurt—and then there was always the specter of scandal arising out of a male agent and a female employee on an out-of-the-office job.

The Bureau was the child of President Theodore Roosevelt, who in 1908 decided to arm the Department of Justice with its own detective force. The attorney general at the time assured a doubtful Congress that the detectives would concentrate on crimes against the United States (like antitrust violations) and not become "a secret political service" or pursue "mere matters of scandal and gossip that could affect only a man's purely private life."

Not until J. Edgar Hoover came along to head the FBI in 1924 were the agents removed from a scandalous spoils system. And Hoover never did stop the collection of personal dirt against individuals whom he saw as threats to either himself or the country. The Director, as he was always referred to, achieved great success against the bank robbers and kidnappers who grabbed the headlines during the 1930s. During World War II, Hoover and the Bureau continued to receive good press. He was the incorruptible cop who headed a superteam. The capture of German saboteurs who landed on Long Island from a submarine made the FBI seem invincible. The office gossip insisted that originally one of the Nazis had actually tried to turn himself in at the New York City headquarters but the agents there refused to believe his story. He had to go to Washington to get somebody's attention.

Hoover continued to rise in the estimation of most Americans when the national climate turned hostile, and sometimes hysterical, toward Communism. In the late forties and early fifties, the Bureau and its director were seen as one of the strongest defenses against foreign and domestic Communists and those perceived as their sympathizers.

In 1950, when I first entered the Bureau, the world situation and the economy had combined to recruit many intelligent men for the jobs of special agents. During the Depression and in the years immediately after the war, Hoover had the luxury of screening candidates closely, accepting only the smartest. The Bureau offered prestige, security, a draft deferment, and a better salary than most civil service positions. As a result, linguistics experts, technical whizzes, people trained in the latest in scientific crime detection applied to become FBI agents.

I was wide-eyed in admiration of the agents. The more I saw of them the more I was impressed by their cleverness and toughness. One night I stayed late at the request of an agent who had been interrogating a suspect in a hijacking. Finally, he confessed. But when a written statement in which he admitted his participation had been prepared and submitted for signature, the accused man recanted. The agent snarled at him, "You little son of a bitch, I'm going to put you through that window unless you tell the truth." We were on the twenty-eighth floor. The man quickly signed the statement. It may not have quite squared with my innocent notions of how agents worked, but it was a case of the good guys beating the bad guys and I admired the effectiveness of the technique.

The big Red scare had now fully infected the country, and the Bureau, both a carrier and a victim, spent enormous energy on the alleged menace. I was sent to cover events such as the annual May Day festivities in Union Square, where I recorded every speech, 170 and more words a minute. Later, this oratory could be introduced as evidence of violations of various statutes aimed against Communists. The government prosecuted Ben Gold of the furriers' union on the charge that he perjured himself by signing a non-Communist affidavit in order to qualify as a union official. I testified in court about Gold's May Day rally statements. He was convicted, but the Supreme Court ordered a new trial when it was shown that the FBI had investigated some jurors and had invaded the privacy rights of the jury. The government then dropped the case.

The most important case for the Bureau during the period was that against Julius and Ethel Rosenberg, accused of having transmitted information on the atomic bomb to the Soviet Union. British Intelligence had seized Klaus Fuchs, a scientist at Harwell, England's nuclear energy establishment. Fuchs furnished the FBI with leads on his American contact, eventually identified as Harry Gold. The trail from Gold led to David Greenglass, a machinist who had worked on the U.S. atomic program at Los Alamos, New Mexico. Greenglass was the brother of Ethel Rosenberg, and she and her husband were arrested as the leaders in the spy ring.

Harry Gold was held in the U.S. marshal's lockup in New York City. I visited him regularly while he read aloud the remembrances of his career he'd scribbled in his cell the night before. It was an unabridged autobiography of a spy. Gold was a meticulous little man, very likable, and with an ability for almost total recall. He remembered dates, events, contacts. He seemed terribly sincere to me and overwhelmed with guilt for what he had done.

My association with the case was revived in June 1953, when I was assigned to go to Sing Sing Prison in Ossining, New York, where the Rosenbergs were scheduled to die in the electric chair. Hoover was positive that as the time of execution neared, the couple would break down and confess.

With me were two high-ranking FBI officials, an assistant director, and the chief of the espionage unit. Sing Sing warden Wilfred Denno gave us living quarters in the servants' section, which was over his garage. He also fixed up a couple of cells on Death Row for us to use as offices; there was even a direct line to Hoover's suite in the FBI building in Washington. He wanted to be kept up to the minute on everything that happened. We came equipped with enough office supplies to last a month, the assumption being it would take that long to debrief the Rosenbergs of all of their information.

The execution had been scheduled for midweek, but the lawyer for the Rosenbergs secured a temporary stay. During that time, we spent our evenings sitting on Warden Denno's porch. I kept my mouth shut, only accepted one drink, and listened. Periodically a maniacal laugh would interrupt the conversation. A former inmate's pet parrot now lived with the Dennos and, aside from the crazy laugh, it limited its vocal expression to "Don't fight, don't fight, I don't wanna die, I don't wanna die."

The reprieve won by the Rosenbergs proved short-lived. A Supreme Court order vacated the stay and the execution was rescheduled for Friday evening. That created some protests, because Friday night is the Jewish sabbath. The government, however, with Hoover pushing vigorously in the background, resisted any further delays.

One complication arose immediately: The executioner lived upstate and the operation of the electric chair was a sideline for him. Nobody could immediately locate him to advise him his services would now be needed on Friday evening. Some Bureau people suspected that the phone wires to his home had been cut. Hoover was furious at the possibility of further delay. He demanded that a helicopter stand by to ferry the executioner to Sing Sing and that state troopers be dispatched to find him.

There was a considerable amount of discussion about the procedures for the execution. Denno explained that when there is a man and a woman, the normal routine calls for the man to go first. But it was his observation that Ethel was much more strong-willed than her husband. Therefore, he thought that if the wife was taken first, led past her husband's cell on her way to the death chamber, Julius might break.

Such an arrangement was proposed to Hoover, but he rejected it. We discussed the predicament of a public outcry if one Rosenberg was executed and then the other decided to talk, especially if it was the woman who died while the man survived.

Meanwhile the two agents with me had meticulously prepared themselves in the event that the Rosenbergs wished to confess. They had brought a series of test questions for which the Bureau knew the correct answers; the Rosenbergs' responses would determine whether or not they were actually cooperating.

On the appointed Friday night we were in our cells on Death Row. Julius Rosenberg was led to the death chamber first. However, we were not in a position to see him or his wife take their last steps. Our presence there was to be highly secret for fear word might get out and the Bureau be accused of some ghoulish intent.

A system had been devised to keep us informed: When an execution had been completed, the chief of guards was to step out into the corridor and signal me with his hand. After a few minutes the chief of guards indeed appeared, as scheduled. He dropped his hand; Julius Rosenberg was dead. In our "office" the line to Hoover had been kept open. The assistant director said, "Mr. Hoover, I have just gotten word that Julius has been pronounced dead." Hoover's response was inaudible to me. He was then informed that Ethel Rosenberg had just entered the room with the chair.

It took an abnormally long time for her to die. There was sweat dripping down the assistant director's face as we awaited the signal from the chief of guards. When he at last appeared and waved his hand, the assistant director spoke into the mouthpiece. "Mr. Hoover, Ethel's had it." There was a pause while Hoover said something. "You know—she's gone," said the assistant director. There was another hesitation. Apparently Hoover insisted that he be formally told, according to the book. "Ethel was just pronounced dead," the assistant director finally said. That satisfied Hoover.

I had waited for the lights to dim as the legend about Sing Sing held. But there was no visible indication when the executioner threw the switch. The electric chair had its own source of power, separate entirely from the system that supplied the rest of the institution. Prisons are extraordinarily noisy places—the inmates are rarely quiet, heavy steel doors slam constantly, bolts clang into place. But that night Death Row was a mausoleum. The whole experience sickened me. Shortly afterward I heard that the chief of guards quit. For me the premeditated death was of frightening impact. I don't think I ever favored capital punishment after my visit to Sing Sing.

We were a different group of people on the ride home. Going to Sing Sing had been almost a lark, a couple of days away from office routine; nobody thought about the purpose of the trip. When we drove back to New York, the assistant director talked about what a narrow, rigid mind Hoover had. It was one of my first glimpses of weakness in a man whom I idolized. Now I was hearing something of his limitations and, worse, how fear of these limitations and of his power was diminishing the work of the Bureau. For example, every statement by an official that mentioned Hoover was summarized and sent to him. On one occasion a supervisor was instructed to boil down to one page an extended speech about Hoover by a judge. The supervisor spent half a day compressing the substance into a single page. It was not acceptable. When he submitted a second draft, his boss demanded to know why the material in the second draft had not been in the first. This went on for three or four drafts.

It was Hoover's habit to scrawl comments in the margins of reports. One file mentioned some individuals associated with a questionable activity. The Bureau director noted "Follow this" in the margin, but no one knew whether the order was to watch the questionable activity or the individuals mentioned. As everyone was afraid to ask Hoover his meaning, twenty-four-hour surveillance was put on both the subjects and the activity.

Every class of FBI candidates received a personal inspection from Hoover, who was extremely concerned with the looks of his agents. After one such screen test, Hoover growled, "Those two or three men that look like truck drivers—get rid of them." Unfortunately the administrators did not know exactly which men in the class offended Hoover's aesthetic sensibility. Rather than risk his displeasure by questioning him more closely, they simply dumped the fifteen who looked the most like truck drivers, just to be sure.

According to my standard that a job which required a white shirt and a tie indicated success, I had made it. My position carried prestige at home; my father would boast to anyone who would listen, "My son works for the FBI." But I was now ambitious. I decided that I'd been coasting long enough. The most attractive avenue of advancement appeared to be an appointment as a special agent. However, I needed a college degree in order to qualify. I entered New York University and, in three years and twelve weeks of night school, earned my 128 credits and a B.S. degree.

I filed an application, which had to include an essay on why the applicant wanted to become an agent. My paper carried the necessary verbiage about "dedication to a life in law enforcement" and a desire to be a member of "this great institution."

Five days after I graduated from New York University I received a letter signed by Hoover offering me a probationary appointment as a special agent in August 1954. I was to be paid $5,500 a year and report for sixteen weeks of training at Quantico, Virginia, and Washington, D.C.

3

The Education of an Agent

QUANTICO'S MINDLESS REGIMENTATION reminded me of the service. Probationary agents had to learn the right way to make their beds, the Bureau way to fold sheets. Five minutes late at mess hall meant missing the meal, and doors were locked at night.

The courses were a mixed bag. We studied the statutes under which the Bureau got its jurisdiction. The Lindbergh law allowed us to come in on a kidnapping after twenty-four hours had elapsed. Bank robberies were federal crimes because the deposits were insured by a federal agency, and hijackings were open territory because of interstate commerce.

We learned the techniques for gathering evidence—fingerprinting, for example—and how to conduct a surveillance. We held interviews with mock suspects.

There were instructions on how to pay informants, how to talk to them. The recipients were to consider the payments as income to be duly recorded on their tax forms, and they had to sign receipts of payment. (In practice, as I learned, this was absolute nonsense.) Informants were forbidden to visit Bureau offices—not to protect their identities, but because they were the wrong types to be seen by the public in Bureau territory.

There were endless lectures on the Communist menace, and we were tutored in the ways of front organizations. On the other hand, there was almost no instruction on civil rights violations or the activities of organized crime.

The weapons training was excellent (although in nineteen years in the field I never had to use a gun). By tradition, an agent did not take his gun out except in self-defense and unless he meant to use it with intent to kill. If the Bureau discovered that an agent opened fire under less extenuating circumstances he was liable for censure and transfer. Even if an agent came upon a robbery in progress, he was instructed to allow the crime to proceed until the stickup men could be grabbed outside the building without gunplay. Later, as an agent, I saw the policy enforced.

However, although the records of the Bureau do not show it, a number of agents have, in the course of a barroom argument or to impress a friend, pulled pistols, put a few shots into ceilings. If an inspector hears of such an offense, the guilty agent faces disciplinary action, but the reason for the punishment will ordinarily be hidden under some innocuous phrase like "embarrassment to the Bureau" or "conduct unbecoming a special agent."

Appearances counted. In a softball game, while wearing a sweat suit, I broke my finger fielding a line drive. The pain was excruciating and I immediately asked the agent who supervised us for permission to seek medical aid. He ordered me to first take a shower, then put on a suit and tie; only then could I see the camp doctor.

We were constantly tested on what we absorbed and on our technical skills. The rate of attrition was fairly high; some said that it depended upon the size of the appropriation Hoover got from Congress every year. Men disappeared because of their poor academic work, failure at the weapons range, for disciplinary breaches, and for just plain not looking like an agent was supposed to. Those who left were "unpersons"; their names disappeared from rosters immediately. The process seemed to occur some time during the night.

After eight weeks at Quantico, presumably when the worst of us had been eliminated and the survivors whipped into presentable shape, we were bused to Washington to personally meet Hoover. It was a critical moment for a probationary special agent. If the top man didn't like what he saw, that was the end, no matter how well one had done in training. You wore a blue suit, a white shirt, of course a tie, and were instructed not to slouch and to give a firm handshake with a dry hand, not easy on such an occasion. It was all over so quickly that ten minutes later I couldn't have remembered the few words of greeting. But I passed the test.

Toward the end of the training period, the class shifted its operations to Washington, D.C. We rented apartments and received instruction at the Bureau's building. The Quantico class-room work had been largely in abstract terms. Now in Washington we heard lectures from agents who had worked on actual cases of robbery, kidnapping, and espionage. The instruction also covered the question of gratuities, rewards, and morals; sin, we learned, was not only against Christianity and mankind, it could compromise loyalty.

We had been issued our badges and identification papers after about twelve weeks. When we completed our training in Washington, there was a small office party—Cokes and peanuts. None of us were anxious to linger in Washington; we were all eager to get to our first office and start work as brick agents.

My first office was Philadelphia, and for the initial three weeks I worked with a veteran of the Bureau, Jim Walsh. He was a beautiful guy, patient with me and hard-working; he guided me through the procedures and then I was allowed to go off on my own.

Several weeks after I arrived, I had my first real taste of how criminals are actually handled. I happened to be in the office late one night, finishing my paperwork. A truckload of whiskey had been hijacked a few days earlier; the cargo had been recovered and the thieves identified. An ex-fighter named Jack Somers* led the group, but neither he nor his associates could be located.

That night an informant telephoned and said Somers and his friends could be found at a fleabag hotel in downtown Philly. Four agents were in the office that night; relations with the local cops were good, and we added two detectives to our party.

At the hotel we split into two groups of three, since the rooms being used by the robbers were on different floors. My trio included another agent and a very tough cop—Mighty Mac Thomas,* we called him. He stood only five eight, but he wore a size eighteen collar. We climbed the stairs to our floor and took up the approved positions around the door of Somers' room.

Mighty Mac hoarsely whispered, "I'll take the door." He hit the panel with his shoulder. Apparently the chain lock was in place. Thomas's charge ripped away not only the door but the frame itself. Plaster, dust, and splinters showered down from the ceilings and walls. Thomas rushed into the room with his thirty-eight out. As the dust settled, we saw one tiny, old, terrified man interrupted in the midst of putting on his pants. "Don't move or I'll blow your fucking brains out!" screamed Thomas.

"I'm only the room clerk," squeaked the man. "You must want the guy next door."

We recovered just in time to catch Jack Somers, alerted by the commotion, as he came out of his room. We placed Somers under arrest in the hall. Thomas told me to keep my gun pointed at Somers, who had his hands raised in surrender. Meanwhile, Mac and the other agent entered Somers' room in search of what the manuals call "instrumentalities of the crime."

The first sight Thomas saw was a girl in the bed. "Would you please leave the room so I can dress?" she asked. Thomas just stripped away the covers. She was bare-ass naked. As she started to put on her clothes, Thomas noticed another man, whom he promptly bounced off a wall. "I'm arresting you for parole violation." The other agent covered this prisoner.

Meanwhile, Jack Somers, who weighed well over two hundred and had Popeye forearms, complained to me, "I'm getting tired keeping my arms up. Can I put 'em down?"

"You better keep 'em up." I was nervous.

"I can't keep 'em up."

I yelled to the other agent, "John, this guy wants to take his hands down."

Mighty Mac shouted, "If he moves, put a bullet in his goddamn head!"

The man Mighty Mac identified as a parole violator whined that we had no legal right to detain him. "Mac, this guy says we're violating his rights," said my fellow agent.

Thomas marched the protester around a bend in the corridor. I heard some smacking noises and a yelp of pain. The two reappeared, the prisoner now holding a hand to his head. Mac Thomas rasped, "You want to give us any more of that rights shit?" The prisoner didn't answer.

Mighty Mac Thomas now turned his attention to the woman. "Are you married?" he asked politely.

"Yes, but I'm separated."

"Okay, I'm arresting you for adultery." He took them all down to be booked.

*　　*　　*

After about a year in Philadelphia, I was transferred to Detroit. That made me a "second office agent," a label that was supposed to carry with it an indication of suitability for more important work.

The boss in Detroit was Charlie Brown, but he wasn't good for any laughs like his namesake in the "Peanuts" comic strip. Charlie Brown was a small man with an even smaller mind. Like most bosses who came from the Midwest or the South, he had this thing about New Yorkers: We were all smart asses. I reinforced the prejudice by being one.

In the mid-1950s the Bureau's major concern was Communist subversion. But Detroit was not a nesting ground for subversives; on the other hand, it did serve as a major truck terminal. Drivers changed, and cargo was transferred and consolidated.

One of my first successes in Detroit involved clearing up a series of thefts from a truck terminal. The place was so big that we couldn't cover it with nighttime surveillance. But we figured that the thieves were probably kids from the neighborhood, since the truckers usually found empty beer cans in the wake of the robberies. My partner and I visited a local high school and talked the principal into giving us a list of the ten worst-behaved students.

The first kid we interviewed professed to know nothing about the robberies. We told him we had found a set of his fingerprints in one of the looted trucks. The boy swallowed the bait and admitted that he and others had stolen sewing machine heads. He gave us the name of one of his associates. From there on it was a chain reaction; each kid gave up another one or two until we had everyone, including the name of the fence. But the fence was smarter. He received a tip about the investigation and when we showed up at his place, he voluntarily submitted to a search. Nothing was in his shop. He refused to confess. In the end, the teenagers received probation. But the thefts at that particular terminal ended; the word spread that the place was watched.

On another case, the well-publicized technical expertise of the Bureau came into play. Another truck terminal had been plagued by heavy pilferage. We broke open several attractive cartons and left them that way, as if they needed to be recoopered. Then we sprinkled an invisible powder on the contents. When the night shift broke, we met them at the gate with a portable ultraviolet light machine. It was great showmanship; you could hear the gasps as we caught maybe half of the crews with dirty hands. It came close to entrapment, but nobody worried about such niceties.

As word spread, the amount of pilferage fell. Some of the trucking firms thought so highly of our work that they offered us jobs handling security.

Usually, I worked with another zealot, John D. Foster. We were book agents, always seeking to perform. In our spare time we cruised around watching for individuals who resembled persons described in the IOs (Identification Orders—"wanted" flyers), which we kept, complete and up-to-date, in the car. One of our better catches was a fugitive wanted for a string of armed robberies of supermarkets in the Midwest. His federal offense was stealing a car. Among the cities that wanted our man was Toledo. The cops in that city were unhappy about some local FBI action so, to appease them, the Bureau surrendered the guy to Toledo. This was the kind of work that helped build one's career in the Bureau.

But there was another kind of effort, which while it did not count among the statistics so proudly released every year, was at least as important toward advancement. In all the larger Bureau offices—New York, Miami, Los Angeles, Cleveland, Washington, D.C.—limousines were available for J. Edgar Hoover's use just in case he ever showed up. The Caddies were, of course, maintained in A-1 shape. In 1956, Railway Express went on strike. At the same time, the Cleveland special agent in charge, reputed to be the champion Hoover idolizer in the Bureau—a title not easily won—happened to be having one of Hoover's Caddies overhauled. The generator had proved faulty and had been sent to Detroit to be rebuilt. It was one of those special heavy-duty generators that helped power a two-way radio and countless other niceties for Hoover's comfort. The Railway Express strike prevented it from being returned, and the SAC had just been informed that Hoover would be wanting his Caddie in a couple of days.

The SAC panicked. He telephoned his opposite number in Detroit, Charlie Brown, to request some special help from Railway Express. Among the assistant chiefs of that organization was a former Bureau assistant director; he personally led a search of boxcars by nonstriking employees for the repaired generator, but it could not be found.

The SAC was now a basket case. He pleaded with Detroit to help him out. Although no spare generator could be located in the factory, Cadillac cooperated fully. They had just finished work on a special job for a Middle East sheik. They removed the generator from the car and crated it. Still, it had to get to Cleveland and we were running out of time. Hoover was never long on patience.

I was assigned to carry the generator to Willow Run Airport outside Detroit. Meanwhile, the office called the airline and won a promise from them to delay the flight as long as possible. We drove to Willow Run with the siren on all the way. I toted the crate to the plane, where the alerted pilot was waiting.

"Two agents will meet you in Cleveland and pick this up," I instructed. "Don't take your eyes off it."

How it could get lost between Detroit and Cleveland, or how he was supposed to handle his ship with his eyes on the generator, never crossed my mind. But I certainly impressed him with the gravity of the matter. He said, "I'm not going to ask what's inside, but because of our instruments, just tell me if it's radioactive."

I shook my head. I was too ashamed to tell him what actually was in the crate.

Although the Detroit scene was not seething with suspected subversives, we, like every other office, participated in the persecution of those known as Communists. We were well informed on harassment techniques: nails embedded in wood that could be placed under a car to cause a flat tire; sugar for gas tanks, potatoes for exhaust pipes. On black-bag jobs, the polite term for breaking and entering, agents brought along itching powder to sprinkle in gloves and undergarments, and an obnoxious-smelling substance called "buck lure" to smear on the fur coats of the affluent radicals. Some agents on the anti-Red squad went so far as to puncture condoms found in the belongings of the enemy. I was never assigned to a unit of this kind of duty, although I did some security and surveillance work. But if it had been my job to pull some of these stunts I would have followed orders; we were all infected with the Bureau's fever about Communist menaces.

On the other hand, few of us volunteered for that sort of thing;

most agents considered work on so-called "fellow travelers" and front organizations as either boring or tinged with unprofessional behavior. Spies, yes; criminals even more so. But there was no sense of triumph in chasing political dissidents. Of course, there were those who were more royalist than the king. From their ranks undoubtedly came such ideas as harassment kits and, in the sixties, Cointelpro (Counter Intelligence Program), designed to confuse or deter individuals in various political groups with anonymous threatening letters, fake phone messages, and planted provocateurs.

In Detroit I received a sharp lesson on the Bureau's preoccupation with form rather than content. All agents were encouraged to file special reports whenever they employed some special investigative tactic that broke a case. Circulated to other offices, these reports acquainted field agents with methods that they might profitably use. John Foster and I had been aware of an embezzlement by a local trucking-company executive. I discovered a way for federal law to be applied to the case and convinced the U.S. attorney to swear out a warrant. Then Foster and I tracked the man down. He confessed to the entire swindle, which actually amounted to closer to $100,000 than the $10,000 originally announced.

Our supervisor agreed that we appeared to have opened up an interesting approach to a common run of thefts, and we filed our case study. Some days later, Foster and I received a command to report to the office immediately. We joked about the coming commendation for our good work.

At the office, Mark Felt (later named as a candidate for the Watergate informant Deep Throat, who figured in the investigations of the Washington *Post* reporters Bob Woodward and Carl Bernstein) interviewed Foster and me. Inspector Felt was then serving as outstanding hatchet man for Hoover. He had scrutinized our report closely, and he pointed out that we had not included in it a paragraph that described our advice to the accused that he was entitled to consult with counsel. In our eagerness, we had simply omitted the phrase, although we had gone by the book in the actual interrogation.

Instead of a reward for our efforts, both Foster and I received letters of censure. That counted for more than just a note home to Dad about bad conduct in class. Any promotion in grade must be held up for six months or more after a letter of censure, and it also would delay a requested transfer. Two or three such letters in a single year put an agent back on probationary status.

In 1958 my two years in Detroit were over; I was being transferred to the New York City office. I was by now a third office man, but, contrary to my New York expectations, I continued to draw the less interesting assignments—chasing draft-law violators and impersonators of members of the armed forces. My work to date would hardly have qualified as significant in terms of crime control in the U.S. At that, though, I was lucky not to draw the worst of all jobs, security checking. Despite the fact that it was close to Hoover's heart as essential in controlling the Red Menace, it was considered the garbage detail of the Bureau.

My most noted success during this tour was the case of a woman who pretended to be a Social Security Administration investigator. In this guise she inveigled her way into the homes of the elderly in Harlem, where she either flimflammed them out of their money or else beat them up until they surrendered their valuables. There were about one hundred complaints filed on her.

We set up liaison with the Social Security offices in New York so that as soon as a report about stolen money came in we were notified. Then Jimmy Young, one of the very few black agents at the time, myself, and Harry Mulhall rushed up to Harlem and sifted through the neighborhood. Once, I spotted a suspect who resembled the description given us and I detained her.

Asked to identify herself, the woman flashed a brass-plate replica of a Social Security card with the name Jacqueline Kelley. "You bitch, we got you," yelled Mulhall, recognizing the name.

It was a pathetic case. Jacqueline Kelley had her own hundred-dollar-a-day drug habit. She was wanted by the Philadelphia cops for armed robbery and in New York for assault. All of us had interviewed white-haired, crumbling ancients in ratty tenement rooms who told the same sad tale about the "investigator" who had ripped off their money, leaving them with two or more weeks to wait for another check. Meanwhile, no money, no food, no medicine.

Jimmy Young used to say that if we ever caught her on the top floor of a tenement, she was going to "fall" all the way down the stairs. But Jacqueline Kelley was just a tub of human misery. Hoover wrote us letters of commendation for her arrest. Yet in spite of the note signed in pale-blue ink, I had no great sense of triumph. Somebody had to go out and stop Jacqueline Kelley, but busting her hardly deterred anyone else—it didn't even pretend to deal with the sources of criminality.

I felt even more discouraged by the necessity to grab people for impersonating members of the armed forces. Harry Mulhall and I collaborated on a number of these cases. In ninety-nine percent of them it was a matter of a 4-F or an underage kid who wanted to put on a show for girls. The impersonators blew it either because they pushed too hard for a reduced admission ticket at a theater or they wore the wrong ribbons and some wise eyes caught the mistake. Usually Harry and I brought the offender up to the offices of the Bureau and read him the riot act about how serious the crime was and the awful penalties involved. We took away every piece of military clothing, right down to the combat boots, and left them only their underwear. Someone in the family had to bring clothes. The GI stuff, including the shoes, we passed out to Bowery bums, after making sure it could no longer pass muster as military.

Harry had worked out a regular ritual. While I read the statute, he would begin by ripping off the chest ribbons, then the epaulets, like some corny film in which the hero is drummed out of the corps. Sometimes our prisoner would burst into tears during our ceremony.

The consequences for someone who was supposed to be in uniform but was not were much more severe. We had a good-size list of guys who had gone AWOL or deserted. Those gone for more than two years we called "old dog deserters." Every agent was given a few of these. Whenever we weren't on a specific case we were supposed to have a shot at an old dog. If you got him right away it was a very clean job. You simply handed him over to the military authorities. But if he evaded you, it meant that you had to do reports periodically.

Some agents had a special knack with old dogs. They would read the file and see a scrap of information that led right to the wanted man. Often I'd confer with one of these experts for some advice on where to look for my old dogs.

Joe Chapman (who later became an expert on art for the

Bureau) and I went after an old dog who supposedly lived in a Brooklyn tenement. When we reached the address, we noticed a rather dignified Hispanic man lounging around in front. Joe asked him whether he had ever heard of our deserter.

"If you are looking for him because he stole a car or robbed a bank, I do not want to be involved."

"Nothing like that," answered Joe. "He's a spy," he lied.

"This is too good a country for that," responded the man indignantly. "He lives on the top floor right."

We knocked on the door of the apartment but there was no answer, only noises inside. We looked over the premises. The fire escape went to the roof, and both it and the apartment could be watched from the hallway. I told Joe to wait there; I would go down to a hardware store and get a spring that I could fashion into a torsion bar, very useful on locks. I came back with the gadget and leaned against the door to pick the lock. But the door swung open—in their haste, the inhabitants had forgotten to lock it.

Inside we found a Cuban girl holding an infant in her arms. She knew enough English so that when we asked for our man she could say, "You kill me, I don't tell you where my husband is." He was obviously not in the flat.

Joe's genius blossomed. "You're not a U.S. citizen. We'll have to deport you, and we'll take the baby and put it up for adoption." Chapman reached for his handcuffs as a demonstration of his sincerity. The woman begged and pleaded, but Chapman dangled his cuffs. She crumbled and telephoned her husband to come home.

It's hard to believe now, but I was so indoctrinated then with the desire to make good that arrests like this didn't bother me. What made it somewhat easier to swallow was that these men rarely served time; the service gave them dishonorable discharges and that ended the matter. One time, however, I played Good Samaritan. I had traced a draft evader through his relatives and found him living with a woman. They even had a couple of kids. The place where they lived was spotless and the kids obviously well taken care of; the man held a steady job. But I had to take him in to the office. While we were there, I remarked that I thought he'd made a mistake in just running out on the draft. With a wife and kids, he would never have been called up. He admitted that she was only a common-law wife. I had a brain-storm; I said why don't you marry her and maybe I can work something out with the U.S. attorney in the case.

A week later I received a telephone call from the woman. She was overjoyed. The man had followed my advice; her children now had a real father and the next boy would be named for me. It made me feel really good, especially when I was able to arrange for the U.S. attorney to drop the case.

Maybe three months passed, and the wife telephoned me. Sobbing, she said her husband had disappeared. Could I, who had been so kind, find him?

I went back to his old haunts, and it wasn't very hard for me to locate him. He explained that before the marriage the woman had risen every morning to make his breakfast; when he came home at night, a hot dinner was on the table and the apartment was neat and clean. Whatever he said, she accepted; there were no arguments. But now, only a few months after marriage, she no longer bothered to prepare his breakfast or dinner; she left the house a mess and screamed at him whenever he showed up. He said it would have been better to have done time than wed this woman. I talked him into returning home—but I was cured of playing the good fairy in the future.

Examination of the Congressional records for the fifties and early sixties to see what Hoover fed to Congress at appropriations time reveal reports and testimony on sex crimes and the spread of pornography and juvenile delinquency. But the dominant themes would be Communist fronts and Soviet espionage. Closer scrutiny reveals nothing about organized crime—for the simple reason that Hoover contended it was a phantom.

During the early 1950s, two FBI agents caught a made guy in midcrime. They behaved like gentlemen, so he relaxed and started to tell them war stories—Mafia war stories. They were astonished at his recitation of the table of organization in criminal circles. They wrote it all down and filed the reports in New York. None of the brass believed a word of it; after all, the Director had announced that organized crime didn't exist. Nevertheless, the material was forwarded to Washington. Apparently nobody there believed it either; it was filed and forgotten.

In November 1957, Sergeant Edgar Croswell of the New York

state police raided a rather unusual convention being held in an upstate hamlet called Apalachin. The convention delegates were the top figures in crime from coast to coast, and they had gathered at the mansion of the Buffalo crime family chief Joseph Barbara, Sr., to settle a crisis.

For the Mafia, 1957 had been a turbulent year. Someone nicked Don Frank Costello in the head, and when he refused to answer grand jury questions on the matter, he received a jail term. In October, assassins bloodied a Manhattan barbershop by shooting holes in crime family boss Albert Anastasia, who had earlier that year deposed one Frank Scalise through similar means. Although none of those present at Apalachin ever revealed the agenda for the convention, it was presumed that they intended to draw up rules for more orderly, less violent successions.

But Sergeant Croswell's raid apparently did not impress J. Edgar Hoover as sufficient evidence to prove the existence of organized crime and racketeering. In fact, local law-enforcement organizations created because of the significance of Apalachin discovered the Director to be an obstacle to their progress. Attorney General William Rogers, Hoover's boss at the time, apparently did wake up; he delivered at least one powerful speech about organized crime and, in 1958, created a special group to combat it. But the assistant U.S. attorney in charge, Milton R. Wessel, received little support from Hoover. Richard V. Ogilvie and Gerard L. Goettel, Wessel's deputies, publicly criticized the Bureau's coolness to the operation.

The FBI files were closed to the special unit, even though it was part of the same government department as the FBI. When some law-enforcement experts proposed a national clearinghouse on organized crime, J. Edgar Hoover played the role of a civil-libertarian hero by adamantly opposing anything that smacked of a national police structure that might subvert local control. Possibly Hoover feared a dilution of his role with a rival organization, especially one geared to a problem that he didn't even believe existed.

Later, when it became increasingly obvious that, even more than Santa Claus, a Mafia did exist, Hoover and his defenders claimed that existing federal statutes prevented action against organized crime. In view of our right to arrest people for auto theft, truck hijacking, and bank robbery, it would seem to me that Hoover's legal adviser would have been adroit enough to stretch the jurisdiction of the FBI against gambling, which moved over state lines; narcotics, which was an international traffic; and a whole series of OC investments that could have been interpreted as subject to federal jurisdiction. At the very least Hoover could have asked Congress for authority to pursue organized crime as a federal offense. With his reputation, he would not have been denied. But he refused to use his prestige in the cause.

"People come to me and ask me whether something can't be done to clean up their cities or their towns," said Hoover in one of his speeches, "to drive out the racketeers and the mobsters. I try to explain that the kind of crime they want to eradicate—call it 'organized crime'—doesn't come within the federal jurisdiction. I tell them, 'Go back home and elect honest men, efficient and hard-working men, to public office.' And they tell me, 'We don't want to get mixed up in politics.' What they mean is that some of the people they would like me to get rid of sit on the respectable side of the table though they are still involved with the rackets. They don't want to face up to this, or to take the risks of the battle, so they tell the FBI to do it."

But that was what those citizens were paying Hoover and the rest of us agents to do. Yet, as late as 1962, Hoover was still dazzling Congress with presentations that showed the recovery of nearly nineteen thousand stolen cars and reported the Red Menace, in the form of the Communist Party U.S.A., to be "an inseparable arm of the international conspiracy against God and freedom which is directed from Moscow." This in spite of the facts that of the five people running the party, three were paid informants, and the operations in this country were chiefly supported by Congress through its appropriations to the Bureau, which funneled funds back to the CP to keep the informants and the party going.

I think Hoover's fears about Communists and the other ideologies he hated were sincere. He got his start in government in 1919 as a young lawyer prosecuting "alien agitators" and "radicalism," in the words of the FBI director at the time. He participated in the famous raids against aliens ordered by Attorney General A. Mitchell Palmer in 1920. When Hoover was appointed FBI director, these activities were not held against him. Communism and other radical beliefs were constant preoccupations of politicians, the press, and the people throughout his lifetime as head of the closest thing to a U.S. national police.

Because of the prestige he had prudently banked over the years, no president or lesser politician felt strong enough to confront Hoover and ask why he stubbornly refused to attack organized crime with the same zeal he had mounted against the "public enemies" of bygone days and the Red Menace. Because the Bureau files held dossiers that detailed minor and major scandals and embarrassing moments that involved hundreds of elected officials and their families, none of the lawmakers cared to make a public case against the Director's dereliction of duty. And, as political dissidence grew in the sixties as civil disorders and the violence of extremists erupted in the streets, Hoover was able to continue his role as the protector of the American way. Also, the more sophisticated dons of organized crime to some extent kept themselves free from the conspicuous notice achieved by other public enemies of the 1930s and thereby aroused no great public hue and cry.

The Bureau's first feeble attempts to keep abreast of organized crime began while I was still in Detroit. Every office participated in an operation called the Top Hoodlum Program for the investigation of the top criminals in their area. Since the Bureau was almost totally uninformed on the structure of the Mafia, the selection of investigators rested on arbitrary decisions by local SACs. Not only were we ignorant of the who's who of organized crime, we did not even have information about the men we picked as Top Hoodlums. One name handed to me in Detroit was Angelo Polizzi. Our files carried no background on Polizzi, and I was forced to use the morgue of a local newspaper to find Polizzi's history.

About thirty years before I turned my attention to him, Polizzi and a friend had been standing on a Detroit street corner when a touring car drove by. A fusillade of shots poured from the car. Five or six bullets wounded Polizzi; his companion was killed. When interrogated in his hospital bed by the cops, Polizzi, who was not expected to survive, professed ignorance of the identities of his assailants. Polizzi lived in spite of the predictions of his doctors, however.

I pulled his arrest sheet from the cops. Polizzi had been grabbed a number of times in connection with murders in the ensuing years. It was obvious that his would-be assassins had now become his targets. Yet he walked every time, released on the authority of a magistrate. Polizzi, for all his notoriety, received a pistol permit. After the Apalachin convention, Polizzi was identified as belonging to the hierarchy of LCN, which stands for Joe Valachi's designation "La Cosa Nostra"; the Bureau adopted the initials as its abbreviation for organized crime.

Outside of putting together a file on Polizzi, identifying some of his relatives and known business interests, and his turf—Windsor, Canada—that is all the Top Hoodlum Program amounted to.

When I got to New York after my Detroit tour I began making contributions to the Top Hoodlum Program there. I checked out court records on births, marriages, and real estate holdings as agents attempted to build files on individuals identified as part of LCN. When the first organized crime squads were created, I asked to be assigned to one. The administrative officer cautioned me that the squads might very well be only a temporary operation designed to satisfy criticism and would be disbanded after the heat died down. Besides, there were no openings on organized crime squads at the moment.

In desperation, I applied to language school. (The Bureau trained a number of agents to be fluent in a variety of languages, the better to monitor wiretaps and bugs, and as further evidence of the need for bigger appropriations.) As a concession to the pressure for attention to LCN, there were openings in the Monterey, California, language school for those considered capable of learning the Sicilian dialect. Yugoslav, Hebrew, Albanian, and of course Russian were among the staples; one agent I knew spent a year learning Chinese, although he never had an opportunity to use his skill on the job.

Even though I have no language aptitude, I scored well on the aptitude quiz, which says something about the value of such tests. But the system at the language school seemed to be an effective way to teach, for our purposes. We memorized dialogues and then recited them, reversing roles. The instructors were foreign-born, and they got across the vernacular as well as the book language. It so happened that instead of training me in Sicilian they taught me the Tuscany dialect.

Even in language school the petty fiction that all agents worked overtime was maintained. Since school lasted from 9 A.M. until 3 P.M., we fulfilled the requisite overtime quota by counting our homework as extra hours. The overtime was credited to the nearest Bureau office, San Francisco.

Although there were no formal written examinations, the instructors wrote reports on us, which were forwarded to FBI offices. The Bureau expected us to be at the top of the class. If there were three agents in a group of fifteen students, they were supposed to rate as the top three. I broke the tradition by being thirteenth in a class of fourteen. The only man below me was a major in the Marines who liked to party even more than I did.

After my wife became bored with life on the West Coast and returned to New York, I stopped trying in class altogether. The instructor complained to the senior agent in the language school, Ed Berkholtz, who promised to straighten me out. When Berkholtz told me I was on the verge of being expelled, I said, "I don't give a damn. Let 'em flunk me out, send me back to being a brick agent."

But Berkholtz was aware that my failure would make the Bureau look bad. And although I continued to be an infrequent visitor to classes, I noticed that the instructor seemed highly solicitous of my well-being. I asked Berkholtz if he knew why. "I told him the Bureau had decided you didn't really need to know the language too well, that you were going to go underground with the Mafia. So long as you had the right mannerisms the brass figured you could hack it. Besides, your chances of surviving underground with the Mafia were so slim that it didn't seem worthwhile to pressure you about your studies." Berkholtz then chewed me out for what he considered my real sin: failure to file daily reports on myself to the San Francisco office and, even worse, not notifying the Bureau that I had changed my address.

In December 1963, I was considered to have completed my language course and I received orders to report to Albany, New York. It was not the office of my choice. I had expected that, with my alleged new skills, I would be sent to a major theater of action, New York City.

The immediate problem with the assignment was my boss in Albany, who formed an immediate dislike for me. His way of doing things became very clear soon after I was assigned to the

Utica Resident Agency, an Albany satellite. I received a tip that the life of a U.S. congressman had been threatened by a former state trooper. The ex-cop's wife was a semi-hooker and had driven him halfway round the bend. Since the woman was a secretary to the congressman, the onetime cop focused his hate on the legislator. It was a potentially dangerous situation, and I immediately telephoned the Albany boss. His secretary accepted the call. It went something like this:

"This is Tony. I'm in Utica. I want to speak to the boss."

"You can't talk to him."

"Is he tied up in an interview?"

"No."

"Then put me through."

"No. He says he doesn't want to talk to you."

Finally, she switched me to the second in command. He and the boss were currently in the throes of a dispute and not on speaking terms, which was a helluva way for the top two men in a Bureau office to behave.

The second in command was well versed, however, in his boss's school of operations. After I had explained the entire situation to him, he asked, "Do you have an *Agents Manual* in Utica?"

"Yes."

"Well, all the answers are there."

And that was the total amount of guidance that I received. The Bureau's way in delicate situations was to tell the agent to take an action on his own, file a report at least, and meanwhile avoid any steps that might embarrass the Bureau. Clearly, the leadership in Albany felt that the agent was solely responsible when anything troublesome arose; if a case did not turn out well, it would be the individual agent who suffered. It's a method designed for second-guessers.

Being in Utica and on my own did give me an opportunity to learn more about organized crime, however. And it was there that I discovered how to be most effective.

While he was in prison, Joe Valachi, soldier in the Genovese Family, had convinced himself that he was a marked man, that Genovese himself wanted him dead. His confessions were already available by the time I arrived in Utica, and it was from them I learned that it was Joe Falcone who ran the town. His boss was

Don Stefano Maggadino, a member of the Commissione, which presided over LCN, and a man who watched over his boundaries like a hawk. Since the Bureau had bugged a laundry owned by Maggadino's Buffalo organization, they could listen in on his reaction to Falcone's report that some New York wiseguys were attempting to set up a card game within Falcone's territory: "Not even Jesus Christ moves into my territory without my okay."

Valachi himself had once tried to move into Falcone's city. To settle the contretemps, a sitdown was called, to be attended by Valachi, Falcone, and Falcone's brother, Salvatore. During the ride to the site, the passenger-side door swung open and Falcone's chief enforcer, John Melito, nearly fell out. Salvatore told Valachi how fortunate it was that Melito was not hurt, since he would have had to deal in kind with Valachi and his henchmen. After the sitdown Valachi decided that he wanted no part of Utica.

Joe Falcone knew all about me, too. When I arrived in Utica, I was immediately introduced to the mayor and to members of the local police department: Falcone undoubtedly picked up intelligence from Utica officials regularly. But I still figured that with a break I could crack his organization and develop information.

Utica was a city that had once expected better things for itself. Situated on the Mohawk River, a way station between the Great Lakes, Albany, and the Hudson River, the place had been a mill town, busy with barge traffic. But instead of settling on Utica, where there appeared to be a competitive situation for labor, the auto manufacturers established their factories in Syracuse and Buffalo. Utica stagnated. Its only vestigial reminder of the unfulfilled future was the railroad station, built to handle the traffic that never developed. It was a monumental pile of Romanesque ugliness. But one evening while I was there it turned into a gold mine of information.

I spotted a hood whom I recognized as a minor satellite figure for Maggadino. He lived in Binghamton and, whatever his business with Joe Falcone, was now glumly waiting for a train to carry him home.

I approached him straightforwardly, introducing myself, and began giving him the needle. "I can't believe a big button man in the Mafia is going to have to take the train back to Binghamton." After we talked for a couple of minutes he admitted he was sore because Falcone's aide, Russell Mancuso, had refused to give him a ride home; such courtesies are expected between soldiers. I played Mr. Nice Guy and offered to drive him. He refused at first, but eventually I overcame his reluctance. On the trip he complained even more about his situation. He was broke; in fact, his life was a stretch of failures culminating in his absence at the great Apalachin bust. He had been scheduled to serve as chauffeur for one of the invitees, but the night before his dress factory had burned down. (I later had reason to believe he torched it himself for the insurance.) As a result of the fire, he had been unable to make the jaunt. He was almost sorry that Sergeant Croswell had not taken him into custody; apparently, to be among those arrested on that day was something like having been with Henry V at Agincourt on St. Stephen's Day.

Johnny Iacco* bemoaned his luck all the way to Binghamton. The only consolation I could offer was the money in my pocket and my profuse appreciation for his having been willing to permit me to drive him when he was not even supposed to be seen with me.

Before I parted company with Iacco that night, I made a date to see him again. I promised that I would obtain more "loans" for him. I also assured him that I had no desire to compromise him; I would not press him for details of anything that was about to happen or had recently occurred.

Our meetings continued, and I eventually turned him with pennies. It took a lot of fighting with the Bureau to extract even the occasional two-hundred-dollar payment to Iacco. And he needed every cent because of an itch for women and a conviction that he could dope out horse-race winners.

When Iacco finally started to talk, he gave me a history of the Maggadino Family, with particular attention to matters involving the Falcones. He solved about eight murders for me (one of the homicide victims was a greedy cop whose appetite had grown too large for the crime family to support). Iacco also informed me of how Gus Grote* had disposed of an old girl friend. Nothing he told me could lead to prosecution; this was all ancient history, because the witnesses—if they had ever existed—were dead or had vanished. But it was nevertheless invaluable, because through Iacco we could put together the dimensions of the Maggadino-Falcone operations, their personnel, and their interests.

Some of what Iacco told me could be checked with local and state police records; the rest was confirmed in the Valachi papers and through other informants.

While I had done everything I could to keep Iacco's role as an informant from the ears of Joe Falcone, I could never be certain that someone would not see us or that Iacco himself would not somehow give the game away. One drizzly night I closed up the offices around eight and headed on foot to the hotel where I was staying.

As I walked on Genesee Street, the main drag, a black Lincoln passed and the man at the wheel gave me a glance. I ignored him, but when I halted at an intersection, I saw a car approaching perpendicular to my direction. It looked like the same black Lincoln. I walked on, and after another block I saw the Lincoln coming toward me from yet another direction.

I figured I was marked. As soon as I reached the hotel, I ducked into the basement and telephoned another agent. He agreed to meet me at the hotel, using a Bureau car because it had a phone in it and I could keep in touch with him.

I now observed the black Lincoln circle the block of the hotel and then park. The driver entered the hotel and headed for the bar. I reached my fellow agent and rendezvoused. For the first time, I felt a little fright; in this instance I was the hunted instead of the hunter.

We spotted our man sitting at the end of the bar. The two of us walked down to him, lifted him off the bar stool between us, and hustled him outside. We asked why he was following me. He denied it, but I knew better. We took his driver's license and recorded the information on it. Then I told him he'd better stay away from me or I'd make the first move. He was the stereotype hit man—black car, careful surveillance, an Italian name and appearance to match.

We released him and then rushed over to the police station and gave the cops the information from the driver's license. They began to laugh like hell. My assassin was a well-known queer, given to cruising in search of bunkmates.

I felt pretty cocky after I turned Johnny Iacco. My second try was Dominick Bretti, who I had heard was a local knockaround tough guy—so tough that he had tried to shake down Joe Fal-cone. That so outraged Falcone that he put out a contract on Bretti. Only through an important uncle was Bretti given a re-prieve, but along with it came a requirement that he not steal so much as a cigarette in Utica.

I happened to be in a barbershop one day when Bretti showed up. He knew who I was. He immediately dropped a dime, dialed a telephone number, and called in a couple of bets. I bounced out of the barber chair, flashed my credentials, and said, "You're under arrest for gambling." Bretti laughed, and that was the beginning of a friendly relationship. But Bretti refused to rat on anybody. I continued to work on him; he didn't mind at all. Bretti never worried about being seen in my company, and he was always offering to fix me up with chicks.

My wife had moved back to New Jersey with our children, and one evening I went to an excellent Italian restaurant, Grimaldi's, to cure my depression. Dick Bretti was at the bar and we began to do some serious drinking. From there we adjourned to a strip joint, and in the last hours of the early morning Bretti offered to drive me to my hotel in his flashy new Cadillac, which was the setting for my stomach's rebellion at all the alcohol it had been receiving in the past few hours.

About a week later I received a telephone call from Dick's sister. The day after our adventure he had been arrested and charged with armed robbery in Florida. While the crime was not something foreign to Dick Bretti's style, it would have been physi-cally impossible for him to have driven from Utica, New York, to Florida in the time since I had last seen him. Bretti's sister told me that Dick was embarrassed to ask me, almost preferred to take his chances in court, but I was really his best alibi.

I telephoned the Miami office of the Bureau, got the informa-tion on the crime, and then contacted the DA. They needed something in writing in order to get Bretti off the hook, so I opened a 137 file (an informant file), making Bretti a TEPCI (Top Echelon Potential Criminal Informant), and described my efforts to turn Bretti. With that written record to show, Bretti walked, a free man.

A month or so later, Dick returned to Utica. He thanked me for helping him, but he wasn't so grateful that he would become a talker. He was the model of the stand-up hood.

* * *

When I arrived in Utica, there were three volumes of files covering Joe Falcone's activities. When I left, there were over ten, put together largely through information I developed from Iacco. I did have one or two other triumphs and I did earn some letters of commendation for my efforts there, but I could see Utica was bush-league stuff. The real game was being played in New York City. And finally, having put in my full two years in Utica, I was transferred back. In January 1966 I began my most productive period in the Bureau.

4

The Wiseguys

WHEN I ARRIVED IN NEW YORK, one of the first agents I sought out was a guy who had served as a translator of Sicilian dialect that showed up on some of the tapes we had compiled in Utica. The Bureau office allowed agents to team up loosely on criminal cases if the two men felt they could work well together. When an agent is transferred to another office, his best way of finding such a partner is to look for the loner, a guy with good cases who is your type of person. The translator of the tapes struck me as fitting the mold. I confided to him that I was not going to spend my time checking out who owned what cars and where they lived. "I'm going to turn guys. That's the only way to accomplish anything." However, although we did share information, it never became a strong relationship—for several reasons, but basically because I preferred to work alone. I sensed that turning someone would require working on a one-to-one basis.

I spent most of my first month in New York associating with winebuyers to orient myself. Then I was assigned to the squad covering Carlo Gambino's organization.

Courtesy of Joe Valachi and other member sources, the FBI had been able to compile a list of people affiliated with La Cosa Nostra families. Beyond the information on arrest sheets provided by local cops, we knew little about them. Our job was to turn them into known quantities.

One of the names given to me was Jackie Gucci*, also known as "Jackie Balls" and, to really close acquaintances, "Dummy." Valachi described him as a real tough guy; supposedly, Jackie had earned multiple notches in his gun in one day. All I had on Jackie Gucci was a 92 case, the Bureau's number classification for an antiracketeering matter. (The Bureau had about 180 such classifications.) The usual technique was to investigate a guy with this kind of rep and try to get him put away on any violation.

Jackie Gucci had recently been released after serving hard time in Atlanta. All told, he had spent over twenty of his fifty-odd years in various prisons. As soon as he was released, his 92 case was reopened. I obtained his last address from the federal probation and parole office. He was living in East Harlem.

One morning I drove up to the neighborhood, figuring I'd make a start by verifying his residence, employment, associates, and relatives. I parked in front of the building and went inside, thinking I would spot his name on a mailbox and then wait for the mailman to come along and verify his receiving mail there.

When I saw Jackie's name on the box, I impulsively pressed the button. The door buzzed and I passed through the vestibule and climbed four flights of stairs. I had no preconception as to how to handle the situation; I just kept moving forward. From up the stairs I could hear him bellowing, "Who is it? Who is it?" I kept my mouth shut and continued to climb.

In the doorway of his apartment stood the killer himself, dressed only in skivvies, his bony, varicose-veined legs looking oddly out of place. When I came face to face with him, I pushed my way inside, mumbling, "It's okay, it's okay, take it easy." I still didn't know what the hell I was doing. I moved through the rooms, opening closets, peeking under beds, checking the bathroom to make sure we were alone.

Meanwhile, Gucci kept rumbling, "What the fuck is this? What the fuck's going on?" He was not much of a conversationalist. I think the fact that he was in his underwear intimidated him. There is a prissiness in some of the older wiseguys, in spite of the violence they perpetrate.

Back in the living room, I finally turned to him and waved my credentials. That upset him considerably and he varied his curses. "Jackie, that's no way to greet a guest. Make us some coffee."

Surprisingly, Gucci agreed. "Okay, but then you get out, you got no right here." He put on a pair of pants and brewed the coffee. All the time, I was still groping for the right way to approach him.

"I could get in trouble for this," Gucci said. "I'm not supposed to talk to you at all."

I began to talk about Utica and some of the people I'd met there. I mentioned his previous history and asked, "How come a big guy like you lives up here in this terrible neighborhood? Your wife had to work while you were gone. She still has to work. They must be really lousy in New York. In Utica, Joe Falcone took care of the people who went away. He sent them cigarettes and money, and even took care of their families. How many times did they send you money?"

Gucci held up two fingers. "Five bucks each time."

"And your wife—she's fifty years old, Jackie. Didn't they take care of her?"

"They never gave her a fucking thing." He was angry. I'd found a sore spot.

"How come they treat you so badly? You were loyal, a real stand-up guy. You could've buried plenty of these people, but no, you were devoted."

"Shit, I shouldn't even talk to you. I should throw you the hell out of here. Forget my name; don't use it against me."

"How did you originally get involved, Jackie?" I ignored all of his protestations of not wanting to talk. And I wound up spending four and a half hours with him. I didn't take any notes, because I had sense enough to realize that our new relationship wasn't strong enough to sustain that, and I asked only about what could be considered ancient history.

Jackie Gucci grew up hating cops. He'd taken his first beating from them at the age of nine. At the age of twelve or thirteen, he'd discovered that one could avoid some police harassment, whether for playing ball in the streets or lifting items in a store, through payoffs. Then he became aware that some of the well-dressed fellows in the neighborhood were never bothered by the law, no matter how they behaved. He quickly learned that these favored individuals were button men and were referred to as dons. Other citizens treated them with great respect.

Jackie Gucci now itched with one mighty ambition: to become a made guy and achieve respected status. He curried favor with the wiseguys, performing errands, working at any odd jobs they desired. In the course of such endeavors he did time twice, but on both occasions he kept his mouth shut and behaved the way a connected guy in the can is expected to. His virtue went rewarded: Jackie became a made guy in the Carlo Gambino Family.

Gucci was one of the raw recruits in the organization, getting made not through an uncle, brother, or father but by his own bloody deeds. As such he was given a full Emily Post course in the proper way for a member to comport himself. Among the valued instructions was the correct way to recognize through conversation whether someone was connected. The proper phrase was "I have a very dear friend and he has a dear friend named . . ." The other individual, if a button man, would respond in kind.

Gucci's first capo was Frank "Cheech" Scalise. Scalise, an ambitious man, operated a vegetable-grocery business in the Bronx. He was also reputed to have been the biggest capo regime in the Gambino Family. Albert Anastasia, not unmindful of Scalise's ambitions and feeling him to be a possible threat as boss of the present Gambino Family, ordered a hit on him. At the funeral, when emotions race unchecked, Scalise's brother apparently vowed revenge. He too was quickly dispatched to join his brother. Then a second brother disappeared, and so ended the menace of the Scalise clan.

By the time Gucci was assigned a new capo, he was in prison. He was informed that his new superior would be Vincent Squillante, a don Gucci knew from East Harlem and for whom he had done a number of favors.

Vincent Squillante broke one of the most honored of all LCN rules: He messed with the women of other family members. And, to emphasize his degeneracy, Squillante preferred to force his attentions upon them while their male partners were in prison. Sooner or later Squillante would probably have been killed by a wronged husband. But even before the males could hold a sit-down to settle his fate, a group of the wronged women arranged a reception for Squillante. When he arrived for one of his forcible assignations, they fell upon him with knives. His hacked-up body was disposed of in a junkyard; the pieces of the corpse were never found. The way he told me this, I suspected that Gucci's wife might have participated in the cutting party.

That afternoon I also learned from Jackie the names of people in the Gambino Family who were unheard of in our files or anyone else's. It was such a wealth of information that I could barely contain myself, even though the specifics would not lead to any prosecutions.

By midafternoon, Jackie's mother-in-law walked in on us. I introduced myself as a life-insurance salesman. She said something about making certain that Jackie was insured for the benefit of his son. The boy was around twenty and miraculously had never been arrested. He had had a tough time fending for himself; again, the organization had failed to produce any aid for the kid—one more grievance for Jackie, one more hook for me.

However, as the day wore on, Jackie's willingness to supply information withered. "I talked straight to you, I was courteous," he said. "I hope nobody saw us together. If you call me I won't answer. I don't want to ever see or hear from you again. Let's part friends. I already made a mistake letting you in here. Let's leave it at that."

I professed great respect for his feelings and for his delicate position. Then I left, making no promises.

At the office, I immediately began telling my supervisor what kind of day I'd had. He was incredulous. He summoned a secretary and had me dictate everything I could recall. The next step was to have a conference to figure out how to proceed from there. I reminded them all that Jackie had explicitly announced he would not see me again. No satisfactory approach could be agreed upon. If we were to exploit the opening, I would have to figure out the way.

I bought two theater tickets for a Broadway show, *Man of La Mancha*, and mailed them to Jackie Gucci in an envelope without a return address. On the evening following the performance, two weeks after I first visited Jackie, I telephoned him. "How'd you like the play?" I asked.

"I loved it," he answered, and then he recognized my voice. "I told you not to call." He hung up on me.

This failure produced a new conference with another notion: ply him with money. That had possibilities, but I didn't believe that a straightforward offer of cash would be sufficient to turn Jackie.

Gucci was on parole; he had two or three years to serve, all from a big narcotics bust that had pulled in, among others, Vito Genovese and Joe Valachi. The chief witness who identified Genovese as a party to the narcotics sale was a Puerto Rican courier named Nelson Cantellops, aka Pineapple. Subsequently somebody put a bullet in Pineapple's head, but not before several of the Genovese Family, including Vito himself, went away. Jackie pleaded guilty, which brought him a lighter sentence than the others and put him back on the street earlier. But he still owed time.

I dropped in on Jackie's parole officer, Gaetano Auriello.* He brought out the file on Gucci and I explained my mission: to violate Jackie, make him either feed me stuff or serve the remainder of his term. In such a situation the parole officer makes recommendations that decide freedom or prison for the parolee. Auriello was a do-gooder and he gave me an argument. "Don't try to use me as a hammer," he yelled. "I'm trying to see this guy rehabilitated."

"Jackie Gucci's got an IQ of less than a hundred," I reminded him. "He's been a knockaround guy all his life, has no trade, and he's fifty-six years old. You think you're going to rehabilitate him? In a couple of weeks he'll be back selling junk to keep himself alive. He's a classic recidivist."

Auriello calmed down. "I won't let you use me to try to turn him. But if you make a case, please call me so I'm not embarrassed." Saving face is not exclusively an Oriental concern. As a veteran of American bureaucratic wars, I can testify that it seems to be the primary concern of most government officials.

I still thought maybe I could make a deal with Auriello. "What if I get Jackie before a grand jury and he refuses to cooperate? Would that be a violation?"

"Only if he's arrested and convicted." Auriello had his limits. However, he did give me the date and time for Jackie's next appointment with him.

The following Tuesday morning I was sitting in Foley Square in a red Mustang, courtesy of a Hertz credit card. I had temporarily convinced the office that surveillance of people in organized crime couldn't be done from those black government-issue jobs with the telephone aerials. Alongside me was another agent, Ed Walsh.

We expected Jackie to drive up, but suddenly he popped up out of a subway kiosk. It was the last way I expected a Gambino button man to travel. It was a good omen; it meant that Jackie was broke.

We decided that Walsh would stay with the Mustang while I followed Gucci when he emerged from his session with Auriello.

After a suitable period, Jackie reappeared and ducked into the Lexington Avenue subway. I kept my distance behind him, and when he boarded the train, I got into another car. It was obvious that he hadn't seen me yet. I walked into his car and plunked myself down next to him. There were hardly any other passengers.

"Hello," I said. He bounced up, ready to leave. But I seized his arm and pinned him. I whispered hints of money plus anonymity, but Jackie reminded me that we had a deal: He had talked to me once and that was supposed to be the end of the relationship. But that was a unilateral agreement—I had never promised not to bother him again. We argued and argued, softly, as the subway rattled up to East Harlem.

At the 110th Street station he rose to leave. "Please don't walk out with me; don't embarrass me." Face is important in the mob, too. I let him go, saying I would call. "Don't waste your time" was his farewell.

Back to the Bureau office, back to another pointless conference, where the most constructive idea was a silly proposal to mail an anonymous hundred-dollar bill to Jackie.

I telephoned Gucci. A recorded message informed me that the telephone had been disconnected. I drove up to East Harlem and spent a day surveilling his building, only to discover that he had moved out. I obtained his new address, in the Bronx, from Auriello.

Ed Walsh and I set up a watch on the Bronx house. One evening around seven we saw Jackie get into his beat-up 1958 Ford and head toward the Whitestone section of Queens. The address he entered turned out to be the home of another button guy, Thomas Massi* aka "Tommy Terror." We didn't hang around that night for fear of being burned.

We continued to stake out Massi's place. One night the pair of them got into Jackie's Ford. Ed and I followed them to a midtown luxury apartment building near the United Nations. They drove into the garage, and we noted that the attendants greeted them. As soon as they disappeared inside the building, Ed Walsh, with the cool of a riverboat gambler, approached the doorman. "Was that Mr. Sullivan who went in? I meant to catch him . . ."

"Naw, that was Mr. Wilson from seventeen-F."

Walsh and I sat in our rented job for several hours watching the entrance to the building, noting the residents (nonresidents could be detected by the way the doorman treated them) and recording the license-plate numbers on all of the cars. Neither Jackie nor Massi had come out by midnight, so we left.

We began checking our files and those of the Federal Bureau of Narcotics for major narcotics offenders. Jackie, of course, was a featured character. In the Federal Narcotics material we noted a mug shot of one man who had visited the apartment building that night. From the license-plate checks we picked up another individual with a strong drug background, a twenty-year junk sentence hanging over him.

This called for a genuine conference, which came to the unsurprising conclusion that the apartment of "Mr. Wilson" was a pivotal point for the junk business, most likely heroin. Either they were cutting the stuff there, distributing it, or pooling the buy money.

On the following day I arrived at the building early in the morning. I took one of the garage attendants aside and explained that I was a detective with the Seventeenth Precinct and we were looking for hot Caddies. Meanwhile I made certain that Jackie's '58 Ford was gone.

Satisfied that Jackie had left, I went to the superintendent's quarters in the basement. Flashing my credentials, I introduced myself to his wife, who told me he was out on an errand. They had at least a nodding acquaintance with the Bureau because a number of U.N. employees and officials lived in the building. In fact, they had on occasion helped agents making security checks on some of these people.

When I had established to my satisfaction that they were respectful of the Bureau, I pulled out a photograph of Jackie, whom she recognized as Mr. Wilson from 17-F. "Is he a spy?" she asked me.

"No, he was put away with a Mafia guy named Vito Genovese for drug trafficking." She recognized several of the other photographs collected from the Federal Bureau of Narcotics. I left, after instructing her to pay attention to the faces of people who came and went and to try to note license plates.

I was reasonably certain now that Jackie and his friends were cutting junk in 17-F. I also asked some agents in the security squads about their experiences with the super and his wife. They vouched for the couple's cooperation with the Bureau, pointing out that they were doing very well running the laundry concession in the building.

The following morning I returned to question the supers and gather the fruits of my labor. To my surprise, the door to their apartment was open. They were gone. None of the tenants or garage employees could tell me why or where, and the building management was as mystified as I by their sudden departure. They had even left their furniture.

I rented a T-bird and took up the watch out near Jackie's house, alone. When he got into his car, he headed out to Aqueduct Racetrack. He paid for parking, drove through the two-dollar lot, and then zipped out the back gate. I reasoned that he had probably made me and remembered that as a parolee he was not to be at a place like Aqueduct. Gucci sped along the Van Wyck Expressway. I pulled alongside, tooting my horn. Obviously unhappy, he parked on the shoulder of the road and waited until I stopped. I walked back and dropped into the seat next to him.

"How's it going, Jackie?"

"You son of a bitch. You fucked me up, showed my picture at the apartment house. Now my boss is mad at me. I'm broke."

"Listen, Jackie, I know what you were doing up there and you're lucky I didn't bust you."

He gave me a very hard eye. "If you tell me what I was doing there, I'll admit it."

I don't claim any great intellect, but when it came to a battle of wits, Jackie Gucci would be overmatched if his opponent was a tree. He knew that I was aware of his history. It couldn't possibly be junk if he was so eager to bet I would be wrong.

There was only one other heavy traffic operations that would pull in high rollers like some of those known drug dealers. "You had a game going in the building with the help of the supers."

"You son of a bitch," said Jackie. "You're smarter than you seemed. You sure scared the shit out of the super. He was on my payroll." That opened the way for a little more talk. Jackie told me that Auriello, the parole officer, had indeed told Gucci what I was trying to do. Actually, I had counted on Auriello's doing just that, because it would make me a much more serious menace in Jackie's mind than if I had threatened to violate him to his face.

"Tell me, Jackie, why are you driving this piece of shit?" I waved toward my T-Bird. "I'll get you a new car—and you don't have to be a stoolie. All I want is the kind of background stuff we talked about at your place. I'll just ask questions and you answer whatever you feel comfortable with."

"What kind of car will you buy me?"

"Anything you want," I promised, although I had a feeling that if he went for the usual Mafia special, a Cadillac, I'd have a hard time down at the Bureau.

"Will you buy me a stripped Chevy? I don't want a Cadillac—it's too conspicuous." He was not totally stupid. I said I'd be delighted to supply him with a Chevrolet. "And can you get Auriello off my back? You got him all hyped up. He thinks I'm going into junk. He's liable to take away my parole. All I'm doing is selling ties. I got a friend who steals them, and I sell 'em to the wiseguys." He showed me a couple of shopping bags with Countess Mara and Oleg Cassini ties in the back of his car.

I created a script for us to feed the parole office. "I'll pay a call on Auriello and tell him I stopped you and thought I caught you selling junk. Only it turned out that you were just peddling ties. I'll be very embarrassed and tell Auriello that I'm dropping the whole thing because it's making me look bad at the Bureau."

Jackie thought it had possibilities. "Call me Sunday morning and we'll see what happens."

The following day, I poured out the sad story to Auriello's delighted ears. I made him swear an oath of silence because this could embarrass me so much I might be transferred to the sticks. I explained how I had followed Jackie. "I saw money change hands, a package passed by Jackie to another hood. I jumped Gucci, threw him against the car, roughed him up a little. Son of a bitch—it was ties, not schmeck! I didn't know what to say. Auriello, I promise I won't bother you again. I'll close the file on Jackie. But if he complains to you, please protect me." Auriello giggled all the way through the story; he was damn near on the floor laughing when I finished.

Naturally he told Jackie everything. But I had it figured right, because this proved to Gucci that I could be trusted to do what I said I would. So we began our relationship.

Every Sunday morning I would load up my car with an outboard motor and fishing poles and pick up Jackie at a place where we could rent a boat. We would circle around and pull up on one of the beaches around JFK Airport. If you walked about five hundred yards from the shore, you had a spot where you could see for a mile in any direction. That gave Jackie a sense of security. As much as he feared being seen by LCN people, Jackie also worried about a cop spotting him and selling him out. That was one reason Jackie preferred Sunday mornings. He believed that the detectives were mostly Irish Catholics who spent Sunday mornings in church.

Jackie constantly fretted over the possibility that his role as an informant might be discovered. He was quite shrewd in the ways in which he strived to keep up appearances. For example, he and Tom Massi had a piece of a homosexual bar. The cops raided the place while both of them were on the premises. Massi lost his temper and knocked one cop down the stairs while Gucci put his arms around a second plainclothesman to restrain him. Along with everything else, the pair faced charges of resisting arrest and assaulting an officer. When Gucci told me about it, I offered to put in a word. He said no; for $2,500 they'd managed to buy off the cops. Giving the plainclothesmen a big score like that improved Jackie's standing among his peers.

He continued my education into the organization. As late as 1966, the Bureau was still ignorant of the ways of the LCN, thanks to the official position taken by Hoover and company over a number of years. We were far behind in our studies. Gucci was an expert on the Gambinos and the factions within the family, which was becoming the most powerful one in New York under Carlo Gambino.

From Jackie we obtained names never mentioned by Joe Valachi—people from Connecticut, New Jersey, and elsewhere, capos whose existence had gone unrecorded in our files and those of the New York cops. Without the roster of players we couldn't hope to follow the turns of the game.

After Jackie Gucci and I got married, the problem was how to keep him out of serious trouble. He did not want to go back into junk—and I can't say I wanted to have an informant who was also a dealer. But Jackie was too old to turn into a nine-to-five clock puncher, and besides, he would be disgraced in his circle of friends. He could survive only through some kind of scam.

He chose to go into the shylocking business, which was agreeable to me. Joe Fingers, Jackie's capo, put up the initial stake for the shylock operation, between five and ten thousand dollars. From a preferred risk, a made guy, Jackie received a point a week interest. Over a year that would add up to a modestly usurious fifty-two percent. Jackie continued to draw street money from Joe Fingers, who probably paid Carlo Gambino half a point for the use of the money. Jackie and Joe Fingers split the half point they kept. But there were many customers who paid more than a point. One client was a stockbroker who was into Jackie for as much as fifty thousand dollars. He paid two points a week. That's about a thousand dollars a week, which should have enabled Jackie to live comfortably on it alone, even after he paid off Joe Fingers. However, the broker's loans fluctuated wildly according to the gyrations of the market. There were also borrowers who came to Jackie for as little as seventy-five dollars. These were tapped-out gamblers who wanted enough to get into a crap game. They had to pay a hundred dollars at the end of the week.

Occasionally Jackie whined to me, "Why do I have to deal with Joe Fingers and Gambino? You have some money, Tony. Let me put it to work on the street and we'll split the profits." That was impossible, of course.

Jackie should have been making at least thirty thousand dollars a year, tax free. Unfortunately, he loved to gamble. When he and Tom Massi started games, Jackie inevitably joined in and lost his dough.

I kept my promise about the car. I told him to buy the Chevrolet of his choice on the installment plan. I would make certain that he received enough to cover the payments, plus something beyond that; the total probably came to two hundred dollars a month. Jackie went to a Chevy dealer with Tom Massi. The two of them thought they were very clever. Each one bought a car exactly like the other's; they even arranged for the license plate numbers to be in sequence. They figured that it would be that much more confusing if anyone tried to follow them.

My biggest worry was that Jackie would backslide and turn feloniously forceful in collecting from a slow payer or a lamster. I had made him promise never to use muscle against someone who didn't pay, but after all, Joe Valachi insisted that Jackie had been a hitter. Gucci would simply laugh about that whenever I mentioned it, but he never denied it, either.

I coached Jackie on how to talk to borrowers in arrears. He would write down the phrases I fed him, like "Don't mistake my patience for weakness." He loved that one.

One day Jackie came to me to complain about a bad debt. He had loaned five thousand dollars to a man who said he owned a bar, only to discover, after the guy skipped, that he was merely a temporary bartender. Jackie asked me to help find him. I said okay, but I never really tried. However, I warned him not to lean on the man when he was found. Gucci protested. "I'm a business-man, not a torpedo anymore." So far as I could determine, Jackie played shylock in unmuscular fashion, never going further than an implied threat. And he loved the business. "I would never have messed with junk if I had met someone like you," he told me. "This is a steady, reliable-type business." It's quite possible that Jackie needed no physical leverage because of his reputation. He had a very cruel, cold stare to his face. With me, however, he was a pussycat. He was so friendly that he wanted me to share his girl friend, who did some hooking on the side.

Jackie once grumbled about his mother-in-law. Working all her life, she'd accumulated about fifteen grand. Gucci wanted to put it to work for her on the street. But she resisted and then fell for a con game with a Gypsy and blew it all. I couldn't find the Gypsy for Jackie, either.

During one of our beach strolls, Jackie asked me to buy him a holster. I really didn't want to know that he carried, but now that he'd offered the information I asked him for an explanation. It seemed that Jackie was seated at the bar in Ed's Tavern in East Harlem, minding his own business, having his one or two drinks. He was a very conservative fellow that way—kept himself from taking on more booze than he could handle. Joe Gurnie, a real bad ass, accompanied by a button man from the Bronx, sat down next to Jackie. Gurnie was not a wiseguy, but he passed himself off as one and he was a very reliable worker for the mob.

On this particular evening, Gurnie happened to be sloppy drunk even before he entered Ed's. He'd done time at Atlanta with Jackie, so when he saw him he called for a round of drinks. Jackie, a model of LCN courtesy, accepted the first drink but begged off the second. Gurnie felt demeaned. "I never trust any-body who doesn't drink," snarled Gurnie. From there, Gurnie erupted into a tirade about how come Jackie had been made while he, Gurnie, was still on the outside. Gurnie went on to the more private areas of Jackie's life, until Gucci could stand the insults no longer. He smashed a drinking glass in Gurnie's face.

Gurnie was five to ten years younger than Jackie and never a pussycat. He came on roaring. Since they were in Jackie's home turf of East Harlem, Jackie did not carry a piece. But he did have a can of Mace with him, and he sprayed Gurnie in the face.

Jackie ran next door to what is known as a social club, a hangout for button men, and asked for a gun. Under the circumstances he figured that he would now have to kill Gurnie. Unfortunately, none of those present possessed a piece, or if they did, they were not willing to part with it. However, two wiseguys from the Gambino organization went back to Ed's with Jackie. Gurnie still had the blind staggers from the Mace, and Gucci's pair of allies proceeded to work him over, stomping him into a bloody mess.

They misjudged Gurnie, however. Still primed with liquor, he scraped himself together and visited his girl's apartment on Seventy-ninth Street, where he cleaned himself up. Then he returned to Ed's Tavern, having somewhere along the way armed himself with two guns. He was ready to hit Jackie and his friends. Fortunately, they had all departed by the time Gurnie arrived. Joe Gurnie sobered up and took his broken body to a hospital. But the issue was not over. Jackie Gucci considered himself to be both mortally offended and threatened by Gurnie.

Jackie consulted with his boss, Joe Fingers, who recommended that Gucci engage the services of one of the surviving old Mustache Petes, Don Cheech, to handle his case. A meet was set up in Brooklyn. As the ultimate boss of all parties, Carlo Gambino, was scheduled to serve as the presiding judge, but instead he sent his underboss, Aniello Dellacroce (literally, "Little Lamb of the Cross"). Don Cheech represented Jackie, while Gurnie's advocate was a Brooklyn capo who backed Gurnie's shylocking operation.

Without dissent it was agreed that the Bronx button man who accompanied Gurnie into Ed's and then stood aside from the action should be censured. Regardless of who was right, he was obliged to help a fellow member in any kind of fight.

That was not enough for the Gucci side. Don Cheech announced, "We still must kill Gurnie. He is a threat."

That was unsatisfactory to Gurnie. Nor did it suit the Brooklyn capo, for Gurnie was shylocking up to sixty thousand dollars weekly on the street and the money would be jeopardized by his death. The capo pledged that his man would refrain from any injury to Jackie Gucci. Don Cheech shrewdly addressed himself to Dellacroce: "And if Gurnie kills Gucci, may I then kill Gurnie's capo?"

That wasn't palatable to at least one of those present. Dellacroce's Solomon-style decision was: If Jackie Gucci came across Joe Gurnie in East Harlem and Gurnie was drinking, then Gucci had a license to kill him. But only under those conditions.

It was not an entirely happy decision for Jackie. He talked of staking out Gurnie's girl friend's apartment on East Seventy-ninth Street, hitting Gurnie when he appeared, and then hauling the body up to East Harlem. But meanwhile, he had taken to carrying a gun in the event that Gurnie should appear under propitious circumstances. And while standing outside Ed's one night he thought he saw Joe Gurnie coming. He backed up against the wall, and the sudden movement jarred the pistol in his pants loose. It slid down and bounced on the pavement right next to a cop on the beat. Fortunately for Jackie, the patrolman ignored the gun. But that was why he needed a holster, to keep the weapon secure in the future. I bought him a holster, which anyone could purchase, as a gift from the Bureau. In the early 1970s Joe Gurnie was found murdered. Jackie Gucci never volunteered, and I never asked about it.

One night Jackie broke his rule about only on Sunday mornings and called me. He had told me that in the early 1950s some people he knew in Boston invited him to participate in a grandiose plan for a robbery. Jackie went up, listened to the preliminary details, and then bowed out because he felt too many individuals were involved. The robbery turned out to be the Brinks holdup. Now one of the minor figures in that crime had approached Jackie with another scheme; this one carried a big payoff and needed only a handful of men. The Bostonian had a kind of special relationship with Jackie; he liked black girls and Jackie could, when the occasion demanded, procure same for him.

Jackie asked me for advice. If he wanted to get more details on the caper he would have to attend a second meeting, but once he went that far he would be obliged to declare himself in or out. Quite selfishly, I urged him to continue as a participant. I assured him that we would find a way to protect him while rewarding him for his efforts.

Jackie attended the second session at a roadhouse off the New York Thruway. We surveilled the place from a parking lot. When Jackie said farewell to his companions and started back to New York City, we waited a bit, then followed him to a spot off the highway, where he filled me in with more details.

An insider claimed that the Republican National Committee had stashed a huge slush fund at the Grosvenor Clinton Hotel in Newburgh, New York. The money was kept on the fifth floor in thirty-two mailbags. Each sack contained two million bucks in cash. The entire floor was guarded twenty-four hours a day. Two people were always present, and they would have to be killed; Jackie's role was hit man. Nobody seemed to doubt his capacity for that job.

We kicked around the ways to proceed. Jackie was willing to go along on the deal, but on one condition: He wanted one of those two-million-dollar mailbags for himself. That was something I was not ready to commit the Bureau to without some upper-level clearance.

Back in the office I sat down with my supervisor and laid out the plot. I offered a plan. The inside man said he would have a pickup parked beneath a window on the fifth floor. The thirty-two mailbags were to be tossed out the window and land in the truck. Jackie and his companions, I said, could stick up the place, but Jackie would convince his associates not to shoot anyone until after the job was done. When the last bag had been disposed of, we'd walk in and place everyone under arrest. Jackie, however, would manage to wriggle free and escape. Then, while I was driving the truck with the evidence to our offices, Jackie would follow me and I would make sure one bag fell off the truck. If anyone questioned the loss of the bag, I would be candid and say it must have fallen off the truck somewhere along the way. Further, in light of the nature of the money, there might not even be any questions about what we recovered.

My supervisor went for the operation. "Don't tell me about any lost bag—I don't even want to know about it. This thing's too big to let slide." The supervisor was the kind of good guy who gave agents enough slack to enable them to make productive moves. I can't use his name even now, because his ways would not be acceptable to the Bureau. In fact, we had to run the Grosvenor Hotel caper undercover within the Bureau. We wouldn't confide in anyone other than the four or five agents who would have to take part. And only one agent aside from the supervisor even knew that Jackie had a mailbag coming to him.

We were dealing with a very chancy thing. There was the possibility that someone could get hurt or killed—or we might slip up altogether and permit a sixty-four-million-dollar robbery to take place even though we knew about it in advance. Bureau instructions specifically state that if an agent becomes aware of a conspiracy to commit a criminal act wherein an innocent person might get hurt, it must be prevented from taking place. But, like most book rules, such restrictions ignore the realities of crime and the criminal justice system. For example, through informants one can learn of a planned bank robbery. It's easy to prevent—just notify the local police of the appointed time and they can park a couple of cruisers in front of the bank and effectively deter anyone from coming on that day. But how long can the cops sit there? If the robbery doesn't go down one day, then maybe it will two weeks later.

And it's nearly impossible to make a case against those who have allegedly drafted a robbery scheme. The best evidence one has is the word of the informant. If you go bust the gang and try to go to trial, your informant not only becomes useless for the future, he's also a prime candidate for a morgue slab. At that, the only case one has is conspiracy to commit a crime, not evidence of an actual attempt to carry out the act. It's damn hard to make "conspiracy to commit a robbery" stick in court, particularly since the only witness is an informant who comes to court usually with dirty hands. He's a vulnerable target for any defense attorney. That's why I pushed for the Grosvenor Hotel robbery to proceed. We could never have touched Jackie's Boston buddy or the inside man at the Grosvenor based on Gucci's knowledge, even if he would have been willing to testify in open court.

Through a license plate check we identified the third man in the deal, the inside guy, who said he was a private guard at the Grosvenor. He had a record that included a rape conviction.

With another agent I traveled to Newburgh to cut in the senior resident agent in that city. We laid out the story, and he was absolutely astounded at what was going on in his backyard. We gave the Grosvenor a careful study, noting the entrances and exits, the ways of access to the fifth floor. We drove out to the home address of the private guard and there, neatly parked next to his garage, was a suitable pickup truck. We drove back to the hotel to talk a bit more. "Just for the hell of it," I said, "I'm going to go to the fifth floor and see if anyone challenges me." I took the elevator to the fourth floor and from there the fire stairway to the top floor. Carrying a concealed camera, I made my way to the site of the money bags.

But when I got there, no one stopped me—and for good reason. The place was empty except for hotel furniture. There were no mail sacks with money; the place wasn't worth the time of a kid burglar.

I asked the Newburgh agent to investigate the inside man, the guard. The agent found out that the finger man was not a guard or any kind of employee of the Republican National Committee. He was just an ex-con who thought a local judge had given him a bum rap for the rape charge. And he didn't feel very kindly toward his parole officer, either. He had intended to bring mail sacks loaded with newspaper to the place to make things look good for Jackie and the Boston contact, who had met the inside man in prison. But he also planned to lure the judge and the parole officer to the fifth floor with the ingenious idea of ripping off a hit man like Jackie; in the course of the robbery, Gucci would kill the judge and parole officer.

When I told Jackie about it, he was furious. "I gotta hit that guy. I gotta teach him a lesson." I told him to cool it and just let his Boston friend know that he'd had problems and would have to drop out of the deal.

For a time, Jackie was an investor in a big Harlem crap game and a monte game with Tom Massi. After Gucci dropped out of the Mafia operation we managed to hit it without exposing him. An informant in Connecticut offered to take us to the site of the game; the cops in Jersey had been rough on gambling, and people from west of the Hudson had been doing their playing in one of the large apartment buildings constructed above the roadway that leads onto the New York side of the George Washington Bridge.

I went undercover for this deal, which meant first that someone had to teach me how to play monte. After I learned the rudiments of the game, the Bureau gave me a big two hundred dollars to play with, which was embarrassing. I saw players holding as much as ten thousand dollars in their fists. The gamblers were an interesting mix: men and women, doctors, bankers, shylocks, numbers operators, even a gunrunner. Once I established my credentials as a regular fellow I managed to introduce another agent as a player. He in turn brought in a third agent so there would be no problem in testifying about the operation. When we busted the game, we got maybe twenty people. Two of those arrested were button men. All pleaded guilty to gambling felonies except for a few of the lesser lights, who were cut loose.

My success with Jackie Gucci meant some good busts for the office and, more important, produced a basic who's who in organized crime. It also freed me from the routine of the company. I didn't have to wear snap-brim hats, dark suits, white shirts with ties, or welts on my shoes, those protectors against soggy feet which automatically signal to the cognoscenti of crime that the fuzz is present.

Jackie Gucci occupied only a small part of my life, actually. I was always busy trying to turn other guys. Shortly after Jackie and I teamed up, I began to focus on another name fed to me, Michael Firenze*, known to his intimates as "Mickey Flowers." He was a relatively new member of LCN and had just been released from prison for an armed robbery stretch. Supposedly Mickey belonged to the Gambinos as a soldier under Tony Scotto.

Based on what I could find in his record and what I gathered from gossip, I decided to check him out through his wife. I figured she had a king-size peeve against Mickey, since it was no secret that he spent most of his time with girl friends. At his legal address I formally introduced myself to her, explaining that this was just a routine check on a recently released federal prisoner; it was part of the system to make certain a parolee lived where he was listed. I didn't think it would hurt me if I innocently needled her on her husband's whereabouts.

She heard me out, went to the phone, dialed a number, and then shocked the shit out of me. "Ask Mickey where he lives.

. . . Ask him direct. Don't ask me." And she passed me the receiver.

I identified myself in the approved manner. He was less than cordial: "What the fuck you want with me?" I told him I wanted to exchange a few words and could I see him now.

"I'm at the Pink Slipper on Eighty-sixth Street. It's my joint."

"I'll be right over. I won't embarrass you. I'll park across the street and you just come out and we'll talk." He wasn't happy about it but agreed.

I had another agent, Charlie Garvey, with me and we pulled over to the curb across from the Pink Slipper. When Firenze walked out, I recognized him immediately from the photographs in our files. "Charlie, maybe I should roll up the window. I think he's going to spit at me."

But Mickey Flowers contained himself, and I invited him into our back seat. I thought I had him easy. "You just told me you own that joint. I could shut it down, break your stones by registering a complaint with the State Liquor Authority. However, I'd rather be friends with you."

"What do you want?"

"I could help you, Mickey." I hoped I sounded sincere. "I could be an umbrella for you and get you some money. I'm not interested in anybody selling a hot watch in your bar. But we could do some business."

The situation was somewhat the same as my initial encounter with Jackie Gucci. I had never expected to catch up to Mickey ten minutes after I saw his wife and have him in a vulnerable position so swiftly. I wasn't prepared to negotiate with him; for one thing, I had another agent with me and I knew that made it much more difficult for a guy like Mickey to relax.

He thought about what I said and then replied, "You call me at the bar in a couple of days and we'll set something up." He walked back to his joint.

"Charlie, he looks like a winner to me," I bragged.

"Bullshit. He's stroking you, that's all."

A few days later I reached Mickey by phone. I gave him the name of a motel and a date. I said I'd tell him the room number after I registered so he could come directly to the room without having to advertise his presence.

I picked out a place on Staten Island, and on the appointed evening I called Mickey and gave him the room number. Then I waited for him. He never showed.

The next day in the office I saw Charlie Garvey. He laughed at me and said Mickey Flowers was just jerking me off.

I called Firenze again and he was very apologetic. We made similar arrangements for another evening. He stiffed me a second time. He stopped taking my calls at the Pink Slipper. I bet Charlie Garvey a cup of coffee that I would turn him.

I started to watch the Pink Slipper. One day Mickey drove off in his car and I followed him, right into the heart of Gallo country, the part of Brooklyn where the Gallos held out in their war against the Profaci Family. It was hostile territory for Firenze.

He went into a building and stayed for about an hour. Evidently he had a broad stashed there. While he was upstairs I locked his car door on the driver's side. When he came out and tried to get in, he couldn't. As he reached for his car keys, I rushed up and grabbed him by the arm and gave him hell.

He was scared stiff when he saw me, not because of who I was but where we were. "Are you crazy? You want to get me killed?" He broke away from me, jumped into his car, and drove off. I followed him, blowing my horn, sticking right on his tail all the way. I stuck with him through red lights, full stops, and traffic for miles before he finally pulled over. He was physically exhausted; his shirtfront was soaked with sweat, and beads stood out on his forehead.

"You motherfucker, you made a fool out of me!" I yelled. "Now either I come into your place and I throw my money across the bar where everyone can see it or you can meet me on the quiet." He accepted the proposition and we arranged to meet at a motel at JFK Airport.

The whole thing almost collapsed because of an officious room clerk. I registered at the place under the name of Tony Damiano. The clerk took my money and then asked to see some identification. I argued that he had been paid in advance, what was the purpose of the ID. He insisted and I blew my cork. I asked for the manager. He started off talking about the motel's policy of verified identifications from all guests. Since Firenze was going to ask for Damiano's room, I wasn't in a position to give up my right name. Anything suspicious would have spooked him. The whole thing was a sham, since this particular motel turned out to have been a favorite meeting ground for a variety of thieves and swindlers. Finally I yelled that my driver's license was in my car parked in the lot and if they wanted to see it they could walk out there with me. My act convinced the manager and he did not press for identification.

When Firenze showed, it did not take long to work out a business deal. Mickey Flowers was pure whore; he would sell anything and anybody for money, including associates in crime. He began with the usual limitations, the no-skin-off-my-ass past history of LCN. He revealed who was responsible to whom, the connections that could be so valuable in figuring out how a load of hijacked whiskey moved or why an individual had been killed.

Mickey entertained me with some stories of how he ripped off people in the trade. He was approached by a guy who said that a Harlem contact wanted a kilo of heroin. Mickey did not deal in junk; not for reasons of morality—it just wasn't his trade. However, he told his acquaintance to get him an introduction to the buyer.

At the meeting, Mickey listened to the black junk dealer's desires and then agreed. "I can supply it, but it's going to cost you twenty-five thousand dollars cash on delivery." That was a bargain price for a quantity of good-quality merchandise; it ought to have alerted the dealer, but he was eager.

"Here's how we'll do it," said Firenze. "You watch the shipping news in the New York *Times*. In a few weeks you'll see that a boat named the *Vera Cruz* will be coming to New York. If it says the ship docks at ten A.M., then you be under the West Side Highway at Fifty-ninth Street at ten P.M., and if it's due at night, then you be there on the morning of the day following. Bring the money and anybody like a chemist who you want to test the shit. But under no circumstances can there be more than two of you—I don't intend to be ripped off."

On the right day and time Mickey drove to the spot under the West Side Highway. In the trunk of his car he had a one-kilo package, all sugar. The black dude arrived with his chemist and the two cars stopped next to one another, motors running. Mickey saw that the package of money looked all right. He reached for the kilo when suddenly an approaching siren interrupted the transaction. "Quick, let's get the fuck out of here," ordered Firenze, slamming the trunk shut. "We can get in touch later if either of us have any beefs about the deal." He raced away and so did the buyer, with his kilo of sugar. What the buyer didn't know was that the approaching "cops" were some of Mickey's friends in a car equipped with a siren. Naturally, the black man never managed to catch up with Firenze. Mickey said his profit came to about five thousand dollars.

On another occasion, a woman approached a pal of Firenze's about paying for a hit. She had a boy friend of whom she was now weary. She had a good job, and she was expecting to marry a well-heeled businessman. Only, the old boy friend refused to get the message. He continued to visit her and to inflict an occasional beating. He was in general a pain in the ass and a threat to her future.

Firenze instructed his pal to tell her that it could be done for ten thousand dollars, payable on proof that the boy friend had been disposed of. Several weeks later, Mickey and another associate trailed the boy friend into a secluded street, took his wallet, and left him sufficiently battered to keep him from going anywhere for several hours.

Mickey and his accomplice then rushed to the woman's apartment and announced themselves as New York City detectives from the Sixty-second Precinct. They flashed gold shields, either facsimiles or stolen. Mickey was a heavyset, gray-haired guy, very tough-talking, who could easily pass for a cop. He told the woman that they had some very sad news for her. A hit-and-run driver had struck and killed her boy friend. Firenze showed her the boy friend's wallet, explaining that they had traced their way to her through its contents. She put on a great act, sobbing and wailing. Mickey reacted very sympathetically. "We haven't been able to reach his relatives, but we need someone to come down to the morgue and make the formal identification of the body. Why don't we come back in a couple of hours—give you a chance to get yourself together and they can clean up the body. The car really smashed him up badly—maybe it was even a truck that hit him. We'll drive you down, then bring you back here."

She expressed gratitude for their compassion and understanding. Mickey and his chum left. About an hour later the original contact arrived at her apartment and claimed the ten thousand dollars. Firenze said he had almost been willing to give up his share of the score if he could have been there to see her face when the bruised but live boy friend showed up.

With every other informant, I found myself developing a personal relationship, no matter how much I tried to guard against it. But I had no such difficulties with Mickey Flowers. He was so venal, and a sexual degenerate to boot. He refused to talk to me on the telephone, not because he feared for security but because he wanted cash on the barrelhead for any information, even a little background on a guy we might be interested in at the moment. If a girl wanted a job in his joint, he was likely to require her to bestow her favors on all his friends.

In the beginning he had been willing to feed us only the background stuff. I soon opened his nose with a whiff of the reward money available for hijackings and he began to tumble those to us. We always protected him, and any other informants, creating an elaborate fiction about how we had a call from a nearby resident about a bunch of guys with a truck at an odd hour of the night, or that we happened to be in an area doing a surveillance on someone and by pure chance we noticed some strange behavior by men in a warehouse.

One night in the late sixties I spoke with Mickey on the telephone. He then went to a lounge in Brooklyn with his son Tommy. Also present was another wiseguy, Charlie Manzione,* who was with a girl that had once been on very familiar terms with Mickey. On the way out of the place, Mickey paused at the Manzione table to pay his disrespects. He whispered a couple of things in the woman's ear; she laughed—they both laughed. Then Firenze left with his son. Tommy Firenze walked on after Manzione came out and started to talk with Firenze. Suddenly the son heard a shot and turned to see Manzione, smoking gun in hand, standing over the body of his father. Manzione took off.

When I first received the news of Mickey's death, I got the guilt sweats thinking word had gotten out that Mickey had rolled over for me, that I was the cause of his death. The only way I thought I could find out anything was through the son. I couldn't go to the cops—I owed Mickey that much. It would be too much of a gamble that the word might get out that stand-up Mickey Flowers had been an informant. I also wondered how much his son knew about his father's business and whether he might have some valuable information.

I called the Pink Slipper and reached Tommy Firenze. "This is Tony Damiano, your father's friend. I'd like to see you." Tommy knew that I had had some dealings with his father, since he'd often answered the telephone at the Pink Slipper, where he worked as a kind of bartender and assistant manager.

We agreed to meet near Plum Beach in Brooklyn, in a parking lot off the Belt Parkway. I drove up in my rented car, and in the parking lot I saw another vehicle; it was an unmarked cop car. I took off. Later I called Tommy Firenze at the Pink Slipper and explained that I hadn't been able to keep our date. However, since I was close by, could he meet me at the phone booth on the platform of the elevated line a couple of blocks away from the Pink Slipper? He accepted the invitation.

About fifteen minutes later, I saw him coming up on the elevated platform; I knew him from photographs we had made of people who went in and out of the Pink Slipper. But he had company with him—two guys who seemed very much like city detectives. I popped into a train that came along. He, of course, didn't know what I looked like.

A few days later, Warren Donovan, one of our old-time agents whose chief business was to maintain liaison with the local police, reported to me. "You know, you've got half the cops in Brooklyn trying to pick you up. They think that a Tony Damiano is involved in a homicide case." Donovan was aware that I used the Damiano alias. When the cops asked Donovan if the Bureau knew a hood named Tony Damiano, he had protected my real identity. All this made me even more anxious to speak with young Firenze.

I staked out the place where he lived. When I saw him enter, I rang the bell and introduced myself as Tony Damiano. "Hey, the cops want to see you," said Tommy. I explained my relationship with his father and the reason I did not want to go to the police. He didn't believe me. I told him some of the more personal details of his father's life, how Mickey had been negotiating to buy another bar and turn it over to the kid. I knew the location they had contemplated and even supplied the name of the fronts used by Mickey to obtain licenses from the State Liquor Authority.

That satisfied Tommy Firenze about my identity and relationship with his father. I asked him about the night Mickey was killed. He refused to give me any names, but he described everything that happened, particularly the scene where his father paused at Manzione's table and engaged the girl in a private conversation that brought giggles from her. Evidently, Manzione became incensed at the liberties Mickey was taking with his female friend and believed they were both laughing at him. He whipped himself into enough passion to confront Firenze outside the lounge. True to character, Mickey Flowers must have responded with another nasty insult and gotten himself killed.

I asked the kid if he'd like to make a few bucks the way his father had, through information. He emphatically did not. He said he had no part in anything greater than occasionally trucking to New York a load of tax-free cigarettes from North Carolina. As soon as possible he intended to sell the Pink Slipper, and his biggest fear had been that the Tony Damiano who kept calling the bar meant to hit him. That's why he had turned the New York cops on my tail.

Anyone working for the Bureau on an organized crime squad couldn't help becoming knowledgeable about narcotics cases. Technically it was not our responsibility but that of the Federal Bureau of Narcotics, a wholly independent arm of the Treasury Department and heavily seamed with corruption. Luckily, I had made friends with one straight agent there named Eddie Guy. We took to exchanging bits and pieces of information. One night Eddie mentioned to me Rico Conte,* newly out of the federal penitentiary after a stiff sentence for junk. Conte still owed a lot of time if he broke any rules of parole. I went through the files we had on him and found a wealth of unused and ignored information. Rico Conte was the wiseguy who in the fifties had spelled out the operations of organized crime to special agents, but whom, under Hoover's spell, nobody had believed. One of the revelations was the story of the blinding of newspaper columnist Victor Riesel for his unsolicited interest in the criminal control of some unions. A psycho named Abraham Telvi had been conned into tossing acid into Riesel's face. The mob then got rid of Telvi.

Conte had in the past given up some fringe people; he was

always careful not to point a finger at any real wiseguys. He was a kind of gentleman. During a hijacking, Conte noticed the discomfort of the driver, who was bound and blindfolded while the truck was being unloaded at a drop. "I hate to see you suffering like this," Conte said to the driver. "I'll take the ropes and blindfold off if you'll keep your mouth shut later."

"I won't identify anyone," promised the driver, who was, as in so many of these incidents, a knockaround guy himself. Everyone got along so famously that the driver even asked if he might be dropped off near his home to avoid any inconvenience. Conte obliged and even invited him to return to the drop in a day or so and have a case of Scotch on the house. When the driver was interviewed by the cops, he gave descriptions of the hijackers and the drop that left the cops hunting in the sticks far from the site of the action.

Conte displayed nice manners and his grammar was superior to mine, but he was a very tough guy. He had led a prison break in New York. Although he was short, bald, what I would describe as near ugly, Conte had a marvelous reputation as a lover. He had lived off and on with a variety of showgirls, including some smashers whose names had gone up in lights.

From what I learned in the file I decided that Conte had the potential to be turned. Eddie Guy assured me that Conte was definitely a made guy. When Jackie Gucci vouched for Conte, telling me that even Vito Genovese respected him in Atlanta, I became obsessed with the idea of turning him.

Conte's last known residence was in Connecticut. The rules forbade me to cross state lines unless I at least notified the office that had jurisdiction there. I went anyway, without informing the New Haven office or the parole people. After my experience with Auriello and Jackie Gucci, I figured to avoid the federal parole people whenever possible.

The address was in one of the slummier parts of town, a shabby tenement building. I rang the doorbell; it was answered by a woman I shall call Anne, whom Conte lived with and called his wife. I asked for Conte without explaining who I was. She invited me in for a cup of coffee and asked me a few questions about how long I had known Rico and from where. I avoided any of these traps by telling her that actually I wasn't personally acquainted with Rico. My brother, I said, had been away with Rico and had asked me to look him up.

I had on my casual clothes—a golf jacket, an old pair of slacks. Anne studied me and asked, "How long have you been out?"

"How can you tell?" I replied.

"I've been around; I know. When a guy pulls a job the hard way it shows," Anne said.

"I'm not a tough guy," I said. "I used a pen, strictly paper." She kept pecking away at my history. "Jesus, you're worse than my parole officer," I complained.

She apologized. "I know it's hard when you come out."

"Yeah, I only have a borrowed car. I've got to get back."

I edged over by the telephone at the door. I wanted a peek at the number. I did not want to have to go through Conte's parole officer in order to get the listing. But Conte had forestalled me. He had removed the card containing the number from the dial face.

"Gee, Anne, what are you, a hooker? You have to keep your telephone number a secret?"

She laughed. "The fucking cops tap the phones all the time, so we try to keep it private." She obligingly supplied the number.

As I was about to leave she asked me to drop her off at the supermarket. Fortunately, I had a rented car; she would have instantly recognized a government car.

A couple of days later I telephoned and Anne answered. I had left as my surname for Conte the original Anglo-Saxon first name of the first agent who had obtained some information from him. I hoped that would trigger his memory for him and help him figure out my purpose. In fact, Anne had nearly caught me at the time. As soon as I told her the name she said, "Go on, you're a wop! I can tell."

I countered with an excuse that since my troubles with the law I now used the surname of my half brother. "That way you don't automatically get the OC after your name on the records." She bought it.

But Conte was never there when I called. I didn't know whether he had doped out my scheme or just did not want to talk on the telephone. I drove up to Connecticut again, but I had apparently just missed him. Anne and I went through the same coffee-in-the-kitchen bit. I wasn't getting to Rico, but I was doing great with his friend. I gave Anne a number for Rico to call. It was a special line in the office that did not go through the regular switchboard; someone answers hello and the caller gives the name of the person he wants.

About two hours after I was back at the office Rico called me. He had apparently not grasped the purpose behind my subtle use of the surname. "I understand you came to see me," he said quite graciously. "Anne vouches for your character—she's one sharp bitch—but I wasn't born yesterday. Nobody leaves their number except fucking cops. Who do you think you're jerking off?"

I confessed my identity. "But you have to admit I managed to sell myself to Anne."

"I'm very impressed," said Conte. He didn't sound enthusiastic.

"What about the courtesy of a little talk?"

"No. I'm old and through with that life. I want to be left alone." He said it nicely, not the way Mickey Flowers would have talked.

"I made two trips up there. The least reward is to be able to say hello to the guy who was the boy friend of—" I gave him the name of one of the really headliner stars with whom he had shacked up.

"You know about her?"

"I know even more."

"Done your homework."

"I'm very conscientious."

It wasn't much of an opening but enough to get him to agree to one meeting at a parking lot in a shopping center. We hit it off immediately. I came in a flashy car that said money all over it. And I went to work on Rico Conte the same way I worked on Jackie Gucci. "I see they really took care of your wife. You go away and they set her up on Park Avenue in a regular palace."

"I came home, needed a stake from friends," Rico answered. "I can't believe how times have changed. The only money they offered was to be a loan. I went to a close old friend down on the lower East Side. He greeted me warmly, asked, 'How are you fixed?'

"I said, 'I'm hurting.'

" 'Could you use a few grand?'

" 'Could I ever.'

" 'Okay, all you have to do is a small favor for me. Go over to see Black Sal in the Fourth Ward [old-timers still cut up the city in terms of the old election districts]. He'll give you something to deliver to a place in East Harlem.' "

Rico became really indignant. "Here I go to see an old friend and he knows I owe a lot of time if I get in trouble and this guy wants me to haul junk. I lost my temper. I told him to shove his money and his package up his ass. I'll never forget that fuck. Someday maybe I'll cop a sneak on [kill] him."

I switched my attack with another routine. "I don't want to know about anything that's going down now. I only want to pick your brain, learn some ancient history, have you educate me. You know how it is with an outfit like the Bureau. They like to make charts, have lines going between the pictures." He laughed, but as a matter of fact, J. Edgar Hoover and his spiritual descendants relied heavily on charts to wow congressmen around appropriations time.

Rico grinned. "Where's my picture on the charts?"

"I don't remember its exact location, but I know it's there." He was proud of the fact that he was a genuine made guy, even if he felt that the organization had forsaken its virtues and rotted.

I asked him about the occasion on which he was made, the ceremony, and who had participated. He laughed again. He asked me whether I paid any attention to the ritual when I was made a Boy Scout. He reminded me that you don't sit around and seriously reminisce about the pledge taken, the knots tied, and who was there. He considered the act of being made as juvenile as the oath-taking of the Scouts. I felt like a fool, because as a newcomer to the study of organized crime, I had spent a lot of time thinking about such empty gestures as the membership ritual. Rico, who in contrast to Jackie Gucci probably had an IQ of 140, was a man who knew the relative importance of things.

I asked him who he was with.

"Three Fingers Brown."

"Who?"

"Three Fingers Brown." He was patient, thinking I might not have heard the first time.

"What was the name?"

"Three Fingers Brown!" Rico was a bit exasperated by my apparent deafness. The truth is I had never heard of Three

Fingers Brown and the information I had put Rico in Carlo Gambino's camp. [Thomas Lucchese, aka "Tommy Three Fingers Brown," had been a founding father of the modern LCN structure. He prospered until he became a family head himself. My ignorance was a measure of the Bureau's innocence about the personas of organized crime.]

"That may be what you call him," I stalled, "but we must have him under a different name at the office."

"Tommy Brown, Tommy Brown." My denseness was irritating him.

I tried hard not to come off as a total schmuck. "Oh yeah, oh yeah, Tommy Brown, of course." I had no idea who he was talking about.

"Who's your capo?" I asked.

"Larry Jo Jo.*" I was smart enough not to profess ignorance about Larry Jo Jo, although we had not a single reference to him in all of our files and this was more than nine years after Apalachin. In fact, it took us a solid year to identify Larry Jo Jo and his connections. With a little more prodding, Rico gave me the names of the other soldiers in his group. Only a few of them had turned up on our charts.

We had talked for about an hour, and before we split I said, "Here's a hundred. This is not a payment as an informer. This is from me." Which wasn't exactly true, since eventually I collected the outlay from the Bureau. "I'll call you in a week or so, after I've digested what you've told me."

Just as with Jackie Gucci, I had refrained from taking notes during my chat with Rico Conte in the parking lot. But as soon as he left, I hurried back to the office to get the information down on paper and show off the fruits of my conquest. As soon as I found out who Tommy Brown was, I went to Guy Berado, the coordinator (straw boss) for the group working on the Lucchese Family. The agents in that unit had been unable to develop any informants in Lucchese's group.

Berado had a desk in the squad room. Other agents sat around him in the open area. "I've got a member source in the Lucchese Family," I announced. Everybody in the vicinity lent me their ears.

"Who is it?" asked Berado.

"Rico Conte."

Berado smiled. "He's not a member. I never heard of him. Who's his boss?"

"Larry Jo Jo."

"Who the hell is that?"

"I don't know any more about his name than that." I cursed myself as an idiot for not having been sly enough to have gotten from Conte the real name of Larry Jo Jo.

"Who else is in the group?"

I supplied a handful of names dropped by Rico.

Berado burst out laughing. "Somebody is stroking you, Tony. These people don't exist. I'd know if they were real. I've worked on the Lucchese Family for years. I can name every member, and there are only fifty."

"You're dealing with the top half of the iceberg," I persisted. "Conte told me they have more than a hundred people."

"Go ahead and write it up," said Berado. "But you're making a fool of yourself."

The experience illustrated one of the serious problems within the Bureau. By 1966 we had become desperate for information about the workings of organized crime. There was a tremendous premium on the development of member sources. If an agent turned someone, he was automatically recommended for an incentive award that brought an extra $150 or $200 bonus and a letter of praise from Director Hoover. The Bureau played its own numbers game, seeking to claim numerous specific penetrations for congressional consumption. As a result, there was considerable pressure to make an informant a member source, even though technically he might not qualify.

On several occasions it was suggested to me that I make so-and-so a member source, even though the individual did not enjoy the distinction of having been formally made. But I resisted, except in the case of Mickey Flowers. When Firenze was about to be made, he was blackballed by another individual, who claimed Firenze had finked to the cops. By the time Mickey Flowers proved himself innocent of the charge, the books had closed. He never was made, but his credentials were so good that he was accepted among the wiseguys as one of them. He was even assigned to a capo when discharged from Atlanta.

With all of this encouragement to produce member sources, and the recognition by outlaws that they could beat or ease raps if they supplied information about organized crime, we brick agents had to be very cautious in accepting the memoirs of volunteers. For example, we had a call one day that there was a prisoner in the Tombs (the New York City jail) who wanted to talk to agents familiar with OC. Another agent and I went to visit the man, who had been arrested for a double homicide. We had just uncovered the graveyard described by Kayo Konigsberg, and the man in the Tombs said he knew where there was another Mafia graveyard. He offered to show us where it was, provided we hung some sort of federal rap on him and removed him from the jurisdiction of the New York cops. I started to check him out. He said he was in the Gambino Family, had been made by Albert Anastasia, and that he'd made nine hits. I asked him how he got started.

"Doing favors."

"Like what?"

"Beating up people—first one was a lawyer."

"How much would Albert pay for a hit?"

"Five hundred."

"Where were you made?"

"Back of a bar. They burned a picture in my hand."

"Where's the graveyard?"

"It's in Staten Island, but I can't tell you exactly. You'll have to drive me to the vicinity. You can get me out on a writ."

"How did you handle your last hit for the Gambinos?"

"Shot him in the head."

The story was too pat. "I don't believe you. You say you're a torpedo, you beat up guys, but you don't look that tough to me."

"Who do you think is tough?" he challenged me.

"Kayo Konigsberg."

"Put me in a cell with him and I'll kill him."

"Hell, Kayo's a beast. You don't know what you're saying. How are you going to kill him?"

"I'll bite him, bite his throat."

I wasn't convinced. "Let's see how tough you are. I'll arm wrestle you." Right there in the interview room we arm wrestled and I flattened him in a couple of seconds.

"I'm in a weakened condition," he protested. "I've been cooped up in this cell too long." We talked some more and it became increasingly obvious to me that he knew all the right words for his song but didn't know the tune. We checked him out with other agencies. He'd done some informing for Federal Narcotics and had given them some good junk pinches. He had some credibility, but he really just wanted to use us to get away from that double homicide rap the New York cops had on him. This was the kind of thing we confronted frequently; the stories at first had the ring of truth, or else somebody skillfully tried to spoon-feed us information that they knew we already had. In either case the material was worthless.

The total number of actual member sources developed nationally amounted to about a dozen, including a couple of names that would shock both the public and the LCN. The other half of the informant problem lay in people like Guy Berado. Experts, self-proclaimed or legitimate, generally react unfavorably to poachers on their territory, particularly if the results diminish the resident sage's claim to omniscience. Berado treated me as an interloper messing with the tidy little charts and reports he prepared to demonstrate his expertise. He was engaged in an exercise perfected by a number of deskbound investigators, the art of report writing. It was a skill that a number of agents developed to protect themselves during J. Edgar Hoover's war on Communism and subversion. An agent assigned to monitor the radical faction of the International Workers Order would periodically comb through ten years of files on what was a moribund organization and dig up enough stuff to splice and rework into a complication on the IWO's activities. The process was carried over into the organized crime program. The agent responsible for a crime family could mine the old reports, add a little new information from the local police plus some gossip from a brick agent, and presto, he presented the Bureau with what passed for a fresh, meaningful look at a segment of organized crime.

Some people rationalized this by saying that the system demanded a report on a case every forty-five days whether or not anything new had occurred. But for others it was simply a manifestation of laziness, time-serving until the pension or private-industry offer came along.

When I or some other brick agent developed material that challenged all of those paper-thin studies of organized crime, it posed a threat to Guy Berado. The fact is, I didn't know enough about the Lucchese Family to have invented anything. When we finally started to dig into our files, we began to come across the

names given to me by Rico Conte. The true makeup of the
Lucchese Family began to fall into place. The agents on the
squad who were sincerely trying to do a job appreciated what I
had uncovered. And as I continued to pick up things from Conte,
they became even more confident in my findings. But I can't say I
ever made a friend of Guy Berado.

In any event, the courtship with Rico Conte had been success-
ful and I married for the third time. Slowly I was giving up the
niceties and rituals expected by my demanding mistress, J. Edgar
Hoover. I no longer had to write reports, but could spend all my
energies contacting and developing informants. But of all the
sources I developed, Conte proved to be the most complete warehouse of material on LCN. He could spit out details and identifications like a well-stocked computer. He recalled conversations,
meetings, infinitesimal details. He had a gift for remembering
faces. I could show him a picture and even if he did not know the
name he would say, "I never met him personally, but I know of
him." Rico would pinpoint the individual's associations and his
place in the infrastructure.

I remember Rico's smile when I handed him one picture. "See
that greaseball [a nonderogatory term applied to old-timers, like
a Mustache Pete]? He was a road hitter," Rico said. "This was a
guy who if Tony Accardo in Chicago had a problem, Tony could
call Lucchese. 'I need a favor. I got somebody to hit and he knows
everybody I got.' Lucchese would send out this greaseball. It had
to be handled that way because neither Accardo nor Lucchese
would assign a hit to some free-lance operator who couldn't be
trusted." This was the kind of work that Jackie Gucci occasionally handled.

Rico explained to me that in some cases a family would only
accept as a member a guy who had a notch. But in recent years,
Conte remarked (as have others), "they were making people who
had never even cracked an egg."

It was Rico who taught me the real nuances of the organization, the language that sounded so innocent but was in fact
loaded with meaning. Because he had floated among several
families, he could teach me the subtle differences. Members from
Brooklyn spoke differently from wiseguys on New York's East
Side. Organized crime went by a number of different names
around the country. To racket guys in Kansas City it was the

Combination or Syndicate, Chicago called it the Outfit or the Arm, New England referred to it as the Office, while Philadelphia used the Big Boys or the Italian Club. The Jackie Guccis anglicized Joe Valachi's "La Cosa Nostra" into "Our Thing." For uniformity, the Bureau reports used the initials LCN. "Wiseguy" and "made guy" signified a bona fide member, but among the elect there were additional locutions such as "goodfellow" and "dear fellow." When two strangers met and it was possible that one or both belonged, the pair would engage in a studied dialogue designed to reveal the extent of one's connections. The key phrase that signaled an individual's connections would be something along the lines of "a very dear friend of mine," et cetera. In the old days candidates for membership underwent a kind of schooling to teach them the proper ways to dress, behave, and talk.

Rico would never admit to me that he'd done anything. However, once we had begun our relationship he constantly reported to me deals that he was being offered. I told him to reject them all, because I knew that he could no longer face going back to serve time. I became so fond of him that I dreaded the possibility that as a favor to me he might become involved in something. He was having a hard time, even with the payments I could get for him. He stayed clean, however, arranging things like vending-machine and jukebox installations. The money behind these businesses wasn't clean, but Conte's work was strictly legitimate.

In 1968 he let me in on an internal scandal in organized crime, a symptom of the breakdown in the old, carefully regulated system. Some renegades had begun to kidnap junk dealers and hold them for ransom. The first individual that they took off was Tony Shoes, a big trafficker in junk despite Vito Genovese's warnings to people like Shoes not to fool with it. Opportunists like Shoes sneaked it, however. Genovese and the other family heads often took a semipublic position against dope. But every family trafficked in it and the boss accepted his cut.

After they snatched Tony Shoes, the kidnappers telephoned his wife and told her that the price for her husband's release was fifty thousand dollars. Apparently she was somewhat miffed at Shoes or else she didn't take the affair seriously. She shut them off. "I wouldn't give you fifty bucks for him." A few days later she received a package. In it she found the head of her late husband. The best that Mario Puzo could imagine in *The Godfather* was the head of a horse in the bed of a man who needed some convincing.

The next to be kidnapped was Joseph "Jo Jo" Manfredi's nephew. Manfredi owned Ed's Tavern, the site of Jackie Gucci's brawl with Joe Gurnie, but Jo Jo was into junk. His nephew, Mike Luongo, operated a gas station and served as an intermediary and heroin deliveryman. With the memory of Tony Shoes's fate still sharply etched in his mind, Jo Jo bought his nephew's life for thirty-five thousand dollars. The payoff occurred in a Queens bowling alley. Actually, Jo Jo himself had nearly been grabbed. The renegades, a mixture of whites and blacks, tried to use phony credentials from the Federal Bureau of Narcotics for the kidnapping of Jo Jo. He managed to run off, but not before they pegged a few shots at him. The last I heard of Jo Jo was that he was serving twenty years for narcotics.

The gang struck again, hitting a couple of Bronx guys for fifty and seventy-five thousand dollars. The organization became very anxious; the word was that the gang had pulled off six kidnappings. A reward supposedly was offered to identify the leader, but whoever the mastermind was, he had so far managed to keep himself hidden.

Putting together the information that Rico and Jackie Gucci had given me, I was able to narrow down the leader's identity to a man who could be shown to have had links to every victim. Joseph Benintende was a Gambino soldier who lived in Queens and was one of the first to be convicted for arranging a fix on a college basketball game. I did some surveillance on him, watching him in his travels to East Harlem, the Bronx, in and out of bars and games.

He noticed me after a while and I made my pitch to him. "I know a lot about you—maybe I could be helpful," I volunteered without committing myself. Joseph Benintende was a neat piece of work; he turned me down, politely but pointedly. But I kept after him. On our fifth meeting I put it to him bluntly. "There's a price on your head. You're the guy who's behind all the kidnappings. Unless we can play my song, I'm going to do a solo about you."

He denied it, laughed at my suspicions. I said I'd give him a week to think about it. I had the feeling that I had reached him, but when he called me it was only to protest even more vehemently that he was innocent of the offenses against his fellow criminals.

I tried another tack. I went to the Twenty-third Precinct in East Harlem. They had a case going against Jo Jo Manfredi and a phone tap on his place, Ed's Tavern. They had recorded the phone call demanding the ransom from Manfredi and giving him instructions for its delivery. I sat down with a detective on the case and swapped information with him, giving him my theories about Joe Benintende. The detective summoned his superior and we kicked the possibilities around. But we couldn't come up with a plausible strategy to exploit my suspicions.

I temporarily gave up on Benintende to work on some other cases. And then his body was found floating in Long Island Sound. The rumor that came through Jackie Gucci was that the cops had sold Benintende out to the mob. I have occasionally wondered whether it was the cops that I spoke with or some others who had figured out the cast of characters. It was also conceivable that the junk merchants had put together their information, come up with Benintende's name, and made the cops the fall guys for selling the information.

The rumor of an open contract, worth fifty thousand dollars, for the kidnap-gang head was bull; so are the claims of hundred-thousand-dollar open contracts on Joe Valachi and Vincent Teresa after they rolled over. If some wiseguy hit one of them, did he drive to the late Carlo Gambino's home on Ocean Parkway in Brooklyn and present a bill? Did he tell Carlo to raise the money by assessing the membership one hundred dollars apiece?

Hits are normal practice in the business of organized crime, just as firings are for legitimate enterprises. The tales of free-lance hitters, like the celebrated killer Joey, are a crock. When General Motors cans an employee, a company personnel officer hands him the pink slip. In LCN, an individual whose work or conduct is bad for the organization is terminated by a member who has been assigned the task as part of his duties.

Of my first three member sources, only Mickey Flowers continued to be an active criminal. Jackie Gucci stuck to a genteel kind of shylock operation, while Rico Conte limited his muscle to pushing around vending machines. And after Charlie Manzione took such violent exception to Mickey Flowers's remarks to his girl friend, I no longer could count on information from an active member. I started to hunt for a new source.

In the office files I came across an active burglar and fence named Julio, who had once performed some services for the Bureau. In the early 1960s he had been arrested in the course of an armed robbery. He fled the state, and the agents who seized him had him ice cold. Julio could look forward to a long stretch in prison, but miraculously he walked. The facts confided to me by the agents involved never made their way onto any official papers that I know of. Julio continued the story and supplied additional details.

The Bureau, and J. Edgar particularly, had been drawing a lot of heat in the early 1960s for failing to protect the civil rights of blacks in the South and to prosecute whites who committed various atrocities, ranging from bombings and beatings to murder. Getting sent to a field office in the South had become something like being assigned to chase Reds, although at least in the latter case you didn't have a hostile population surrounding you.

One of the prime hates of the racists was Medgar Evers, who lived in Jackson and was Mississippi field secretary for the National Association for the Advancement of Colored People. On June 12, 1963, as Evers walked from his car toward his house, he was struck in the back by a rifle bullet. He managed to drag himself to the house, where he fell dead in front of his wife Myrlie and their three kids.

By 1963 the Bureau had begun to buy some information in the South, and the agents on the scene were able to learn the names of several people involved in the plot to murder Evers. But they couldn't come up with the evidence on who actually fired the rifle even though the local cops had found the 30.06 with its shiny new telescopic sight in a vacant lot, near the thicket from where the sniper ambushed Evers.

The local agents had questioned people but they hung tough. Meanwhile, Attorney General Robert Kennedy was putting the heat on Hoover, who, in turn, raised the thermostat for his subordinates.

In New York, two agents who had been talking to Julio about his interstate flight case made him an offer. If he would assist the investigation in Mississippi, he would be the beneficiary of the best the Bureau could do for him. They guaranteed a walk on his case plus any reasonable fee for services.

Julio and his girl friend flew to Miami Beach. He left her there to soak up some sun and build an alibi for him in the event that he would require one, and drove to Mississippi. He checked into a Jackson hotel and then went to a particular store. The manager of the place had been identified by agents as a member of the local White Citizens Council. Supposedly he had played a major role in the conspiracy that took the life of Medgar Evers.

Julio explained to the store manager that he was newly arrived from Chicago, would be working in Jackson for some time, and wanted to buy a TV set. He haggled over the price but finally came to terms. Julio then instructed the manager to hold the set while he arranged for a place to live. Further discussion with the manager revealed that the store would be open until nine that evening. "Could you wait for me even if I'm a few minutes late?" asked Julio. No problem, said the manager, happy to consummate a sale.

That night, about twenty minutes after nine, Julio drove up to the store. The manager had waited for him, as agreed. There was no one else in the store. "Could you put the set in my car, please?" asked Julio. "I have a bad back and can't lift anything." The manager obliged, carrying the set out to the sidewalk beside Julio's car, and then locking the store door. "Put it on the back seat," instructed Julio. "The trunk is filled with my clothes." The manager opened the back door of the car and pushed the set in. As he leaned into the car to secure the TV, Julio shoved him hard to the floor and jumped onto the back seat. He stuck a pistol in the man's ribs and told him to lie there and keep his mouth shut. An agent who had been crouching invisible in the front seat sat up and put the car in motion.

They drove south for several hours. Another automobile, filled with agents, tailed them. The manager fell silent after his first few questions brought him only a dig in the side. In fact, Julio slapped him hard and frequently. He began to whimper and complained he might throw up. Julio replied, "If you do you'll eat it." Finally, they arrived at a safe house, a deserted building somewhere in the lonely bayou country of Louisiana.

The agents took up positions around the house to guard against any unlikely interruption. Julio led his prisoner inside to what passed as a kitchen, sat him down in a chair near an open window, and tied him up. The appliance-store manager began to whine for his life and Julio cut him off. "I work for the Grand Dragon of a Chicago chapter of the Klan. He's very put out by this action of yours down here because it wasn't coordinated with him. Tell me the whole story of how this happened so I can give him a full report. Then I'll let you go."

Apparently terrified, the bound man gave Julio an account of the assassination. When he finished, Julio said, "You sit here and don't try to escape. I'll be back in a few minutes." Julio walked outside to confer with the agents. Through the open kitchen window they had heard every word. They rejected the story—the names weren't right and the facts didn't jibe with what they knew. Julio returned to the kitchen. "You just gave me some bullshit! Now let's have the truth," said Julio, threatening him with violence.

Once again, he listened to the story, and so did the eavesdroppers. For the second time Julio counseled the prisoner to have patience and mind his manners while he took a brief stroll. Outside the agents said, "He's stroking you—that's not the way it happened."

For a third time Julio approached his captive. But now he came on very strong—his pride was hanging by a thread. He took his .38 and stuck it in the mouth of the store manager. "Listen, prick, this is your last chance. You either tell me the absolute truth or I will blow your head off. I don't have any more time to waste."

Genuinely frightened now, the man poured out a new version of the Evers murder. When he was through and began to beg for his freedom, Julio conferred with the agents, who said this last description fitted perfectly with the facts as they knew them.

Julio returned to the kitchen. "Okay, now you repeat all this for me, slowly, while I write it down." When the statement was completed, Julio had the trembling prisoner sign it. Then he was packed into the back of the car and driven silently back toward Jackson. On the way, Julio went through his wallet and removed eight hundred dollars in cash. Before entering the city, the car slowed and Julio dumped the author of the confession out of the car.

On the following day, several FBI agents paid an official visit to the store manager. They informed him that a known criminal had been seized that morning at the Chicago airport. During a search of his person this document with the Jackson man's signature on it had been found. Would he care to explain its meaning? He copped out completely, admitting to his role in the conspiracy.

The actual marksman, Byron De la Beckwith, was arrested. The official word from Hoover's office after Beckwith's arrest was that as a former U.S. Marine, Beckwith had been traced through a latent fingerprint left on the "Golden Hawk" sight of the rifle. That was pure hokum; a partial print can't be used to find a person; you need all ten fingers in order to have enough details to cull out a match from the millions of prints in the file. In court, it all came down to nothing; two juries refused to convict Beckwith based upon what admissible evidence the Bureau could dredge up.

When I heard the story and confirmed it with Julio, I was ashamed that the people I worked for had to go outside the Bureau to find someone to perform their dirty work. An agent could have done what Julio did, but using him of course reduced the potential for scandal about the behavior of agents on the job.

And to boot, the Bureau welshed on their end of the deal. After Julio went home via Miami, the New York agents told him that their bosses were intoxicated with delight over the results of Julio's odyssey in search of the truth. They agreed to give him a walk on the interstate flight rap, and told him to name his price.

"My expenses came to about twenty-three hundred dollars," said Julio, "and that covers the air fares, the car rentals, motels, and meals for the four days it took. I beat that creep out of eight hundred, so all I want is the rest of what I laid out, fifteen hundred."

Everyone sobered up quickly. The rosy flush of success faded as the bureaucrats faced up to the problem of how to handle a fifteen-hundred-dollar cash payment to their outside consultant on the case. Any large informant payments required an okay from Director Hoover personally, and nobody cared to advise him of the background on how the Evers murder was solved. The feeling around the Bureau was that Hoover labored under the misapprehension that our sources provided us with stuff because they loved us, because they had suddenly seen the light and converted to the path of righteousness.

And so, a bitter Julio told me, he was never paid as promised. He was sore at the Bureau, but at the same time he was quite pleased about his work in Mississippi. He had some of the old-time Sicilian attitudes ingrained in him; it was considered very bad form to hit anyone in front of the innocent members of the family. "They shot him where his wife and kids could see him bleed to death," said Julio. "Only a degenerate would pull a stunt like that." I asked Julio what he would have done if the store manager had continued to lie. "I'd have pulled the trigger. I'd have felt bad using the agent's gun, but I couldn't turn him loose after that."

I tried very hard to convince Julio to return to the fold, telling him I would get him his money. And in that I succeeded, using new information that he had furnished me as a guise. I got authorization to pay him fifteen hundred dollars, the Bureau's outstanding debt. He accepted the money and signed a receipt for it. But he refused to become involved any further with the Bureau because he had lost faith in its integrity.

There was an interesting footnote to the whole affair. When I turned in the receipt to the office, the girl in charge of the books insisted it was not Julio's signature. I tracked down an agent who had once dealt with Julio and given him some minimal payments to demonstrate good intentions. He admitted to me that he always felt abashed at asking an informant for a receipt, so he had faked Julio's signature. That, of course, opened up an entire new area of potential corruption in the Bureau, one I had never considered. Subsequently, I have heard of several instances where agents pocketed the informant's money, in part or whole, and gave the office a phony receipt. At least one agent was quietly dismissed for this offense.

Although Julio refused to go on being an informant, he did tell me that if I ever wanted to turn a Soviet spy in the United States, he would be happy to take on the contract. "And if he doesn't become an informant, all you'll have is one less live spy." He was reflecting a prejudice shared by all members of LCN. They have the same passionate hatred for Communism as did J. Edgar Hoover. Most of them understandably profess a great love for the

United States and its economy. Only under the free enterprise system, with all of its paper instruments and decentralized control of goods and services, could organized crime operate. I'm not suggesting that a socialistic arrangement would eliminate large-scale crime; it would probably only change the structure of organized crime without eliminating it. But the opportunities available in the free enterprise system help explain why organized crime was prepared to cooperate with the CIA and take out Fidel Castro.

I never counted Julio as a real source. His information did not have to do with LCN, but with my employers. Occasionally I'd run across his name in connection with a crime, but I wanted no part of him. As far as I was concerned, he'd earned a lifetime pass from the Bureau. Of course, I told myself that if it ever happened that I caught him red-handed, he'd have to go.

Having struck out with Julio, I sought another busy entrepreneur in the mob, Nick Billeti,* aka "Bullets." Billeti was nominally part of the Gambino Family, but he was almost a free-lance operator, with his own crew, including a cousin who was very close to Carmine "the Snake" Persico. They specialized in hijackings and burglaries, and they fenced their spoils on the side. Billeti was known as a stand-up guy, afraid of no one. He also never hurt anybody unless forced to. He had once taken down a truck with Mickey Flowers. When everything had been unloaded at a drop, Mickey Flowers took out his gun and pointed it at the driver, explaining to Billeti that he thought it would be better if there were no witnesses. Billeti told Mickey Flowers that he would whack him out if the driver was shot.

When I discussed Billeti with my supervisor, he suggested that we put some pressure on him, because he had a girl friend and his wife might be very upset if she learned about this. I refused to play that game; I decided to warn Billeti that we were going to keep the heat on him until he would be unable to do any business at all. Sooner or later we would violate him and make him serve hard time.

Unfortunately, around this time J. Edgar Hoover was making one of his periodic efforts to cut costs. He ordered that there be no more rental cars used in surveillance work. We were up against very sophisticated individuals who were hard enough to fool with a smooth car; it was impossible to sneak up on them with a Bureau vehicle.

Using an official car, I trailed Billeti for a few miles until there could be no doubt about what I was doing. When I pulled him off the road he gave me the usual bad-mouth, but I patiently explained that I was going to be after him constantly. I had done my homework on Nick Billeti, and after I gave him the standard numbers about how I could be of some service to him, I rattled off a list of jobs that I knew from other sources he had been involved in. He heard me out and refused to commit himself to anything, but when we parted, he gave me a telephone number where I could reach him. I gave him a code name I would use.

We held a second meeting on a deserted dock in Brooklyn. I offered him something more than money and an absence of harassment. He had a brother-in-law doing time. I made some calls to the proper authorities and the brother-in-law's application for parole was approved. You had to play your cards very carefully with the parole people. It was too risky to play your hand face up by laying out the precise arrangement that was contemplated and exactly who on the outside was involved. I usually told the parole official only that this favor could result in a significant number of arrests for the government. Once my candidate had been sprung, I waited until the first big case by the FBI appeared in the newspapers, maybe six months later—a kidnapping, bank robbery, or gambling bust—then called the parole office and implied that the whole thing came about through the release of my man.

Having obliged Billeti on the matter of his brother-in-law, I organized a third meeting. I told him I would make two calls to him; the first conversation would ostensibly include the name of a mutual friend, which actually would be the name of the hotel, and the second call would mention the price of an item, which would be the room number. In the initial call I said that my associate "Mr. Pierre" would be arriving in New York that day for the deal. On the second call I said that we figured the price on the shipment of shirts to be $12.77.

I came to the Hotel Pierre well prepared. I had a number of photographs of people that I wanted Nick to identify, and I had forms for debriefing an informant tucked away in my overnight bag. When there was a tap on the door, I took a small screwdriver that I carry attached to my key chain and began unscrewing the very fancy brass knob. When Billeti came in I said, "These knobs are great, just what I need for a house I'm building." Billeti was very amused at the idea of an agent trying to steal a hotel doorknob, and that put him at ease.

When I took out the photographs for him to look at, however, he balked. "I'm a rat if I'm caught here at all," he said. "If I get killed, I deserve it."

"Look," I pleaded. "I've gone out on a limb for you on your brother-in-law and I've spent the Bureau's money on this hotel room. Just give me enough so I can justify the effort."

But he was adamant about giving me any help. I was getting desperate, but I clung to the fact that he had shown up, which would seem to mean he had potential.

"What do you weigh?" I asked him.

"Around two ten." Billeti was an ox of a man, like a short piano mover, thick neck, huge biceps, very little flab.

"Okay," I challenged. "I weigh around one seventy and the heaviest thing I ever carried is an FBI report. I'll arm wrestle you. If you put me down, I won't bother you ever again. But if I put you down, we're getting married."

"Shit, pull over the fucking table and let's get it over." I knew he had pride in his own strength; he was the kind of guy who never asked anybody in his crew to do anything he wouldn't do himself.

We made very strict rules—the elbows had to stay on the table at all times and feet on the floor. Then we went at it, for what seemed to me at least ten to fifteen minutes. I thought blood would spout from my fingernails, so tightly did he squeeze my hand. He almost had me down several times, but I had one secret advantage: Although I'm thin, I have a very long forearm. My brother also outweighed me by thirty to forty pounds and I could always pin him. Arm wrestling is a matter of leverage; the lever is the forearm and, as Archimedes said, give me a long enough lever and a platform to stand on, and I can move the world.

Anyway, it was long enough to fight Billeti to an excruciating standoff. Finally I said, "We're like a couple of schoolboys fighting over a girl." It was a way for both of us to gracefully slide out from possible defeat.

Billeti then measured my bicep against his. "Son of a bitch, mine's two inches bigger," he swore. But he was looking at the wrong end of the arm for the key to arm wrestling. It was the same trick that helped me humiliate the punk who thought he could take Kayo Konigsberg.

We hadn't resolved anything. Suddenly Nick said, "I like you. I enjoy your company. Let's make a marriage, as you call it." In return I promised him that I would protect him to the best of my ability, and that included not only his identity but a safeguard against the routine harassments of the Bureau and any bum raps.

Through Nick Billeti I got word of an impending major hijacking. He had learned that in the haul would be a truck with $500,000 worth of watches. Billeti told me the location of the drop, and we set up a surveillance on the place. The FBI operation was to be a combined attack, involving both the organized crime units and the hijacking squad. And I was given the power to say when we would hit the drop.

From our vantage point we saw the first truck move into the garage. After it sat there for a while, two Econoline vans arrived. Each one carried off twenty-five to fifty cases of Cutty Sark Scotch. Agents trailed the vans to see who the fences were. Everybody wanted to move in right away, fearing that if we waited the swag would all disappear. However, I insisted that we wait, that my source had said better things were on the way. Ed Best, my supervisor, backed me up and I continued to run the show.

In the first thirty-six hours that the liquor truck was at the drop we saw over five hundred cases removed. Cars drove up to the place and took away small loads. We jotted down the license plate numbers and took pictures. By the second morning after the Cutty Sark arrived, everyone was getting very antsy. The supervisor of the hijack squad raised a very valid point with Ed Best. There we were, observing the distribution of stolen cargo, and we had failed to act. There was a distinct possibility that we would lose much of this load even if the so far unseen other truck did come. The carrier of the Scotch would have a terrific bitch about how we conducted business at their expense. Ed Best brought the matter up with his boss, SAC Dick Baker. "There's more on the way," said Baker. "That's the answer. You wait like Tony says."

Around noon of the second day, another big trailer truck arrived. This was one from a container ship with a load of women's clothes, maybe $50,000 worth. As that stuff began to ship out of the garage, the pressure to hit the place grew much greater. Dick Baker called me. "You've got what you wanted, Tony. There's two good loads."

"Be a little patient. We'll do better." I had great confidence Nick Billeti's tip would prove out. Baker agreed to a limited extension of time. About two hours after I spoke to Baker, another giant truck rolled down a one-way street from the wrong direction. The driver was so excited that he missed the garage opening and sheared off part of the sidewall of the building. We checked out the license plate with the New Jersey state police. They had only minutes before gotten a report of the truck; it contained $380,000 worth of nonprescription pharmaceuticals. Nick Billeti had been wrong about the precise nature of the cargo but correct on everything else. It was a very big catch for the Bureau when we finally did bust the scene.

The principals behind the entire operation were in the Joe Colombo Family. Colombo was wild with rage when he heard how he had been thwarted and that some of his troops had been arrested. To protect our source, we indicated to the press that an elderly woman with insomnia had been disturbed by the racket in a nearby garage during the late-night hours and complained to the Bureau about suspicious behavior. From Billeti I heard that Colombo got so mad he wanted to put out a contract on the old woman if she could be identified.

Protecting Nick while making use of his information was a major piece of work for me. Hy Gordon, a notorious Miami fence, came to New York one day about a load of jewelry in the hands of the Colombo Family. One piece was a very valuable and distinctive necklace. We knew all about the stuff; we even had photographs of some items. Billeti heard about the deal from one of his associates. After Gordon inspected the merchandise, a price was agreed upon. Delivery was by courier to a grocery store that served as a front. In the approved manner of the trade, the courier inventoried the load to make certain no one had pocketed anything, paid out $32,000, and then left with over $100,000 worth of gems in a plain manila envelope. Nick told me all about the deal, but I could not figure any way to grab Gordon or his courier without jeopardizing Nick.

About a month later, a guy from the jewelry exchange who occasionally told me interesting things remarked that he had recently been in Miami, where he'd seen Hy Gordon. "He's got some beautiful shit down there, including this necklace with emeralds and rubies in a display case in his home. He tried to sell it to me, said it was ice cold."

That gave me an idea. I called a brick agent in Miami and explained that Gordon was sitting on a load of hot valuables. If the agent, Joe Yablonski, could legally get into Gordon's home, he would see the necklace. and I would send by air a photograph of the necklace for identification. Once Yablonski spotted the jewelry he could return with a warrant.

Yablonski had the perfect answer. For some time the Bureau had been routinely interviewing people who flew to certain islands in the Caribbean. Yablonski was certain that Gordon was a frequent visitor to the islands.

Everything worked perfectly. Yablonski gained admission to the house and asked him a few innocuous questions. Gordon, as expected, gently stroked Yablonski about his travels. Yablonski also gazed upon the jewelry in the display case; he recognized the necklace. From Gordon's house, Yablonski went directly to the offices of the U.S. attorney and secured a search warrant. Gordon's activities were well-known; he was the subject of frequent surveillances and investigations, but nothing of an evidentiary nature could be gleaned. Till then, that is.

Joe called me from Miami. "Holy shit, we've already identified the loot from two other armed robberies and there's a locked closet that I need a special warrant for." Then came the complication. "Gordon took me aside," Yablonski said, "and he told me, 'If you help me, I can give you enough information to make you the next director of the FBI.' He'll give up a lot of people." Sure he would, and one of the leaders in the list undoubtedly would be Nick Billeti. I explained to Yablonski that it would be a disaster for my source if Hy Gordon rolled over. I told him to get the special warrant for the closet but to be noncommittal while he dealt with Gordon.

In the meantime I set up an emergency meet with Nick Billeti and told him the developments. Nick told me he had dealt directly with Gordon in the past and that Gordon could bury him. Nick also told me another item of interest that could be of help. I rushed back to the office to send a teletype to both Miami and the Bureau in Washington informing them that the higher-ups in LCN were very fearful of Gordon's rolling over. Since most of them at one time or another had dealt with him, they had decided to kidnap Gordon's only child, a young daughter. When the Miami agents received the teletype they immediately followed the book. They notified Hy Gordon and the Miami police as well as the Dade County sheriff's office. Gordon's daughter was hustled off to be placed in hiding. Gordon then decided he knew better than to become an informant. He preferred to take his lumps and keep his mouth shut. He was sentenced to ten years; after serving a few years in Atlanta Penitentiary he died there.

To help Billeti retain his good standing with LCN, I created a phony charge against him. During an abortive hijack attempt, the robbers were forced to make a hasty escape. One of them had jumped from a second-story window and was seen hobbling off with what looked like a broken ankle. When I got the report of the incident, I remembered that a few hours before, Nick had been complaining to me about his cousin, an active criminal, having torn some ligaments while horsing with his kids. Our liaison man quickly informed the New York cops that an informant had just advised us that Nick and his cousin had been involved in the crime mentioned in the papers. They were both picked up but released after they demonstrated alibis that explained even the coincidence of the injured ankle. In Nick's circle an arrest of any sort counted as a kind of merit badge. The ploy was akin to Jackie Gucci's refusal to have me intercede with the local police when he and Tom Massi were busted at their fag bar and assaulted the cops.

In spite of my precautions I constantly feared that Billeti would get himself into trouble from which I couldn't save him. I knew that he was not the kind of guy who was going to settle down and sell vacuum cleaners for a living. On the other hand, I tried to get him to keep his distance from any crimes done by guys in his crew. He turned me off. "How can I ask them to do anything if I don't lead them, Tony?"

But he was smart enough to look into every proposition with great care. As the Bureau and local cops put more heat on organized crime, the number of finks increased. There were dozens of small-timers and some medium-sized operators who were willing to set up somebody else in return for a reward of money or a walk from something hanging overhead. Nick would telephone me occasionally and in a kind of offhand way ask me about people who had approached him. There were, for example, a couple of guys from Connecticut with a juicy proposition. They knew of a watch salesman who carried better than fifty thousand dollars with him on his rounds about the country. He could be taken quite easily on a specific date in Phoenix. The only complication was that he carried a gun and one would have to be prepared to shoot him. I contacted our New Haven office and sniffed around for information on the pair who had invited Nick to join them. New Haven was very guarded in its remarks about them; I instantly smelled a trap for Nick and advised him to wriggle out.

Protection of my informants was a major concern for me. Standard procedure for many of the smaller fish hooked by the law is to offer to serve as bait for someone bigger or more notorious. Nick Billeti was known as an active guy; there were plenty of cops and feds anxious to put him away. Because he was such a stand-up individual, there was also a bunch of LCN people who would be happy to see him sent away. Between cases manufactured by some slob who thought he could buy his way out with a story and setups that verged on entrapment, Nick Billeti was in as much danger from going away on a bum rap as on a genuine one.

At the same time, I had to face the possibility that an informant could use his status to get the agent in a box, where he either had to see a big case go down the drain or else permit his source to make a healthy criminal score. The opportunities for abuse were there, which made me, as the top recruiter of member sources, very vulnerable to talk about agents who gave bad guys licenses to steal. And there were a few guys in the office who were critical of me.

Working with Nick Billeti posed real dilemmas for a brick agent assigned to organized crime. Agents could penetrate the so-called subversive organizations without much trouble, but that wasn't possible with LCN and it still isn't. There is no way that an agent can develop over the years the history and the references that will enable him to become a functioning member of organized crime. In addition, in order to establish the proper credentials, an undercover agent would be forced to commit a number of crimes, possibly including murder. Critics of Bureau technique point to the ease with which agents have worked their way into upper-echelon posts within political movements, but that, after all, does not involve breaking the law.

Recently an FBI agent named Dick Genova somehow managed to become a chauffeur for the successor to Don Stefano Maggadino, one Sam Pieri, in Buffalo, but that was the exception. And Genova, a superagent, was able to make only limited use of his position.

On the other hand, the Bureau for too many years crippled itself with an attitude that one could deal with organized crime by operating from a sterile bastion instead of getting into the mud where LCN thrived. There was a never-ending battle with the Bureaucrats to justify the pennies we spent on informants who helped us recover millions of dollars worth of stolen goods. At least one could take a cost-accounting look at such deals and come up with a lot of black ink on the right side of the ledger. However, that was only part of the true accounting that we had to face. Because we agents could not go truly undercover, we had to rely on the Nick Billetis. They were not making their contributions because they revered the Bureau or had suddenly become converted to the path of righteousness chartered by Director Hoover. Far from it. They worked with agents because it was profitable for them: They avoided prison, got reduced sentences or parole for friends and relatives, maybe enjoyed some revenge against guys who had betrayed them, and picked up informer fees and some very substantial sums in the way of rewards paid by insurance companies delighted to refund five percent in return for saving the other ninety-five percent liability.

Their motives for assisting us didn't really concern me except as I was able to find a weakness and exploit it until I turned them. But the most troublesome aspect, as with Nick, was the worry that I handed out a license to steal. Billeti realized how valuable he was to me, and he knew I would try to protect him if he was caught. I had to take the position of never wanting to know of anything that he was going to do ahead of time unless it was for the benefit of the Bureau.

Nick Billeti seemed to like to test the temperature of the water whenever he contemplated a major crime. He asked once about what seemed to him to be a very easy job. An armored car made a regular stop in lower Manhattan to pick up money from a couple of banks, which were on opposite corners of the street. The practice of the guards was to park the truck in front of one bank, remove the sacks of money, and stow them in the vehicle. Then, instead of making a U turn on a busy street or going around the block, the guards walked across the street to the second bank. They carried the bags of money from that bank all the way back across the street to the truck. They were very vulnerable to an attack and could not count on any help from the man inside the armored truck during the time they returned from the second bank. Nick asked me what I thought of the possibilities. I told him under no circumstances to try it. Perhaps he was only teasing me when he came with such schemes; after all, he was savvy enough to know that I was never going to approve of any of his criminal operations in advance. But I also gave him a security blanket. I could argue him out of attractive propositions that carried great risk.

Every informant received from me a standard sermon on how far I would go on his behalf. If he did something that I was not warned of in advance and he was caught, there was no way that I would back up a story in which he claimed to have been performing a service for the Bureau. I also said that if he was caught with his pants down while pulling a score, I'd personally see the trial judge and say that the defendant ought to be viewed as akin to a crooked cop, someone who enjoyed a position of trust and who had a relationship with a law-enforcement agency and then abused that arrangement, and that he should be sentenced accordingly.

Arrangements to meet with informants depended upon who initiated the meeting. My sources could of course call me at the office or at my home. If I was around at the time it was easy to set up a rendezvous. But if I was unavailable, things became complicated. It might take three or four tries for us to connect. When I felt a need to consult, I had to be careful about any messages I left at a guy's home or his place of business. Our relationship was secret even from the wives and girl friends.

The actual meetings, aside from the strolls on the beach with Jackie Gucci, occurred while we were parked on streets or on a dark pier, in the reference section of the New York Public Library, main branch, at any number of museums in the city, or in shopping-center parking lots, where nobody paid attention to a couple of men waiting in a car while wives did some shopping. Rarely could we stick to a place for too long. Sooner or later my source would think that he recognized someone; once, a man driving by did actually lean out and say, "Hiya, Nick."

When I first began to deal in informants, the policy of the Bureau authorized me on my own judgment to make an initial two-hundred-dollar payment to a source. After that, every additional amount was supposed to be cleared through the Bureau in Washington and justified by a report. When we first began to pay so many bucks for so many facts from connected people, it was all on a COD basis. The Bureau would modify the arrangements after a source proved to have a constant stream of information and it was recognized that it would streamline matters to have regular sources of intelligence on a salaried basis. The pay scale for informants I handled ran from two hundred dollars a month to as high as eight hundred dollars a month for a productive operator. In addition there were lump-sum payments in truly outstanding cases for as much as five thousand dollars. Periodically I would have to submit a report that explained in detail the value of these "Bureau employees." Naturally, everything was on a cash basis; you were not going to find any button man walking into a bank with a check made out from the accounts of the FBI.

I once figured that Nick Billeti actually earned $65,000 over an eighteen-month period through our relationship. The Bureau salary accounted for only about twenty percent of his take. The rest came from varyingly grateful insurance companies and others whose valuables were retrieved through Nick's help. Negotiations for reward money required fancy choreography. Bureau policy officially forbade agents like myself from serving as the middleman between the insurer or trucker and an informant. But no alternative was feasible. The informants could not afford to disclose their identity to the outfits willing to compensate them. The routine was for a source to tell me where a $200,000 load of imported perfume could be found. The informant would ask for a $20,000 "finder's fee." I would reach the people who were liable for the loss and tell them we had a chance to get back their stuff but it would cost $20,000. Very often they tried to knock down the price. I'd say that I would check with my informant and see if he'd go for it. A half hour later, without even making an attempt to reach Billeti, I would go back to the company and say that $15,000 was the absolute minimum. The terms would be accepted.

After we hit the drop and made at least one meaningful arrest, the maneuvers would continue. The insurers had to pay off in cash. Bureau regulations also barred me from handling this money, and that was one policy I was careful to follow; there was too much risk that I could be accused of skimming the reward. However, most informants had no desire to personally meet their benefactors, and they rarely did. Beards stood in, receiving the cash from the insurance company rep and passing it on to someone else. None of the intermediaries knew why the money was being paid and they were ignorant of its final destination.

Occasionally the companies welshed on the agreement. With the tears now dry, a controller would chisel on the amount. In such instances an informant could only curse and rage about the lack of honor in the world, but he certainly wasn't going to sue for the stipulated sum.

The big payoff only came if the stuff had already disappeared and we couldn't locate it. In the case of the three-truck job that Nick tipped us to, we could only come up with a $2,500 reward for him.

I resisted the temptation of some easy cash as a kickback from my sources after they collected their rewards. I admit to having accepted a bottle of whiskey occasionally. One large unintentional windfall happened when Billeti called me on a Sunday morning. "I heard something about the game between the Jets and New Orleans this afternoon." I didn't follow pro football, and Billeti's information had nothing to do with a dump—although rumors concerning pro football point spreads sent us out checking leads occasionally. Billeti talked about the weather in New Orleans and an undisclosed injury on the Saints. "Get something down with a bookie," Nick urged.

"Where am I going to do that? I don't know any place I can put down a bet."

"If you want, I'll do it for you."

"Okay, put me down for a big one."

I watched the game that afternoon, and the Jets made me a

winner easy. Later in the week, I saw Nick and he started to count out hundred-dollar bills. "What's that for?" I asked.

"Your bet."

"When I said a big one, I meant one hundred."

He laughed. "You're lucky the Jets won, because if they lost you'd sure as hell owe me a grand!"

The longer I worked with my sources the more complex our relationships became. It was easy enough to keep my distance with Mickey Firenze, but Nick Billeti was a man whose company I enjoyed. I knew him as a stand-up guy who kept his word, a true man of respect. I lost a guy I thought of as a friend when he died in his own bed of a massive coronary at age fifty. But all the time that I worked with Billeti I had to reassure myself that our relationship was not the ultimate perversion of the whole law-enforcement idea. In my mind, what we did was justified on the grounds of the greatest good. I knew that I was perpetuating the career of a criminal, but I believed that the information Billeti gave us was worth much more than what he managed to steal. It was a case of two steps forward and one step back.

My fifth member source grew indirectly out of my association with Nick Billeti. One of his troops was serving time at Lewisberg Federal Penitentiary in Allenwood, Pennsylvania. He mentioned to Nick a fellow inmate, Gino Asturi* who was in the same cell block and was doing very bad time. Asturi could not take being cooped up; he wept at night, and he had confided to Nick's man that his kids at home were getting into a lot of trouble without him to keep them in line. Gino may sound like a flabby kind of guy but he was actually a reasonably hard-boiled soldier—his Lewisberg vacation came from a bank robbery. It's just that some men can serve their time more easily than others. Gino walked around like a rumbling volcano.

Billeti passed on this information during a casual conversation and then forgot about Asturi. But I didn't. I knew him to be an associate of Carmine "the Snake" Persico. All of us at the Bureau itched to put Persico away. He had worked hard to earn his nickname. He had the disposition of a cobra that had been stepped on, and he was more lethal than any of his namesakes. We had a laundry list of things that could be attributed to Persico but no evidence to take into court. Vicious and cold-blooded,

Carmine Persico was ready to kill for love as well as money. He once asked Joe Profaci, then head of a Brooklyn-based crime family, for permission to hit a guy who was fooling with Persico's girl friend. Profaci turned down the application. It was okay to whack out anyone who messed with a wife, but a girl friend was considered by Profaci to be open stock.

Once I heard that Asturi couldn't hack his cell time, I reasoned that he might serve the Bureau. A resident agent near Lewisberg knew the warden of the place well, so I asked him to explain to the warden that I wanted a confidential talk with Asturi. Asturi had worked as a stonemason. If the warden could invent a pretext that his fireplace chimney was breaking up and could bring Asturi out to fix the bricks, he would have the cover I wanted. It would be impossible to interview a guy like Asturi inside the prison and not have everyone in the place know that an FBI agent had been snooping around.

The warden cooperated fully. When Asturi entered the house to work on the chimney, he found me. Asturi could have passed as the elderly, mousy bookkeeper for a small business. Slightly built, with wispy gray hair, he asked nothing more from life than opportunities to lean on a bad debtor, to pick up a piece of hijack action, or to move in on a modest extortion target. Then it was back to the bosom of his family. He personified the type who rapped people on the skull with a piece of pipe and then went home to gently pat his grandchildren on their heads. My advantage came from the fact that doing time interfered with his warm paternal instincts.

Once the warden left us alone, Asturi agreed to talk. I led him gently, pointing out that I knew how rough prison was on him: the problems at home, the failure of the organization to do the right thing financially while he was away . . . Maybe in the old days of the Mustache Petes they took care of the fallen, but my experience generally was that the new breed of leaders in LCN didn't give a shit what happened to button men and their families once the guy got put away for any length of time. . . .

"If you'll give me some inside stuff to help us put away Carmine Persico, I'll get you out of here and I'll see that you can take a walk on anything hanging over you." In fact, Gino Asturi did have a pending local indictment for another escapade.

He wasn't hard to convince in that atmosphere, and he filled me in on the details of a job he had gone on with Persico. They broke into a government-bonded warehouse where one of the gang had been assigned to shut off the burglar alarm. He fumbled the job and the alarm rang. Fortunately, they managed to silence it before anyone was aroused, and the robbery went off smoothly. Gino agreed to testify in court about the theft, even to take a lie detector test. He was not fond of Carmine because of his attitude after Gino was sent away. "Even if this doesn't go down, I'll give Persico to you on something else," said Asturi. "But there's one condition: I have to clear it with my wife. She's coming to see me this weekend and I'll have her call you Monday." He thanked me profusely for how I had approached him, for having spared him any embarrassment.

On Monday, Asturi's wife called. "Please don't do anything with my husband," she pleaded. "I'd rather see him once a month in the can than in a coffin. I won't let him do it."

There wasn't much I could say except that I would honor my promise not to hassle Asturi any more and to keep our meeting confidential. I went through a few very anxious moments when I had to tell the U.S. attorney that the case I thought I had against Carmine Persico had collapsed.

I forgot about Asturi for around two years, until the State Liquor Authority came to us with a complaint about some hoods trying to move in on the owner of a cocktail lounge. The proprietor resisted. His stubbornness was rewarded with a firebomb thrown at his house and the beating of one of his employees. Among those implicated was Gino Asturi, who had been paroled in time to become involved in this venture. The Authority had passed this item onto Denis Dillon, head of the Eastern District Strike Force—the federal group drawn from several agencies to combat organized crime—and Dillon in turn called on the Bureau for an extortion investigation.

With another agent I went to Asturi's home in the early morning. Still in his skivvies, Asturi was assisting his wife with breakfast and getting some of his grandchildren off to school. He recognized me immediately, and I told him why I was there. However, I said I would not demean him with handcuffs in front of his family and we wouldn't disrupt the family routine until the children left for school. We then left the house and waited for him outside.

On the way down to the Bureau offices I sat in the back seat of the car with Gino. "I'll never forget that you did not use the information I gave you at Lewisberg and that you kept your promise to me," he said. We talked a bit more and he agreed to see me the following day in a parking lot.

Gino revealed that Persico was behind the attempt to move in on the cocktail-lounge owner as well as being a prime factor in a number of other crimes. Joe Colombo had already organized his campaign against the Bureau for maligning people of Italian background. The protest had involved writs to halt surveillances, testimonial dinners, rallies, and picketing outside our Manhattan offices. Gino reported that the pickets had served as a blind for a Colombo-Persico undercover operation. They had taken photographs, ostensibly of themselves but in reality of every person who entered the building. Then the pictures had been scrutinized by members of the various families and a rogues' gallery of FBI agents was created. Carmine's troops had also photographed the people in close proximity to their home turf. These shots were in turn compared with the faces recorded around our building. It was fortunate that long before Colombo's picketing, I and a number of other agents handling sensitive matters made it a practice when reporting to the office to enter and leave the building through the basement on another street.

From Asturi we learned that Carmine normally kept a small arsenal at his upstate New York home in Saugerties. We set up a stationary surveillance there and observed the Persico gang perfecting their shooting skills in a deserted area near the house. We captured them—Carmine's brother, Allie Boy, with some of his friends. All were in possession of pistols. In the house we found a variety of guns as well as a deadly silent crossbow, which allowed us to bring added charges against the Persicos.

Gino filled me in on other significant details of the Persico brothers. Many years before, Carmine had murdered a man. A witness who became known as the Blue Angel surfaced to testify, but before Carmine could be convicted, the Snake's older brother, Allie Boy, stepped forward, took the rap, and got life imprisonment, of which he served eighteen years before being released. A helluva lot of brotherly love. As could be expected, the Blue Angel was murdered by an "unknown" assailant a few years later. Subsequently, I discovered that other law enforcement agencies had the same information on the Persicos.

Allie Boy, whose real name is Alphonse, was a strapping, handsome man, while Carmine was scrawny and ugly. His hand was twisted from a bullet wound and he had also been shot in the face during the long war with the Gallo brothers in the 1960s, when they challenged the authority first of Profaci, then of Joe Colombo, who succeeded Profaci. Carmine generally was given the credit for having attempted to garrote Larry Gallo. The accidental appearance of a neighborhood cop saved Gallo, although he was left with a permanent croak in his voice and eventually died of throat cancer.

The Persicos were involved in a spectacular case that boosted my stock with John Malone, the assistant director who was head of our New York office. To resolve the matter we also received help from both Nick Billeti and Gino Asturi. In 1952, two brothers made the mistake of stealing the jewels of Regina Pacis (Queen of Peace), a votive shrine at St. Rosalia's Church in Brooklyn. Capo Joe Profaci, like all crime family heads, had a fine appreciation for rendering unto Caesar and to God. Perhaps because the theft brought a lot of heat from both the law and the public, he ordered the jewels restored and said, "I want one ball from each of those guys brought to me." Profaci was not denied either wish; the multilated corpses of the thieves were found later.

Now, in the winter of 1972, a pair of junkies not too concerned about what they did so long as it would stake them to a few more bags of heroin, and who were certainly not students of history, ripped off the Regina Pacis jewels. Their search for customers brought them to a gin mill. Nick Billeti occasionally frequented the place and heard about the goods being offered. He telephoned me with the information.

Although the swag amounted to little more than penny-ante stuff in the scores of organized crime, I saw a magnificent opportunity. "My God," I said. "John Malone is a friend of the archbishop. If we can get these things back, Malone will be the happiest kid in town." Billeti further advised me that he had been told the stuff had been offered to Charlie "Moose" Panarella, a Carmine Persico loyalist who was very tight with Allie Boy.

I went to John Malone and Bob Franck the SAC for organized crime with the news. Malone was all for putting the arm on anybody who was mentioned and thereby recovering the stuff. I had to explain the criminal facts: Any precipitous moves on our part might cost someone his life.

Information from Gino Asturi now came to be very much of an asset to us. Through Asturi we had learned that Carmine Persico's son Larry had become a pill popper. His father considered this an almost fatal breach of discipline. He ordered his older brother, Allie Boy, to keep a lookout on the kid, who was around eighteen. If the boy didn't shape up, Carmine wanted him hit, and Allie Boy should be the hitter, which is one more indication of the Snake's basically lovable character.

Some months earlier, my supervisor, Sean McWeeney, after having learned about the Persico Family troubles, had gone to Allie Boy and offered to play Good Samaritan, to keep an eye out for the youth and protect him if possible. Sean McWeeney had been able to reach Allie Boy because he had been the arresting officer when the Persico gang was nabbed in Saugerties. On that occasion, Allie Boy had been very appreciative of Sean's gentlemanly behavior. He was accustomed to much rougher handling from the cops when they came to call. "You want to talk to me," he said, "subpoena, even arrest, me—regardless of the purpose— all you have to do is call me."

We worked out a script that incorporated all of these elements. Sean telephoned Allie Boy and said he wanted to meet with him to discuss the problem of the nephew. I drove Sean in a Bureau car to Prospect Park in Brooklyn on a bleak afternoon. Shortly after we arrived, a sartorially splendid Allie Boy appeared, chauffeured by one of his goons. He and Sean then proceeded to stroll through the park, impervious to the cold drizzle.

Face to face, McWeeney abandoned the nephew subterfuge. After mentioning that he had learned the boy had taken a disastrous trip on LSD, he came to the point, the Regina Pacis jewels. "Mr. Malone, the director of the New York office, is extremely interested in the recovery of these precious pieces," said Sean. "While they have some value, they will be easily recognizable if sold in their present form. Melted down, the worth is much less." In fact, the value of the Regina Pacis jewels is based largely upon their sentimental and religious significance. McWeeney switched to flattery. "We know your importance among people in Brooklyn, and you and your brother undoubtedly have great influence in such matters. If someone would telephone our office and simply tell us where the jewels are, we would be content with just a recovery. There would be no effort to arrest anyone. In fact, we would not even desecrate the jewels by dusting them for fingerprints." Allie Boy was very receptive to the notion, and we felt that if we could sit on Malone long enough and keep the New York cops from barging into the act, the whole thing would play nicely.

Through the grapevine we heard that Panarella, Allie Boy, and some other heavies had not so casually met in a restaurant. One of those present was heard to say, "I'm glad we're not going to break these things down. It would be a sin." That made it sound as if everything would go fine. But the outcry from the parish and the diocese had stirred up the local detectives, men no less religiously inclined than John Malone. They issued statements about an imminent break; in fact, we heard that they had actually zeroed in on the two junkies who took down the stuff. Once the pair opened their mouths and told where they had dumped it, our friends Panarella and Persico would abandon the project and the jewels would disappear. Indeed, one rumor indicated that the possessor of the gems had passed up a switch to Panarella when he discovered the law following him.

On Saturday morning an operator at our offices took a cryptic message for Sean McWeeney from a male voice. The instructions were to go to a locker at the East Side Airlines Terminal. The Bureau operator reached McWeeney at his home in New Jersey, a good fifty miles away. He telephoned me, since I lived much closer, and I reached Bob Franck. He and I went to the terminal and located the man in charge of the lockers. He flatly refused to open up until the twenty-four hours granted to each user had elapsed. We could not persuade him differently no matter how much we coaxed or threatened with our FBI credentials. Fortunately, we found Dennis Dillon of the strike force. He secured a search warrant. We opened the locker and there were the jewels.

As expected, John Malone went berserk with joy. He personally telephoned the archbishop with the good news. He put on an elaborate press conference in his office with everything neatly spread out so that the news photographers could get good copy. The Holy Grail was nothing compared with this.

Everything had worked out perfectly. Malone instructed Bob Franck to secure incentive awards for himself, McWeeney, and me. In fact the switchboard operator who took the anonymous call was herself awarded a letter of commendation, a tribute to one of the unsung heroes. Such was Malone's joy.

Gino Asturi tipped me to one of the more sensational inside Mafia cases, the kidnapping of Manny Gambino, son of Joseph Gambino and nephew of the boss of all bosses, Carlo.[1] Through a close associate of Carlo Gambino's, Gino learned that Manny had been snatched and a ransom note received. Included with the note was a photo taken from Manny's wallet. The kidnappers instructed the family to deliver the money to the parking lot of a Molly Pitcher restaurant in New Jersey. Joe Gambino, Tommy, another son and brother of the victim, and a nephew drove out to the Molly Pitcher with a bag full of currency, only to get lost and then arrive at the wrong Molly Pitcher. When it came to following the script of their own kind, the Gambinos showed they were as clumsy as anyone else.

I telephoned Manny Gambino's home, identified myself, and asked to speak to him. His wife Diane answered that he wasn't home. I questioned her as to when he might be expected. She responded that she had no idea.

I confided to Manny's wife that we had picked up rumors of her husband's disappearance, and I inquired if she had any indication that he had been kidnapped. Still she denied that anything was amiss, as any loyal mafioso wife would do. I asked to speak to her father-in-law Joe Gambino. Not only wasn't he around, Diane Gambino had no number where I could reach him. That ended my first approach to the Gambinos.

At our offices there were several conferences to consider what

[1] After the 1930s assassination of Joe "the Boss" Masseria and Salvatore Maranzano, each of whom had tried to make himself the supreme commander of LCN, it was agreed that a separate-but-equal status would be accorded the heads of the five New York families. However, in the 1960s, as his power grew, Carlo Gambino became recognized as more equal than the others. De facto, rather than de jure, he was known as capo di tutti capi, boss of all bosses.

the Bureau's role should be. Although I had been given the information by one of my informants, I was not on the Gambino squad, but the Colombo. Dick Baker had been made an assistant director and transferred to Bureau headquarters in Washington. The new SAC, Frank Hitt, said official courtesy required that Jim Mulroy, head of the Gambino squad, be placed in command. Hitt obviously did not approve of me or my methods, and he was unenthusiastic about my making any pitch to the Gambinos. However, he did grudgingly agree to allow me to make contact with them.

I waited a day after the first call to Manny's wife and then made another. I hinted that I had more than just some casual details on the affair, that through wiretaps we knew quite a bit about the kidnapping and were prepared to render assistance.

Diane Gambino stubbornly insisted her husband had not been kidnapped, but her voice told me that she was under enormous stress and she was hanging on my every word. Finally she cracked to the extent that she took my name and telephone number to give to her family attorney, in the event any emergency should arise.

About two hours later, the attorney called me. He assumed a noncommittal line: "I understand you have some information that indicates Manny Gambino has been kidnapped." I said that we had indeed heard this was the case and then baited him with references to reliable, confidential sources.

"What will you do about it?" he asked.

"We are powerless to act," I said. "Without a complaint from the family or some corroboration, there is nothing we can do"—not wholly true. I sympathized with the reluctance of the family to call in the FBI, but I assured him with my best Eagle Scout sincerity that in our eyes Mr. Gambino was neither more nor less than the Lindberg baby. We had an obligation to find him if he had been kidnapped. I went so far as to tell him that we all realized that Manny Gambino was a reputable citizen with a legitimate business—which was a lie. He was heavily into shylock operations and other Gambino rackets. But even if he were the worst criminal in the world, we would do everything possible to restore him to the bosom of his family.

"Let me talk to the family," said the lawyer.

Silence was all that came out of the Gambino household for

two days. Finally the attorney called me and said the Gambinos had agreed to avail themselves of the services of the FBI in an effort to save Manny, who, they now admitted, had been kidnapped.

I hurried out to Manny Gambino's house in the Whitestone section of Queens. It was a newish one-family attached house of fair size furnished elaborately in crass plastics, vibrating colors, expensive schlock. In the crowd I managed to find the lawyer and Manny's brother, Tommy Gambino. I again gave the customary guarantee on the kidnapping: Top priority was the safe return of Manny Gambino. They had just received word that another telephone call would be made that would spell out new instructions for the ransom. One of the principles taught all agents is that on the scene, an agent must dominate the situation. I did my best to live up to the requirement. I laid out for Tommy Gambino and the attorney exactly what procedure we were to follow. When the call came in, an effort should be made to keep the other party on the phone for as long as possible. With the permission of Tommy and the lawyer, we would tape the call and also make a try at tracing its origins. They agreed. Tommy Gambino was to tell the kidnappers that because he had a bad heart he would need someone to accompany him when he delivered the ransom. I would be the individual with him.

The attorney suddenly raised a stunner: He asked that the FBI put up the money. I explained that we never advanced the cash in a kidnapping or extortion case. We wouldn't prevent the family from making payment of a ransom, of course. If they wanted to gamble with funny money or a false bankroll, we would supply the appropriate materials. But never the real money.

At that moment, in the chaos of the Gambino home, Frank Hitt arrived on the scene to introduce his own confusion. Hitt listened to my plans and then engaged in a whispering session with his number-one man. Frank Hitt had been upstaged by a brick agent. I was ordered to sit outside in a Bureau car and wait for further orders. The situation deteriorated. The lawyer yapped about how the Bureau discriminated against the Gambinos by refusing to front the ransom, and Hitt was sore because he thought any cooperation with the Gambinos jeopardized the purity of the Bureau.

As politely as I could, I excused myself to the Gambino clan and slunk off to sulk in a Bureau car. The FBI presence was supposed to be discreet, as for any kidnapping, but we had a near rush-hour mob of agents going in and out of the Gambino house, plus cars spotted around the neighborhood. The nearest ones were parked a block or so away, but anyone watching the house couldn't have missed the government-issue cop-type cars; for one thing, the motors had to be kept running to service their radio systems.

I dropped into a car about a block from the house, brooding over the insult to my pride. After an hour of consoling myself with private diatribes, I received a radio message ordering me back to the house.

Frank Hitt and company had not reassured the Gambinos. Wails, screams, and curses stippled the smoky air. The family had decided that I was someone they could trust. The phone message with further instructions had indeed come through. But it had been too brief to trace beyond the general territory of Staten Island. Tommy Gambino insisted that I be permitted to travel with him for the ransom payoff.

Frank Hitt drew me to one side. He instructed me to lie on the floor in the back of the car. Using a walkie-talkie, I was to keep in touch with the cars that would follow the payoff vehicle at a discreet distance.

The kidnappers had asked for $200,000, but the family said that the most they could scare up was something under $50,000. The mafiosi had decided to try to buy back one of their own at discount prices. Possibly the Joe Gambino side of the LCN was suffering hard times. And, too, there was also the possibility that $200,000 in ready cash as a ransom could lead to future unpleasant questions from the Internal Revenue Service.

Just before we left, one of Manny's sisters, who had taken to occasionally banging her head against the wall, fell to the floor at my feet and screamed, "Please, Tony—I've lost one brother already. Make sure you bring back my other one!" I tried to reassure her that we faced no danger, but her fears were not lost upon Tommy. Since the kidnappers had been told Tommy would have a relative with him, and I had been ordered to remain hidden on the car floor, we had to take a third person; Tommy insisted on his business partner. We used a Cadillac Eldorado that belonged to Tommy's partner. I noticed that Tommy owned a 300 SL

Mercedes; the frozen-clams casino business was apparently thriving.

The initial instructions ordered Tommy to wait near a telephone booth at the corner of Eighty-second Street and Madison Avenue in Manhattan for further orders. As we drove into the city I asked Tommy if he had a gun. Both he and his partner were shocked. Was I out to arrest them on a Sullivan Law violation (carrying a concealed weapon in New York State)? I explained that in a kidnap case it might be better if we all had guns in the car.

Tommy Gambino became noticeably more uneasy as we approached the telephone booth. He wanted to use the car as a kind of security blanket and wait in it until the telephone rang. However, there were no parking spaces near the booth, and I counseled that it would look better if he left the car and walked to the booth. For all we knew, one of the kidnappers could have been watching us. Someone for sure was watching the area: a small army of agents. They jotted down the license plate numbers of every car that drove by and relayed the information to our offices, where a swift check was made on the registered owner. It was a necessary exercise but futile in this instance.

The wait for the telephone ring was a long one. At last Gambino received the marching orders. We were to cross the George Washington Bridge, take the first exit on the Jersey side, go north on the Palisades Parkway, pull in at the first gas station on our right, and wait next to the four pay telephones in the place for further instructions.

We followed the plan exactly. I kept in contact with the backup cars, cautioning them to stay far enough off the pace in the event that anyone was observing the action when we pulled into the gas station on the Palisades Parkway. The kidnappers had chosen their site well; the telephone area in the station was brightly lit, but the rest of the place was closed.

Tommy Gambino was not cut out for this kind of work. He had started to stammer, and I began to have worries that he might develop into a genuine cardiac case. But we waited and sweated until one of the phones rang. Tommy received his final instructions. He was so tongue-tied with fear when he came back to the car that he had trouble communicating with us. Finally we were able to learn that we were to drive about a mile farther, until we saw a metal rail on our right. At that point Tommy was to leave the car, heave the plastic bag with the money over the rail, and drive away. If all went well, Manny Gambino would be returned to his family by morning.

I told Tommy that we would follow the directions but in slow motion, hoping the delay would give our teams in the area a chance to get into position. Tommy was near panic and not easy to reach, but I convinced him to drive past the railing as if he did not see it, then pretend to realize he had gone too far and back up. When he'd done that, Tommy left the car with the bag, flung it over the rail, and rushed back to us. "Let's get the fuck out of here!"

I asked Tommy to go slowly in spite of his obvious desire for more speed. Then in the rearview mirror he spotted some headlights. "They're following us—they're going to grab us, too," he wheezed.

"Just pull off at the exit ahead," I told him, and then I passed on the latest development to the backup car, still several miles away. I wasn't uneasy. It wouldn't make sense for them to grab us.

"Holy Christ, they're going to overtake us!" yelled Tommy Gambino as he noticed the car gaining on us.

"Stay in the center of the road until the exit," I directed. "I'll take care of it if there's trouble." As we swung into the exit, the car behind us whizzed by, just innocent late-night travelers.

The trip back to the Gambino home in Queens was uneventful. We arrived at about three in the morning. On my walkie-talkie I heard some of the exchanges between the agents back at the drop site. Sean McWeeney and his partner had been in the vicinity but had not been able to get to the drop before the bag disappeared. The kidnappers, as we later learned, had been very smart. The railing actually marked that part of the parkway that passed over another road. Anyone following us on the parkway would not have been able to get to the underpass road in time to catch the perpetrators. However, McWeeney was close enough to observe a van cruising the area and write down the plate number.

When we entered the Gambino house, Tommy was still stammering. I announced that I had just witnessed a very brave deed, performed by a man who had done everything he could for his brother, including risking his life. A kind of wake party followed;

the booze flowed and sandwiches were passed around as agents and members of the LCN and their families broke bread together. We all shared the same disappointment. Tommy later took me aside and thanked me for my words on his behalf and swore that if I ever needed a favor I had only to call him. He also confided to me that they had inserted a religious picture in the plastic bag along with the money, hoping an icon might stir some humanitarian sentiments in those who held his brother.

Whatever sense of relief had developed, it all began to ebb as Manny Gambino had not shown up by seven A.M. An hour later I borrowed the Eldorado and with Tommy went back to the place where he'd tossed the money over the rail.

Under some bushes I found the torn garbage bag. Neither money nor religious picture was there. I placed the money sack inside another plastic bag, to preserve any fingerprints, and then we drove to the FBI offices in Manhattan. Tommy requested that I not force him to come upstairs for an interview and I granted his wish.

Manny Gambino did not come home, and the Bureau organized a routine investigation of the kidnapping. But the fact that most of Manny's associates were extremely reticent about conversing with agents on any subject was a severe handicap.

I didn't work from that angle. Instead I went with agent Charlie Garvey to see Paul Ginder,* whom I had discovered through a hijacker who turned government informant. In our offices after his arrest, Ginder, with his checkbook and deposit slips, had behaved like a perfect gentleman. What he was willing to admit to us in our offices and what his records showed turned out to be not very incriminating as far as we were concerned, but the information we developed was enough for the IRS people to go after him. I was called to testify against Ginder, and I saw him at the courthouse before the trial, introduced myself again, and began to make conversation. I asked him if he knew where the hijacker was. He said no, with some surprise. "The son of a bitch disappeared after I lent him four hundred dollars from my own pocket," I griped. Ginder laughed and sympathized with me over my loss. Actually, as a government witness whose life was considered in danger, the informant had been relocated and given a fresh identity. I did know where he was.

"I'm sorry about this," I told Ginder. "I can't perjure myself with my testimony, but when the U.S. attorney is finished with my direct examination, tell your lawyer to ask me what I think of you as a person. I'll say that I feel you're a gentleman, a decent guy, courteous, and pleasant."

"I appreciate the offer," replied Ginder. "But I wouldn't let my lawyer embarrass you into a public statement about my character."

"No, don't feel that way," I argued. "I'd only be speaking what I feel is the truth, and I would be glad to do the same for anyone else in your position."

However, when I was under cross-examination, Ginder's lawyer not only failed to ask me what I thought of his client, he also vigorously impugned my veracity, suggesting that my testimony about Ginder was part of a conspiracy of liars aimed at incarcerating his client. Verbal push came to verbal shove and it ended with both of us shouting at one another before my part in the trial ended. The U.S. attorney never interfered; he was enjoying the fight.

Later I ran into Ginder in the hallway and he apologized to me. "That son of a bitch. I'll fire him. I didn't want him to start in on you."

"Hell, he was just fighting for you, Paul."

Among the things I had learned during my investigation of Paul Ginder was that he was close to the high and the mighty in the Gambino Family. He would be a logical source of information now. I telephoned his house and the maid told me he was away but would be back late that evening. I arranged with Garvey to meet me out there. Ginder lived on a country lane in a Westchester village. As I drove into the road, I saw Ginder backing out of the driveway. I blocked him off, then got in the seat next to him. Ginder remembered me immediately from the courthouse scene and our other encounters.

"Hey, I beat that tax case" were his first words.

"Yeah, I know, but I didn't come all the way out here to congratulate you. Manny Gambino's been kidnapped—we'd like to find out who did it. I'm not asking you to be a stoolie or to become an informant. All I want is some background information that might clear up the case and find Manny, or what's left of him, and whoever snatched him."

Ginder thought this quite reasonable, and he laid out what he had picked up on the street. Actually, he handed the case to me. Manny had fallen in love with a show-biz blonde. He wanted to leave his family because the girl refused to have anything more to do with him unless he gave up his wife and went full-time with her. Manny was advised by his betters in the clan to grow up and forget the blonde. In his circles it was okay to have a mistress but it was bad form to leave your wife, particularly if you were a nephew of Carlo Gambino.

Manny also had business problems. He had too much money out on the street, possibly because he was trying to maintain two households. The bankers at home were restless about this aspect of Manny's life. One of Manny Gambino's clients was Bob Sentner, a heavy gambler who was into Gambino for $100,000. "The man to look up is Bob Sentner; that will solve the case," said Ginder.

The whole thing came together with that name. The license number of the van spotted by Sean McWeeney revealed it to be a rental to Sentner. It took five interviews with him over a period of months before we finally reconstructed the entire venture. The snatch began as a hoax. Manny Gambino worked out the scenario with his debtor Sentner, a friend of Sentner's, J. E. Kilcullen, and two others, William Solin and John Harrington. Midway through the plot, Gambino's accomplices began to have their doubts. They could see that if things went sour Manny Gambino would give them up, either on a contract to LCN friends or to the law. There was an argument in Gambino's Cadillac and Sentner settled the dispute with a bullet in the back of Manny's head.

Before we located the body or finally charged Sentner with the killing, we discovered Manny Gambino's car parked at Newark Airport with bloodstains on the seat. Because it had been necessary to wait a period of time before the body could be safely stashed, rigor mortis had set in. As a result, Manny Gambino had been buried sitting up, a condition not uncommon in rub-outs that occur while the victim is in a car. The chosen burial site was to be a New Jersey dump near Earle Naval Ammunition Depot.

At one point during the investigation I talked to Tommy Gambino, in the hope that he might be so grateful that he would assist us in other matters. He arranged for a head-to-head session with Moishe Kessler, who had been very close to Manny Gambino and was someone I'd been anxious to meet for a long time. I met him at a glorified hot dog stand near Flushing Airport. Kessler grew up in the Brownsville section of Brooklyn when it was still a Jewish ghetto. As a youth, Kessler knew the local heroes: Abe Reles, Louis Lepke, Gurrah Shapiro, and other Jewish hit men who had performed so efficiently that they were known as Murder Inc. It had been Kessler's dream to succeed into their ranks, but by the time he reached maturity most of them had been murdered, executed, or jailed. Moishe carried on like a wiseguy, and in terms of talents and inclinations, he was eminently qualified. But his ethnic background prevented him from enjoying actual membership. He was very thick with people in LCN.

Kessler could behave like the crudest of beasts, but at our meeting he was on his best behavior. "Never in my life," protested Moishe, "did I ever believe that I would cooperate with the FBI. But I love Manny Gambino like a brother and I would give up my life for him. I'd do anything to help." But the material he gave out was all stuff we knew or which he politely fabricated.

A couple of years after the kidnapping incident, Moishe Kessler was busted in a very curious affair that involved smuggling plastic explosives out of the country. When a U.S. attorney appeared on the scene to process the arraignment, Kessler blustered, "You can't touch me, I'm CIA." The prosecutor thought that was a novel chunk of bullshit. But now, neither he nor I is quite so sure. One of the lesser accomplices in the Gambino kidnapping had once been a CIA employee, and another had been a Green Beret. One can draw connecting lines between Kessler, who received a mysteriously light sentence for a heroin rap, his claim of CIA immunity, and the backgrounds of Manny Gambino's kidnappers. And it has been gossiped that the Gambinos were the avenue of communication between the CIA and the underworld. It would be logical of the CIA not to deal with the hired help when they might go directly to the boss of bosses, Carlo Gambino.

Frank Hitt had opposed our intervention in the Gambino kidnapping because he seemed to feel that if the Bureau performed a service for someone in organized crime, even if it was something mandated as our responsibility under the law, the Bureau would be desecrated. But that overlooks the fact that the FBI is there to help everybody. If a beneficiary happens to be LCN, okay; he might turn out to be a worthwhile route to further penetration of the ranks.

Of course, every extreme has its opposite. There were those agents who treated major figures in organized crime as their equals or, worse, with servility. They seemed overwhelmed by the power and arrogance of top-echelon people in LCN.

The Bureau's official position was to be courteous, but not lose sight of the fact that he's the bad guy and you're the good guy. My own attitude was to keep courtesy just above the minimum. I wouldn't flake a man (plant incriminating evidence on him), nor would I bounce him around. But if I happened to see him on the street, I'd be happy to drive through a mud puddle and splash his nice clean suit.

5

The Scammers

ORGANIZED CRIME OPERATES through its own fronts, legitimate-looking businesses that are wholly owned subsidiaries, and through a large contingent of larceny-minded individuals who retail the stuff ripped off by wiseguys. They peddle stolen securities grabbed from mailbags and brokerage houses, jewelry from heists, whiskey, counterfeit money, securities, and art. They rarely engage in rough stuff and can be categorized as white-collar criminals. They too serve as valuable informants, tattling upon others in the same swindles as themselves and supplying intelligence about the wiseguys with whom they deal.

Usually better educated than the mob guys and smoother in dress and speech, they move easily between the underworld, powered by muscle, blood, and violence, and the upper world, where larceny wears a nylon glove. Most of the big numbers of LCN know better than to live in conspicuous fashion the way the rackets guys of the thirties did. Flaunting their wealth, Lucky Luciano, Dutch Schultz, and Owney Madden only embarrassed the law into pursuit of them. By comparison, the scammers are somewhat anonymous individuals who can live it up. They don't arouse public indignation with their white-collar crimes and they don't hurt people. They are freer to indulge themselves—which is an asset, because it is among the jet-set country-club types that their enterprise flourishes best.

In 1968, Congress, chivied by J. Edgar Hoover's excuse that the Bureau couldn't strike at organized crime because the violations too often fell short of federal offenses, passed a broad statute to cover shylocks. Technically, it went by the heading of "extortionate credit transactions." The original law was so all-encompassing that the Justice Department laid down guidelines for us: There would be no prosecution for usury unless the sums involved amounted to substantial money and the lenders threatened, implied, or committed violence upon their clients.

Allen Magid was our first customer, and we learned a lot about how not to handle such cases from the experience. He was about thirty-five years old, short, stocky, quite intelligent, and possessed of an excellent memory. He had been in the roofing-and-siding business. Some miscalculations on his part plus the vagaries of the stockmarket put him into a financial pit. Having exhausted the legitimate sources of money, he began to draw from the shylocks of the mob. When Magid couldn't pay off, he became a pusher for swag from heists, stolen government checks, and phony securities. He even became a shylock himself.

Unfortunately, Magid's outgo continued to exceed his income. His contacts in crime beat him up and threatened his life, but they squeezed him too hard. He went to the Garden City, New York, branch of the FBI and turned himself in. He offered to provide evidence and testimony against his tormentors in return for protection. Since most of Magid's dealings and experiences involved New York City figures, and Garden City did not want the workload such a source creates, he was shipped to our office. We moved Magid to a hotel and put him under guard. As part of the protection, the Bureau hid his wife and kids at a motel in New Jersey. The instructions to the agent who accompanied the family to the location specified that the affair be handled discreetly. However, as Magid's wife registered, with the agent standing idly by, the motel manager suspected something unusual. He started to ask questions and the special agent, who was new to the job, lost his cool. He whipped out his credentials and growled, "This is a matter of national security. No more questions, please." Any chance of having the Magid family party pass unnoticed vanished. However, the manager was so struck by the notion of national security that he lavished every kindness possible upon the group.

Magid himself proved to be a mixed blessing. We all made the catastrophic mistake of believing that with his information and testimony we could get convictions against the crew that were indicted. Putting all our faith in Magid, we didn't go out and collect corroborations; at the very least, we should have sent Magid back into the street wired.

When the accused had their day in court, Magid, with his

prodigious memory for names and facts, was a spellbinder on the witness stand. But Allen had neglected to tell us that he had a psychiatric record. The defense counselors ripped into his story as a dealer in swag and stolen securities, his role as a shylock himself. Then they zeroed in on his psychological troubles. Magid's credibility was demolished. We lost every case that went to court. Furthermore, the government was still obligated to the expense and trouble of creating a new identity for Magid.

The Magid experience and several similar ones soured me on the pursuit of shylocks. It became obvious to me that the chief complainers were guys who had blown their stake and wanted to use the Bureau to wriggle out of the deal they had made with the devil. They decided that a shylock was something dirty only after they couldn't meet the payments. Nobody forced these guys to borrow the money; while I disapproved strongly of the use of force to collect from or to discipline slow payers, I couldn't see that there was a hell of a lot to be said for the deadbeats who tried to wipe out debts by giving up benefactors to whom they had turned in a moment of need.

Although Magid's information was worthless on the witness stand, he passed along some excellent material on other crimes. An associate of his, William Lieber,* managed a diamond and jewelry exchange. Lieber, in hock to shylocks like Magid, arranged to get off by setting up a robbery of the exchange with a couple of connected guys. They promptly cheated him out of his share of the $400,000 plus in jewelry taken. Desperate, Lieber contrived a neat caper. He had in his possession the labels from the stolen merchandise. He proposed to a would-be wiseguy that an approach be made to the owners of the Long Island exchange. The stuff had been woefully underinsured, and the wiseguys could offer to return it all for $100,000 in cash and the jewelers would still be better off than they were.

In due course, the wiseguys met with one of the owners and showed him some tags that came from the stolen property. The only problem for the proprietors was raising the cash. Some cash came from Lloyds of London, the insurer, some came from the jewelers' own bank accounts, and the rest was scraped up in loans from friends and relatives. At this point, thanks to Magid's information, we entered the case. It was fortunate for the exchange owners that we did, because Lieber's confederate, being unable to actually turn over the swag, had intended to take the cash and kill the jewelers.

The whole affair again demonstrated the problem of closing in before a crime had actually been committed. There was no charge we could stick against Lieber. The wiseguy who planned to kill the jewelers escaped. But we couldn't have afforded to let things go so far that someone would be killed. Later, we hooked Lieber for fraud in a loan application.

We traced the stolen jewelry to a Colombo man's house on Staten Island. When agent George Moresco and I arrived with a search warrant at the home of Sally Boy Mangimelli, the family was just getting up. While we searched the house, the wife excused herself for a few minutes to drive a youngster to school. She returned and offered to make coffee. I got tougher. "Give us the stuff or I'll take the place apart, piece by piece."

Obviously, Sally Boy had recently made a big score. He'd been the operator of a broken-down luncheonette that had just closed. But this was a brand-new house and everything in the place, from the pillowcases to the clothes in the closets to the furniture, was spanking new. It was as if these people had left their previous residence with nothing but the clothes on their backs and a sackful of money.

When I raved a bit more about what I would have to do to the place, Sally Boy resignedly said to his wife, "Okay, we may as well turn it over." He was actually a pleasant, seemingly accommodating man, but he had the reputation of being a mean bastard.

"What do you mean?" asked his wife.

"You know, hand it over," ordered Sally Boy. He grabbed one of the schoolbags and tossed it to me. Inside were a gun and about five thousand dollars in currency.

"We want the jewelry," I insisted. Sally Boy said he knew nothing about any jewelry. Moresco and I combed the house thoroughly and found nothing.

The visit to Sally Boy's place was a bust. Even the case against him for illegal possession of a pistol by a convicted felon was thrown out of court after his lawyer successfully argued that the weapon could have belonged to one of the older children's friends who had stopped by the house on the way to school.

Eventually, most of the swag from the Long Island Jewelry

Exchange showed up; it was part of the stuff Agent Yablonski found in Hy Gordon's house in Miami through the tip supplied to me by Nick Billeti.

I did much better with a source given to me by Mark Ross, the New York parole officer. Mark told me of a character who had just been released after seven years—one of his periodic stretches for various scams—whom I shall call Sidney "the Schemer" Roth.* He was a well-connected Jewish hood.

The Schemer's behavior wasn't hard to understand. His father was an old-time racket guy who worked for Jacob Shapiro and Meyer Lansky. Old man Roth was an early entrepreneur in narcotics, a violation of a statute known as the Harrison Act, but one day the law came after him. Sidney was in his early teens. His father slipped him out the back window with enough cash and documents to get him to England, where there were relatives.

By the time the Schemer reached his majority, his father was dead and Prohibition had furnished big opportunities for the ambitious. Schemer returned to the United States to be pleasantly surprised. His father had maintained his reputation for never having caved in under pressure and never having informed—a real stand-up guy. That was a precious legacy for the young Roth. His name opened doors for the ambitious youth. The Schemer went to work in gambling operations for Frank Costello and after repeal of Prohibition he marketed legal booze for Joe Profaci.

He was accepted by the powers in LCN, whose attitude was that a smart Jew makes money. Unfortunately, Schemer had a weakness: a passion for out-of-the-money horses. He was the kind of guy who, owning a nightclub, would go out and in a single evening drop fifty thousand dollars at a crap game, wiping out his title to the club.

He had a thing for the R. H. Macy's department store, using stolen credit cards and rubber checks. One technique was for him to sidle up to a girl at a cash register and say that he was from the store's security unit. "See that fellow there?" He would point to an inoffensive character several counters away. "I'm watching him. He dropped his credit card. Lemme see your sheets with the stolen card numbers." She would oblige, and he would make certain that the numbers of the cards he had were not on the "hot sheets." Then he would raid other departments of the store.

At one counter a girl looked at the name listed on some traveler's checks he was passing, "Suburu Yokahama." "What kind of a name is that, Turkish?" she inquired.

"No, my father was Japanese but my mother was Jewish," said Schemer with a straight face. (Because of the Japanese name, he had struck a bargain on the credit card and the four thousand dollars worth of traveler's checks, paying only ten cents on the dollar instead of the usual twenty to twenty-five cents.) Schemer so charmed the saleswoman that she accepted a bottle of perfume from him, which he bought with the stolen card.

Quite often he would go up to a salesgirl and hand her a card from which he had gotten considerable mileage. "Here, turn this in," he'd say. "You'll make fifty bucks on it because it's hot."

By the time Mark Ross introduced us, Schemer was close to sixty. He moved like a flaming rocket one moment and a burned-out stick the next. One day he would borrow ten dollars from me; a week later he would be able to show me that he had twenty thousand dollars and would be happy to pay me off tenfold. I would accept only my tenner back.

Turning Schemer depended on being on the scene at the right moment. A connected guy, Joe Woods,* had been grabbed on a heavy drug rap. Schemer happened to be in a position to testify for the prosecution. They offered him a tempting deal. If he performed as a friendly witness, the remaining five-odd years of parole ahead of him would be trouble free. With forty years of conning as his autobiography, a man like Schemer Roth doesn't change his act. And unlike Jackie Gucci's naive counselor, Gaetano Auriello, Mark Ross, the parole officer in this instance, knew it. And so did the feds who approached him. It would not be difficult to violate Schemer Roth, because he couldn't stay in bounds under any circumstances. That's what made the offer so tempting to him. It would be a license to misbehave.

But when Roth went on the witness stand, he confounded the prosecution. In no small part because of Schemer's convenient memory, Joe Woods beat the rap, and later the hood soaked Schemer with expressions of gratitude.

"You stuck your neck out for me. A good tree bears good fruit," said Joe, referring to the long-departed Roth senior. "I thank you again."

"I'm on the balls of my ass," said Schemer. "And the government is peeved at me. Can you stake me?"

"Of course," generously offered Woods. "Here, go buy yourself a hat." In the trade a "hat" is a small gift, varying according to the level of inflation. The offer from Joe Woods was a measly fifty dollars.

Thus, when I approached Schemer he was really pissed off at his old friends in the mob. He swallowed my pitch, and the promise of a small steady income, eagerly. For starters, I managed to quash a bad-check rap, which was the immediate result of Schemer's failure to procure a stake from Joe Rogers. It was against the house rules for an agent to approach a judge. But in Schemer's case I figured a small sin by me was a cheap price to keep Schemer on the street working for me.

Keeping Schemer out of the can was not easy. One night I was having a reunion with some old friends from Utica at the Waldorf-Astoria when I was paged for a telephone call. At the other end of the line was a patrolman from the Fifth Precinct, the East Greenwich Village area. He explained that he had stopped a car for a routine identification check. The car was hot and the driver had in his pockets no less than sixteen credit cards in various names, none of them his own—which happened to be Sidney Roth. However, when the policeman informed Roth he was taking him in, Schemer argued. "You can't arrest me. I'm on a very big case for Special Agent Anthony Villano."

"Can you verify his claim?" the cop asked me.

"You could check it out with the director of our New York office, John Malone, if you like, but it is true. We'd prefer that Roth's name not be mentioned indiscreetly. Why don't we work it out that you've made a good recovery from a civil standpoint? You've got back a stolen car plus the credit cards. Let Roth go and I'll make him behave."

The officer accepted the bargain with a gentle reminder that we owed him one. "If I ever can, I'll make you a hero," I promised. (The quid pro quo in these relationships was to give the locals a case that technically might also be ours. For example, we had thrown to the police the crap game once operated by Jackie Gucci and Tommy Massi. We could have busted the game, since it also ran afoul of federal statutes, but this was our way of repaying favors from the city cops.)

The Fifth Precinct cop put Schemer on the phone, and I gave him hell for both his stupidity and his cupidity. "I got you off.

Now, just walk out of the station house. Walk very slowly—but after you reach the pavement, run like the thief you are."

But there was no limit to Schemer Roth's chutzpah. "Wait a second—how about telling them to give me back the Cadillac and some of the credit cards?"

"Schemer, if you don't get the hell out of there and start running, I'm coming over and personally beat the shit out of you." He left, complaining.

Roth's girl friend, Rita, was the most long-suffering woman in the world. While he was away or flat on his ass she worked as a waitress to keep them alive. Then he would steal her tips. Even when he tried to give her a good time, she wound up suffering for his crimes. As a vacation, Schemer took Rita to Las Vegas. While there he played with stolen American Express checks. Roth used to buy the checks from Times Square hookers or pimps who stole them from the johns. The going price was about one thousand dollars for four thousand dollars worth of checks.

As a consequence of Roth's transactions at the gaming tables, I received a call one morning at three A.M. It was Schemer. He and Rita were in Nevada's Clark County Jail, charged with possession of stolen Amex checks in Las Vegas. Unfortunately for Roth's venture, the hooker from whom he had bought these pieces not only fleeced her john but stabbed him as well. Everyone was watching for these checks.

As soon as Schemer outlined his predicament I shut him up. I knew that all the telephone calls from Clark County Jail are recorded by the sheriff. I also figured that a Jew caught trying to rob Las Vegas would get fifty years from the 400-percent Americans who own the state. "Don't talk any more; don't call me," I cautioned Roth. "I'll do what I can from this end."

My boss, Dick Baker, knew a vice-president of American Express and agreed to approach him. The plea was that Roth was a very important source and could be counted upon to give us, and Amex, two for one and possibly better by helping to retrieve two loads of stolen checks in return for a pass on his own mischief.

American Express was agreeable, but Clark County wanted its pound and a half of flesh. They would release Roth and Rita only upon receipt of a thousand-dollar bond and a promise that

Schemer would never sully the incorruptible atmosphere of their casinos again. That meant the bond would be forfeited. There was no way I could promote the Bureau into putting up the bond. It had to come out of my own pocket. Dick Baker was concerned for my financial well-being.

"Will Roth be good for the money?"

"If he hits a horse, and I reach him before the next race." Still, I wired the bond.

Schemer called me from Las Vegas as soon as he left the hospitality of Clark County. "Could you meet us at the airport? I've only got thirty bucks in cash left." I was nagged by the fear that he would hang some more paper if I left him on his own, so I said okay.

At the terminal Rita was still shaken. "You can't imagine what it's like being locked up with all those hookers!" Schemer, however, was his usual ebullient self. He took me aside and handed me seven hundred dollars in cash.

"I thought you said you only had thirty bucks."

"I did. But before we went to the airport I went to the casino and run it up to seven hundred. If I could have stayed longer it would be seven thousand."

He also gave American Express its first payoff for the favor. "When they grabbed me I had only four hundred-dollar checks on me. I hid another five thousand dollars in Amex checks behind the cabinets in my room." I immediately contacted American Express, and the company was suitably grateful for the subsequent recovery.

Another narrow escape for Roth took place at Kennedy Airport. This time the Port Authority seized him. The officer who spoke to me considered Roth a terrific catch. "He's got to be one of the biggest thieves around. He's selling airline tickets for fifty cents on the dollar, using stolen credit cards to get the tickets. We calculate that he's ripped off the airlines for a couple of hundred thousand. But," said the Port Authority cop, "he keeps saying he's inviolate, that he works for you."

"Do me a favor," I pleaded. "Don't book him until I get there."

I hurried out to the airport. Every law-enforcement agency in the territory appeared to be on hand for a chance to put Schemer away. The local precinct cops, the downtown Manhattan DA's office, the Secret Service, the postal inspector—they were all there to put the arm on him.

As the center of attraction, he was having a ball. He was such a marvelous bullshitter, spieling his sea stories and simultaneously opening his listeners' noses with offers of fancy gifts. "What size shoe you wear, ten and a half D? I'll mail you four pairs of handmade alligator shoes. They were made for me but they don't fit right. What's your shirt size? Could you use a stereo?"

When I showed up, he greeted me warmly and asked for a moment to speak to me privately. The request was granted, and Schemer started by removing his shoe. "Here's some phony IDs and other evidence they didn't find." He handed me the stuff. I protested that he was making me into a coconspirator.

"Hell, when they left me in the bathroom, I flushed twenty years of evidence down the pot. I dumped another ten out the car window. They had five guys in the car that took me to the offices here, and I was handcuffed—I still tossed the stuff out the window."

The truth is Schemer Roth was working for me out at the airport. Cargo thefts were running into the hundreds of millions. With his connections and ability to move in the right circles, Roth had not only tipped me to what was going on, he also had taken to hanging around the terminals and hangars to observe the people involved. Unfortunately, while working on my business he was also occasionally slipping into some of his scams on the side.

The airports had become open territory; no single crime family enjoyed a monopoly. There was ample room for everyone, including a lot of free-lancers. Schemer originally got into the operation when a man in a bar offered to sell him some swag. Roth came to me and said, "I think maybe this is coming out of the airports." I encouraged him to build his relationship with the salesman. He did it so well that he came to be accepted within the inner circles of the gangs looting the cargo shipments. Because of the nature of the thefts, I found it necessary to enlist the support of the U.S. postal inspectors. I was nervous about the organization; it's too political to be trusted. One postal inspector, however, Stew Jones, was excellent at his job, and with his cooperation we began to wire Schemer to gather evidence.

Based on the intelligence from Schemer I was able to get him a walk from Kennedy and the Port Authority cops. And he continued to supply me with vital intelligence on how things were done and who was involved.

One of the biggest thieves was Bobby Cudak, a ramp man for Northwest Airlines. With a handful of confederates, Cudak ripped off hundreds of bags of registered mail, sacks with highly negotiable stocks and bonds, jewelry, and air freight cargos of pelts and rare-metal ingots. In fact, one bag contained thirteen million dollars worth of negotiable securities. The security was so poor at the airports that Cudak and his crew hauled their stuff away in trucks. Schemer Roth, performing his own surveillance, watched Cudak load up a yellow van and tracked it. We obtained a warrant and busted Cudak.

Once we had Cudak and talked to him about the million years of various counts that he faced, he began to cooperate. He gave up the fences and his associates. There was very little honor among these particular thieves; every one of them had been cheating on the other. Through Cudak we picked up the Schaefer brothers—James, John, Charles, and Edward—and they rolled over and gave us William Ricchuti.

Most of the principals, including some of the LCN members, went before a Senate subcommittee investigating the role of organized crime in the stolen securities racket. Cudak and James Schaefer appeared as cooperating witnesses; the mob guys kept their mouths shut.

As in most thefts of this nature, the gangs often received inside information on which flights carried valuable cargo. When alerted that something valuable was due, Cudak and company had only to squeeze mail sacks to feel if there was another bag inside, a sure sign of registered or precious items. Truck hijackers get their tips from drivers and dispatchers. Only occasionally does somebody goof and wind up, as one crew did, with 300,000 Ping-Pong balls.

Schemer Roth also played a part in saving the skin of another informant for us. A garment-center guy I knew, and whom I'd softened up and then turned over to another agent, was in trouble with shylocks who belonged to big wiseguys. They had come to him with a proposition: He could continue to pay the "vig" (usurious interest) or he could get off by participating in a hijacking they had planned.

The guy—Harry Shroder*—telephoned his contacting agent, Dick Witkowski. The plan was to burglarize an unspecified warehouse, load up a couple of trucks, and then take the swag to Scranton, Pennsylvania, to a drop owned by Joe Colombo. Shroder was to be in on it because he knew textiles and they needed some advice on values. Witkowski asked me for advice to pass along to Shroder. Aware of how badly the Bureau wanted Joe Colombo, we decided to let Shroder go along. As soon as the trucks made it to the Scranton drop, he could duck out and give us a call. We would have a crew standing by to hit the place— and maybe we would get lucky and come up with Colombo himself.

It was all arranged for a Friday night. About two A.M. on Saturday I received a telephone call about Shroder's disaster. As part of the operation, he had driven his Eldorado Cadillac to the New Haven, Connecticut, warehouse that was being robbed. He followed the trailers right into the building. Everybody started to load the trucks but, unfortunately, nobody had remembered to turn off the burglar alarm. In came the cops. In the ensuing bedlam, a big goon hired to load and unload the trucks fled right through a plate-glass window. Shroder lammed through the opening in the glass, on the goon's heels.

Shroder staggered through the woods and brush until he finally made it to a taxi stand, where he hired a driver to take him all the way home to Manhattan. He then called Witkowski and wanted to know what he should do. Witkowski consulted me. I advised that Shroder report his car stolen, have his wife say that he was in Philadelphia, and go there, meanwhile sending his wife and kids to Atlantic City for the weekend. Witkowski agreed and passed along the instructions. But there was another call Sunday night. Obviously Shroder hadn't followed the game plan.

Since his Eldorado had been found so neatly parked in the New Haven warehouse, FBI agents had shown up at Shroder's house. Because, as he later explained, he was afraid of his wife, he had failed to clue her in. There he was, still home, nursing the ankle he'd injured in his flight through the woods. As instructed, he said his car had been stolen; he had reported this to the local cops. When asked politely by the agents for a photo of her husband, the wife obligingly handed over a perfect reproduction. He was in real trouble now; after driving him for almost two hours, the cabby would sure as hell recognize him from that photograph.

On Monday morning I went to the SAC and filled him in on the story. We had to protect our informant and ourselves. I volunteered to go to New Haven and throw myself on the sword. I would talk with the prosecutor and the chief of police, both of whom were very highly regarded by the Bureau there. I intended to explain the whole deal—that we had hoped to catch the head of one of the major crime families in a robbery, or at least find his Pennsylvania drop and make a full recovery. The SAC accepted my proposal.

I traveled to New Haven to see the authorities. Sympathetic as they were, the prosecutor and police chief pointed out that the warehouse belonged to an influential corporation. The presence of the Eldorado could not be ignored. I offered a solution: I would produce "Harry Shroder" for a police lineup; the cops and the cab driver would look him over and see that this was not the man they had seen on the day of the attempted robbery. They agreed. Now all I had to do was find the right stand-in for Harry Shroder. But none of Shroder's friends or family would take the chance. "Not even when I offered my brother-in-law a thousand bucks," complained Shroder.

I knew somebody who would do it just for the hell of it: Schemer Roth. "Give me your wallet and leave one hundred dollars in it," I told Shroder. My only problem was that Harry Shroder was forty-two, fat, nervous—a typical garment-center tycoon. Schemer was sixty-four, gray-haired, slender.

On the ride to New Haven, Dick Witkowski and I prepped our stand-in. "Project yourself as a forty-two-year-old, fat, tired garment-center businessman." Schemer then proceeded to commit to memory Shroder's background, his children's birth dates, his wife's maiden name, and all the other details of their lives.

At the police station, only the chief and the prosecutor knew the deal. We identified ourselves, including our Mr. Shroder. Fortunately, the agent who obtained the photograph of Shroder had never bothered to show it once it was learned the subject himself would make a lineup. The witnesses, the cops, and the cabby looked at the lineup. They all shook their heads no—except the cabby, who suddenly yelled, "I know that guy! I know that guy!" I died, but then he said, "I know him, but not from that night." He had ferried Roth to a racetrack one evening and had never forgotten him. Few people did. Now I had to pull Schemer out of the police station—I saw him huddled with a detective who was a ham radio operator. Roth was about to con him out of an order for electronic equipment, just so the trip shouldn't be a total loss.

On our way home, we stopped off for a celebration dinner at a fancy restaurant in Connecticut. I was just able to catch Roth as he tried to pay for the meal with a hot credit card. And when I finally left him off, having retrieved Shroder's wallet—minus the hundred-dollar fee—I discovered that Schemer had tried to retain one of Shroder's credit cards.

In other instances I went undercover with Schemer's assistance. Once he gave me an introduction to the owner of a flashy discotheque in the suburbs of New York who was peddling blank signed bank checks. I met with Ira Rimmer* at the Commodore Hotel. He seemed to fancy himself as a kind of Mr. Lucky, straight out of the movies. Not to be outdone, Schemer passed me off as the fastest pen on the East Coast.

I started out by moaning that it was a pity I hadn't met Rimmer a week earlier. "I had a load of Scotch that went for forty bucks a case."

"Christ, I'd have taken all you had."

"What about twenty-dollar gold pieces or uncut diamonds?"

My new friend became even more interested in me. "I'll give you some bank checks," offered Rimmer. "You can lay them off for merchandise like you spoke of. All we want is fifty cents on the dollar." This was what I was after, a ring that was hanging paper all over town. "I can't tell you the contact's name," he warned me, "but I can get the checks cleared with no trouble."

"You get me the first check, and if it passes, we'll all get rich," I promised. My cover story was that I was notorious in East Harlem, a good territory to use, since it was kind of open turf. He couldn't check me out with any single source.

We agreed to meet at his "joint" several nights later. Rimmer was at the bar with another man, the Mr. Big of their operation, when I came in. Rimmer didn't even introduce me. Mr. Big gave me a look over.

"I'll see you in the john," said Rimmer to his partner, who departed. After a few minutes passed, Rimmer instructed me: "Take a look in the second urinal."

It's not exactly the kind of place I would've preferred to find my fortune, but I couldn't be choosy. I fished out the envelope, and inside was a signed blank cashier's check.

"Okay, I'm putting it in for $442," I advised Rimmer. "Then we'll see how this goes."

I went to a branch of Chemical Bank, where I knew the manager, and explained the plot. I asked him to put the piece through, that we would guarantee the cash recovery. The people at Chemical accommodated me, and three days later I spoke to Rimmer. "Did your man see the results of my handiwork?"

"Sure did, only it's a girl." That narrowed the identity of the source but not enough to make any arrests and go to court.

"Okay, my next one will be for three hundred thousand. We'll drop a couple like that and then sign off. Meanwhile, can you use a portable TV? I've got three color Sonys and a couple of stereos in case you're interested. If you give me an address, I can deliver."

He bought it all and gave me the girl's address. "Okay," I told him, "it'll take a couple of days. Now how about the next piece for tomorrow?" He was as eager as I. However, I begged for a location other than his joint, on the grounds that the place was too fancy. We settled on the Commodore bar. The deal required me to put up half of the original $422 check plus a couple of thousand up front on delivery of the next check, the balance to come after it cleared.

We had the Commodore sprinkled with agents. The instructions were to pinch him before I handed over the money. Otherwise the cash would become part of the inventory of his possessions and not retrievable until after the case was disposed of. The best evidence was for him to possess the check at the time of arrest.

At the bar, Rimmer slipped me the envelope. I peeked inside, saw that it was the genuine article. "Here," I said, handing it back. "Check the number so your girl is sure to know what to look for." As he studied the number, I pretended to reach inside my jacket. That signaled the other agents to grab us. (Whenever I played an undercover role as a criminal it was always part of the drill for me to be busted, in order to protect the informant. Sometimes I would be in the pen with the other guys when a cop or agent would come around and say something like "You, Tony Damiano [my alias], there's a warrant out for you from Los Angeles for homicide. Get your stuff; we're sending you to L.A.")

While we were handcuffed and starting on our way to the FBI offices, I had a brainstorm. "Listen," I whispered to Mr. Lucky, "I'm in bad shape. I've got big time hanging over me, and this means going away for a long stretch. Do what you want, but I'm going to cooperate and give it all up."

Rimmer started to sweat. "I'll lose my joint and my liquor license." I tried to look sad over his problem. Naturally, as soon as they took him in to be interviewed he spilled everything—the idea was to be the first one to cooperate and strike a bargain. He gave up everybody who was involved in the deal.

A lead from someone I'll call Sally Anne,* an angry hooker who'd been caught with stolen credit cards, opened up a maze. She'd spent some time with a toughie named Sonny Red Indelicato. Having gained Sonny Red's confidence in bed, Sally Anne learned some details of Sonny Red's range of enterprises. Since Sonny Red had a lifetime parole hanging over his head, he was a character that Mark Ross had suggested I work on.

Out of prison, Sonny Red was the "go-for" of Joseph Yacovelli (Joe Yak), underboss and ultimately the temporary successor to Joe Colombo after Joseph Gallo's black gunner destroyed his brain with a bullet at the 1971 Columbus Day celebration of the Italian American Unity Day rally. At the very best, Sonny Red was supposed to support himself in the shylock business and stolen securities.

Back in the early 1950s, Sonny Red had been sitting in a car outside a social club. Inside, a friend of his, Carmine DiBiase, aka Sonny Pinto, was in a card game. DiBiase's opponent was a chum named Mike Errichello, aka Mike English, but DiBiase had a pronounced aversion to losing. He left the club, came back a short while later, and put a bullet in the head of his pal English, who'd had the poor judgment to win and fall asleep at the table. DiBiase was about to take off when he noticed a witness to the killing; he put a couple of bullets into him. Outside, DiBiase hailed a ride with Sonny Red. The witness, however, survived.

The cops caught up with Sonny Red, accused him of being an accomplice to a homicide, and made it stand up in court. That bought Sonny Red a life sentence. DiBiase, on the other hand, managed to hide out for eight years before he was caught and tried. DiBiase was convicted on his own confession but the decision was reversed. A retrial brought him an acquittal. During the eight years, although the cops couldn't find him, DiBiase had been available enough to be made, while poor Sonny Red, who was eventually paroled after doing his time, wasn't around for any swearing-in ceremonies.

Based on Sally Anne's tip about Sonny Red we obtained a warrant to search his sister's house in the Mulberry Street neighborhood of New York, within stone's-throwing distance of some favorite LCN hangouts. Sally Anne claimed Sonny Red stashed his shylock records and stolen securities in a bedroom drop. I went through the bedroom by the square inch and found nothing. It was a helluva kick in the ass for me, the supersearcher, not to be able to locate the drop.

She also mentioned a second and adjoining apartment that was theoretically empty. Using the same warrant, we went through that place. It was not actually vacant; there were piles of old furniture and a wardrobe full of Oleg Cassini clothes, probably plucked from a hijacking. We found a gun and a neatly kept notebook of shylock records. Only it didn't belong to Sonny Red; it was his thirteen-year-old nephew's account book. The kid had not only listed the debts of five and ten dollars as well as the vig; he had even created his own family. He listed himself as the boss with lines drawn to other names as caporegimes, under which appeared boxes containing names and addresses of the boy soldiers.

Sonny Red's sister, the mother of this budding godfather, started to scream at us, and I waved the pubescent loanshark's composition book at her. We went back to her apartment and really tore the place apart. In the midst of the ransacking, the boy showed up. "Who's in charge here?" he said.

"I am," said one of the New York detectives.

"That gun you found—it's not my uncle's. It's mine; I found it in a trash basket," the kid announced.

We had struck out entirely with Sonny Red. The Manhattan DA looked at the gun and the shylock records and said, "You think I'm going to prosecute a thirteen-year-old kid for this? Hell no."

I didn't see any way to go after Sonny Red until Sally Anne came to me again with both a squawk and some information. Two mutts, Joe Wagonwheels and Billy Sea, had stuck her up at gunpoint, roughed her up, and relieved her of two thousand dollars worth of merchandise and stolen Amex traveler's checks. She brooded about her injury until she picked up a piece of information. Joseph Yacovelli had a black-sheep brother, Charles (Charlie Yak), who was in business with another guy. They dealt in stolen credit cards and penny-ante stuff, bargain-priced items from hookers and pimps. Sally Anne did business with them only when desperate. Nevertheless, she had heard that Joe Wagonwheels and Billy Sea had stuck up Charlie Yak and his associates and thrashed them so badly that Charlie Yak required hospital attention.

The squabble offered potential leverage for a move on Sonny Red and company. It was conceivable that at issue were shylock rights to certain territories. But I needed to know the truth about the stickup of Charlie Yak. I wired Sally Anne. She contacted Charlie Yak's partner and led him like a blind horse.

"I thought Charlie Yak's brother was a big man, a guy who could protect you."

"He is big. I guarantee that Joe Wagonwheels will pay for this," said the aggrieved voice on the recorder.

"It sounds to me like you guys owed them money."

"Naw, it was nothing like that. It was strictly a stickup." It was no fantasy about Joe Yak's taking revenge. Joe Wagonwheels and Billy Sea disappeared permanently soon after.

Meanwhile, Carmine DiBiase, Sonny Red's old friend, paid off another grievance for the Colombo Family: He was the trigger-man who shot down Joe Gallo in 1972, when he tried to forget his cares with an early-morning snack at Umberto's Clam House.

The fingerman for the Gallo hit was Joe Luparelli, a typical knockaround guy who had tried all his life to become made but never quite showed the right credentials. By having spotted Joey Gallo in an exposed position, Luparelli thought he would improve his status with the family. However, after the assassins holed up at a Nyack, New York, apartment owned by Joe Yak, Luparelli detected what he thought were signs of hostile intent on the part of his companions. One night he suffered extreme stomach pains; he knew about witnesses already in the hands of the cops who had been mysteriously poisoned. He awoke from a troubled sleep to see Carmine DiBiase standing over him, perhaps measuring the angle of fire. While the Nyack party sat at a glass-topped table, Luparelli was chilled to overhear DiBiase make a joke about him. DiBiase held his hand under the table, formed a gun shape, and smilingly pointed it at Luparelli.

The threat to Luparelli may have been only a paranoid's vision, or else his sense of security was poor. But one day the fingerman excused himself to get a pack of cigarettes in town and then didn't stop running until he put three thousand miles between himself and DiBiase. But even in California, Luparelli felt that the executioners would inevitably find him. He turned himself in at the Bureau field office in Santa Ana.

Luparelli asked to be turned over to Denis Dillon of the Eastern District Strike Force. But the decision was that while technically Joe Gallo's death could be a federal rap, the case most properly belonged to the local cops. Luparelli wasn't enthusiastic about the transfer, but he was no longer in a position to call the shots.

Unfortunately, the chief of New York City detectives, Al Seedman, made the same kind of mistake we had made with Allen Magid. He banked his hopes on Luparelli as a witness and arranged for surveillance of the four hoods still ensconced in Nyack. A workman at Nyack later made a positive identification on Sonny Red as a visitor to the hideout. Seedman would have been much better off if he had put Luparelli back in place—out on the street, where he could be covered. Added evidence against DiBiase and company might have been gathered, because nobody else at Umberto's admitted to having seen or recognized anyone. To make matters worse, the quartet at Nyack managed to drive off and disappear—DiBiase had already demonstrated once that he was an expert at this sort of thing.

Before the whole case fell apart, I did have an opportunity to interview Luparelli, and I managed to penetrate deeper into the maze opened by Sally Anne. Luparelli knew all about the stickup of Charlie Yak by Joe Wagonwheels and Billy Sea. Luparelli had managed to find Wagonwheels and bring him to that dusty apartment next to the one occupied by Sonny Red Indelicato's sister. There, Sonny Red, Carmine DiBiase, Joe Yak, and others fell upon him with ice picks. Luparelli assisted in the burial of Joe Wagonwheels in a nearby garage. I called Mark Ross and said, "I think we've got Sonny Red."

We and the New York cops dug up the garage floor. We found no corpse, just the stink of death. The New York medical examiner, Milton Helpern, looked over the hole and said he was convinced that there remained in the dirt signs of the putrefaction of a human body—the residue was too much to be from rats. But we had nothing to use against Sonny Red, who continues to be free on the street.

There was a falling-domino syndrome, particularly when you dealt with the white-collar scammers who served time hard—unlike the button men, who accepted prison as a kind of tax they paid for the right to operate. Button men rarely traded in an associate in return for a walk. But the scammers often caved in and offered up anybody they thought might interest us.

Don Jones, one of a handful of superagents in the FBI, had been transferred, and as his last official act he introduced me to an informant named Barry Kahn.* Kahn operated ostensibly as a kind of investment banker, but in reality he was better versed in the negotiations of hot paper.

At forty, Barry Kahn epitomized one variety of con artist. As a teenager he hustled for fast-buck operators who blitzed Harlem blacks into signing up their children for music lessons. Barry would stop parents with kids on the street, ask the children a couple of questions, and then announce, "This boy is a prodigy; I can tell from the sound of his voice and his basic understanding of music. It would be a crime to deny him a chance to develop that musical talent."

Kahn graduated to the sale of phony oil leases, operating mostly in the Midwest and the South. Traveling with veteran hucksters who coached him in the trade, Kahn played a variety of parts—geologist, oil tycoon, lawyer—in the scripts that suckered rich and poor into parting with their cash.

In New York City, where he blossomed into an active securities swindler, Kahn blew every dollar in a jet-set lifestyle. He sniffed enough coke to have a permanent case of the sniffles. He picked himself up with amphetamines, let himself down with either booze or barbiturates. He always had to wear the latest fad, breaking out in Nehru jackets, denim, leather, and beads.

When Barry drank, it had to be at some name-dropping joint, like Elaine's or P. J. Clarke's. If he owned a car, it had to be a Ferrari or an Aston Martin. His friends were the most expensive hookers in town, big-score cocaine importers, and, of course, the better-class securities hustlers. His wife had divorced him, but Barry remained devoted to their five-year-old boy; his idea of a birthday party was to rent a piece of an expensive New York City restaurant for a luncheon for the boy and his friends. The tab would run around $250, which the place would have a tough time collecting.

Kahn's office was like a circus held in a bordello. He spent much of the day screaming over the telephone at various creditors, including department stores that were disturbed by his credit-card extravaganzas and utility companies that wanted to shut off his services. When the management at his apartment house called about the fourth month's overdue rent and indicated that they were about to evict him, Barry yelled, "I'm going to throw a party there with ten Puerto Rican hookers! We'll put on a show that will empty your whole fucking building—your whole fucking building, you hear that?" In case the listener wasn't paying close attention, Barry had a trick of banging the telephone speaker on his desk in a way that rattled the eardrum at the other end of the line. Such confrontations usually ended with his promise to send a check as a partial payment.

Various thieves would visit his office with propositions for trading U.S. Treasury bills, pre-World War II German bonds, certificates belonging to the bluest chips in American corporations. When he was not bargaining with these individuals, Barry passed the time grabbing at the anatomy of his latest secretary, usually a hustler temporarily retired from her customary trade.

When it got down to serious business, Kahn's character radically metamorphosed into Mr. Responsible. Self-taught, he knew the world of finance beautifully. He knew what paper was worth and how to exploit it. He could talk to bankers, brokers, and private investors in a soothing, authoritative tone that inspired confidence. He was actually a very shrewd, intelligent guy who could have done well had he not been committed to hustling.

When I met him, he was close to being buried again for his sins. He had done eight very hard months once. With his way of life, he couldn't accept a second and probably longer term behind bars. It wasn't difficult to secure his cooperation.

After I won Kahn's confidence, he cracked to me that he was approached to "middle" some stolen securities. At the time I was deeply involved in the Joe Colombo gambling operation and instructed Kahn to keep me advised. "You better tape any calls," I told him. "We will need the evidence." Finally, arrangements were completed for the transfer of cash for the paper. Kahn told me where it would all come down. I complimented him on his good work and then ordered him to stay the hell away from the Plaza Hotel lobby, where the deal would be consummated. His presence would not be required. We would be able to arrest the people involved for possession of the stolen securities.

For some inexplicable reason, however, Kahn decided to show anyway. He was like that, a character who was unable to resist being in on a large scam; possibly he even thought he might be able to skim off a few bucks before agents arrived on the scene. Instead, agents from another unit using their own informant spotted Kahn, took off in a wild car chase after him, and busted him on the sidewalk in Times Square. When they brought Kahn in, I gave him hell for disobeying me and then I spoke to Joe Sullivan, the SAC in charge of general criminal matters. I explained that Kahn had been very good news for us and that he had helped make this case. Sullivan heard me out and allowed Barry to be cut loose. "But he owes us one," said Sullivan, and I passed the word to Barry.

A short time later Barry Kahn notified me that another "investment banker," Cy Greenberg* had asked if he knew a banker who would cash a $100,000 ice-cold Treasury bill for which Cy would pay a twenty-percent "commission." I might not be a Wall Street genius, but even I know ten-dollar bills will never be legitimately wholesaled for eight dollars.

I persuaded Barry to invite Cy Greenberg to bring his T bill to Barry's "main man," a banker at the Royal Bank on Lexington Avenue in New York. Naturally, the officious banker turned out to be an agent and the "ice-cold" T bill was hotter than a Bronx tenement in July.

Cy Greenberg did not look forward to prison any more than Barry Kahn. But Greenberg was another type altogether. There was nothing flamboyant about him. After he consummated a crooked deal he, like Gino Asturi, only wanted to enjoy the pleasures of his suburban home. Also, as distinct from Kahn, Greenberg spent much of the time engaged in legitimate deals. I immediately prodded him for his supplier, and he finally gave me the name of a lawyer. Greenberg and I made a call to the lawyer, with Greenberg stressing that he had a very anxious buyer. When the counselor arrived and showed his hand, I busted him too. A few words about his dark future induced the lawyer to give up his source, another legal eagle. Lawyer number one called lawyer number two to say that I wasn't satisfied with only the $100,000 piece that I was shown; I wanted a million, since we were aware that the theft involved about two million.

When lawyer number two arrived to dicker over the million, I put the arm on him and coaxed him to give up his source. He revealed that Tony Rollo, a mob guy, was the brains behind the entire deal and was parked in a Buick nearby with some friends. We had already staked out the area with agents. They grabbed Rollo and the two torpedoes as well as additional hot paper.

The entire operation was completed within a single day, involved a fantastic recovery and, later, five solid convictions. All this came from Barry Kahn's tip. About a month later he telephoned me with the bad news. "I just got busted by your friends for that thing at the Plaza." Kahn had been released on his own recognizance, but the case had already been filed with an assistant U.S. attorney.

When I protested to my supervisor about the treatment of Kahn, I was told to talk to the securities squad, particularly Harry Gossett, a solid, hard-working guy who had the case. "Shit, Harry, what gives? You know the deal Sullivan made with Kahn," I lamented.

"Don't talk to me, Tony. See Joe Gamble. He's the new boss here. [Gamble replaced Sullivan, with whom I had made the deal.] I'm only an Indian."

Gamble lost his temper when I tried to intercede for Kahn. "Goddamnit, he's stealing us blind. He doesn't give us cases; he can't have a license while he's screwing us."

"We made a deal. It was agreed that if Kahn gave us a good case, we'd call it fair and square on the Plaza Hotel. And he did give us a very good one."

"That was Sullivan's deal. I'm not bound to it," said Gamble.

"Bullshit. You can't break the Bureau's word. If you continue this charade, I'm going to testify for Kahn in court." At issue was my career in the Bureau against my word to an informant. As far as I was concerned, the answer was the bottom line for whatever ethics or morality I could claim.

Gamble really didn't believe me at first. "You son of a bitch, you would testify for that fucking thief?"

"Right's right, and I never met anybody so unprincipled as you."

"You either retract what you just said or I'm going to get you fired."

"I'm going to talk to the U.S. attorney on the case."

"Take Gossett with you," insisted Gamble, which suited me fine. The more witnesses I had to Gamble's stunt, the better I liked it.

The U.S. attorney, Bobby Lawyer, was very negative on the matter at first. "The indictment naming Kahn will be filed tomorrow. The grand jury has already heard the case."

I related the previous events, the bargain struck at the office, and the contributions Kahn had recently made. That failed to sway the U.S. attorney.

"If it goes to court, I'm going to testify for Kahn," I said.

Bobby Lawyer smiled. "That'll make it interesting, the FBI testifying against the FBI." He wouldn't budge because, he explained, the reports he had seen all pointed to Kahn as the moving force in the swindle.

"I think maybe I have some evidence that will change your mind."

"My mind is made up, but I'll listen," Bobby Lawyer smiled patiently. From his office I called Barry Kahn. I was praying that he had followed my instructions and recorded the calls that had to do with the Plaza Hotel deal. Fortunately, Barry had wired up his phone. He brought the tapes down to Lawyer's office immediately.

It was a revelation for the prosecutor. Barry Kahn obviously was not the prime mover but only a fellow propositioned by the others. The discrepancies between the tapes and what the prosecutor understood were plainly audible. "Screw this," Bobby Lawyer sighed, "I'm nolle processing the whole case. It's the most fucked-up deal I ever saw, with informants working against informants."

Gossett, who had listened to the whole business, now had the unpleasant duty of letting Joe Gamble in on the latest development. "They're going to drop the whole case," he said on the phone. "Kahn had some tapes he made."

Gossett listened to Gamble and then turned to me. "Tony, Mr. Gamble wants you in his office in twenty minutes with those tapes."

I hid the tapes until Gamble accepted the futility of his position.

A third individual, less a scammer than an innocent dupe, proved to be a valuable source and aid in several cases. Marvin Nadborne operated a used-car lot in Brooklyn. His business was just piddling along when one day he was approached by a fellow from the neighborhood who offered to supply cars at bargain prices. Nadborne and his new friend became partners. The company did smashing business, until the feds came along and roped in Marvin and his associate as dealers in stolen cars. He pulled a five-year suspended sentence. Nadborne, I am convinced, was ignorant of the machinations of his confederate.

Marvin had one weakness: He liked to gamble. Without his used-car business behind him, he swiftly ran up some debts and then turned to the loan sharks. As the bites became increasingly painful he was smart enough to realize that these jaws would never let loose. He went to the law for help. Eventually, Marvin was directed to me. I saw immediately that he could be very helpful. A small mountain of a man, Marvin had that essential salesman's gift, the ability to convince a prospect that he was about to be offered an item at a bargain price. Marvin could make it with the mob guys; they would trust him to produce revenue. I had learned my lesson from the experience with Allen Magid. Instead of simply pumping Nadborne dry of his knowledge, I placed him where he could continue to supply intelligence.

As a schmuck in hock to the shylocks, Marvin was able to get in on a scheme for bank loans to connected guys who then put the money out on the street at shylock rates. An official in the bank who okayed the loans received a kickback for his services. We broke that up and then Nadborne became involved with a hood named Patty King in a scheme to dump half a million in counterfeit. Unknown to King, Nadborne, through my intercession, spelled out the caper to the Secret Service, who grabbed King and company with all their merchandise.

While awaiting trial, King got in touch with Nadborne. "We've gotta lot of weight for that load of fugazy. I gotta sell something and then split. You know anything about selling drugs?"

Nadborne said he might be able to find a buyer. King pulled out a bill of lading for two drums of Serenace, an extremely powerful depressant made by Lilly and Company, insured for $284,000. It was not the kind of drug that Nadborne had expected King to be handling. It had been stolen from JFK Airport while bound for Japan. Neither King nor Nadborne had any idea what Serenace was, but Marvin promised to look for a purchaser.

Marvin Nadborne reported this conversation to me, and we then worked out a cover story for him to lay on Patty King. The insurer was committed to a twenty-five thousand dollar reward for complete recovery of the drug or ten percent of anything short of the entire shipment. Marvin was to tell Patty that I was an East Harlem drug peddler who had boasted that if I had enough stuff in one place, I could sell it, that there were "people around who'd buy horseshit if it's packaged right." Patty had told Nadborne the price was $300,000, that the drugs weighed about forty pounds, and that he wanted $150,000 cash up front.

Nadborne conferred with Patty King, who did not wholly trust our informant. King realized that someone had given him up to the Secret Service with the phony tens. "If you're a rat, I'm going to put a bullet in your head," he remarked to Nadborne not very casually during the Serenace discussion. "And if anything goes wrong on this," he reiterated, "I'm going to fucking waste you." Unabashed, Nadborne argued price with King and was finally able to haggle him down to $150,000, with $100,000 cash up front. It was always extremely important to fight over the price when making an undercover buy; otherwise the seller assumed you were either a cop or else intended to pay for the merchandise with Monopoly money.

When Nadborne brought King's suspicions to me, I figured that

Marvin was coming to the end of his usefulness. "If this thing goes down, it will be advisable to have you leave town for good," I told him. We arranged contingency plans for his immediate relocation.

I checked into the Summit Hotel in Manhattan under my alias, Tony Damiano. In my room Nadborne called King at a number where he could be reached. When King got on the line, I took the phone and yelled, "You're out of your fucking mind! You want a hundred grand in cash up front and I can't even sample the drug you got. It could be bicarbonate of soda."

King proposed that we bring the money to a place in New Jersey where we could inspect a sample of the merchandise.

"Sure, sure. We'll walk in with the money. You'll hit us over the head and rip us off. I've got my chemist registered here and I've got the money. Figure out a safe way for us to test the stuff. No trips to lonely places."

Patty King protested his good faith but claimed he needed to check with his people. A short while later he called and asked if we'd be agreeable to a trip to a private house in Brooklyn, where my chemist—who was Ed Pistey, another agent—could examine the drugs.

My answer was still no. We could not take a chance on being in any isolated surroundings where we could be easily taken. "The way you talk, it's all beginning to sound to me like a scam. You don't really have anything to sell. All you want is a crack at the one hundred gees."

King pleaded for patience. "Wait a minute," he said and covered the speaker on the phone. When he came back on the line he asked if my chemist and I would accept what he called a "public place" in Brooklyn as a place to analyze the drug. If we were satisfied, then I could telephone an associate to deliver the cash.

We made King wait while we considered all the angles. Around twelve forty-five in the afternoon we called him again and said okay. Instead of telling us how to get there, King said he and a buddy would come to the Summit and drive us to the "public place."

It took a little over an hour for King and his chum to arrive. In my room were Marvin Nadborne, Ed Pistey, who played the chemist even to wearing a white smock, which he borrowed from a nearby hospital, and Special Agent Dick Witkowski, who passed as a guard for our money. We had carefully strewn currency on the table and left open an attaché case stuffed with greenbacks. Actually it amounted to all of five thousand dollars; the insurance company was very chintzy on advancing us show money. But we arrayed it artfully enough, with ten-thousand-dollar wrappers and bill-size cuts of newspaper, to widen Patty King's eyes. As soon as he got the scent of it, I slammed the case shut. There was a brief interchange about procedures, and then Patty King asked me to step outside the hotel room. In the corridor he turned decidedly unfriendly. "I think you're a cop. I'm going to search you."

"Be my guest," I said, removing my jacket so he could pat me down more easily. I held the jacket in my hand while Patty ran his hands over my body. Ordinarily I carried my pistol in a belly holster that fitted snugly unside the waistband of my trousers; that way there was no bulge to betray what I carried. But on this occasion, my .38 was in the pocket of the jacket I was casually holding. He, of course, found nothing. If there had been trouble, I figured I could grab the gun in my coat.

Instead of appearing insulted by his actions, I voiced my approval. "That's good. You keep thinking that I might be a cop and then you're going to be very careful on how you do things."

"Okay, we'll leave the money here," explained Patty. "When you're satisfied with the drugs, you can call and release it."

"Let's leave Marvin behind, too," I said. "I don't trust him. You, me, and the chemist is all we need." I wanted to cut Marvin out of the action wherever possible. We already had U.S. marshals out guarding his home, ready to pack up his wife and kids and ship them out of town as soon as the operation ended.

On the way out I remarked to Patty, within earshot of Nadborne, "Has this guy got a wife and kids? Because I'm telling you, I had to go to every shylock in East Harlem to come up with this hundred thousand and it'll cost me a hundred and ten thousand. If I get crossed I'm coming out to his house and do a number on his fucking family."

"Don't get scared if you see two torpedoes with me when I bring the money," Marvin then chirped to King. "He's got guards for his hundred gees." That explained away the agents who would be seen with Nadborne when he showed up at the site of the Serenace.

Waiting outside in the car used by Patty King was a man introduced to me as Jerry and later identified as Jerome Meistrion. In his capacity as a scientist, Agent Ed Pistey remarked that this drug possessed very poisonous fumes if inhaled. He hoped we would not be working in an area of large drafts or big exhaust fans, such as a garage. Jerry reassured him that the "public place" was a butcher shop with a back room ideal for our purposes.

Around three in the afternoon we arrived at the shop, which was on the edge of the black ghetto, Bedford-Stuyvesant. King now accepted a secondary role in the scheme. He waited outside in the car while Jerry took charge. He led us into the rear of the butcher shop, where we met Paul Esposito, described as the owner of the package we had come to buy. Jerry confided to me that in the future it would be wisest to deal directly with one another in order to "cut off all the fat." (Standard procedure among the honorable thieves of LCN is to undercut one another whenever possible. Both Bobby Cudak and Jimmy Schaefer had given us innumerable instances of double and triple crosses on the goods looted from the airlines. Cudak and Schaefer cheated on one another, the fences cheated them, the mob guys encouraged everyone to slice out any associates.) Jerry and Paul proposed that I eliminate Patty's and Marvin's shares in any future deal, and, in fact, they expected another package worth even more. We agreed to hold new negotiations that evening at a bar on Fifty-first Street in New York City.

From a two-suiter bag, our buddies brought out two polyurethane bags with the Serenace. Ed Pistey had come prepared to do a medicine man's act. He played with pieces of equipment that he carried in an attaché case. While he performed his "tests," another partner in the packages, Irving Shick, was introduced. Shick appeared to have rank over everyone in the place.

Ed Pistey whispered some gibberish in my ear and I said to Shick that the drugs appeared to be as specified, although without a full lab setup it was impossible to be sure.

Paul assured me that I should get four million dollars on the street for the Serenace, and would I now call the Summit Hotel and arrange for the delivery of the money. I got Marvin on the phone. "Get your ass in a cab and bring the money to the H and H Meat Market at 1421 Broadway, Brooklyn." I asked to speak to "Ski," the agent pretending to protect the money. "You two guys go with him; don't let this fucking guy get lost with our money."

The sellers were a bit anxious; they wanted to know what kind of car would be used. I explained that a taxi would carry Marvin, the guy Patty King had seen in the room with him, and another guard for the cash. Shick stipulated that only one individual should enter the market.

Paul Esposito was staring at Ed Pistey. "Your face is familiar," he said. "Do I know you from somewhere?" I could see another bad scene coming.

"Maybe you've seen me around Flushing Avenue, where I work for Pfizer Pharmaceutical," suggested Pistey.

"Yeah, no wonder. I had a numbers business in that area. These guys"—Paul pointed to a couple of go-fors—"were runners there for me." Tranquillity was restored.

The taxicab with Nadborne and the two agents pulled up outside and Patty King accosted the trio. King explained that only one member of the party was to enter and he himself would remain outside. Nadborne and the two agents conferred. We needed King in the store to make the case solid. Witkowski and Jim Nelson, the other special agent, had no idea whether there might be ten guns inside the butcher shop. We wanted as many of us in there as possible. Properly coached, Nadborne pleaded, "Patty, these fucking guys say they will kill me unless you go in there with us. They say how do we know you haven't worked over their boss and it's all a trap. If you go in with them, they feel they're protected."

Patty King bought the argument. I met Nadborne in the front of the store. "Ain't no need for you to be in here." I wanted him out of any possible line of fire. I carried the suitcase of money to the rear of the store with Nelson right behind me. "Open it! Open it!" the hoods yelled at me. "Let's see the money."

We snapped it open, showing the yellow pages of the Manhattan telephone directory inside. Pistey, Nelson, and I announced, "FBI—you're all under arrest."

We had the neighborhood full of agents and they came running into the place as soon as Nadborne appeared back on the street. A local cop became curious about the commotion and asked what was happening.

"FBI matter," said an agent. "Just tend to your own business."

The patrolman became annoyed. "I'm a cop—who are you telling to mind his own business?"

"Get out of here or I'll arrest you for interfering with federal agents," snapped our man. The officer grumbled and left.

It must have made quite an impression on the neighborhood, which was basic black. We marched out five hoods, all properly manacled, and we could hear murmurs in the crowd . . . "What's going on, man?"

As we passed through the crowd Pistey made it a point to say a couple of times, "In addition to other things, they were selling adulterated meat."

Even before we had the gang down at our offices for processing, the U.S. marshals at Marvin Nadborne's home were notified and began moving the family, carrying only a few bags of clothing, to a hideout on Long Island and from there to Washington, D.C., for a week.

The insurance company had promised Nadborne twenty-five thousand dollars. When the chairman of the board was notified of the full recovery and what it cost, he took it upon himself to thank the Bureau for its splendid work and then said that although they never paid more than a five-thousand-dollar reward, in this case they would be willing to pay ten thousand. Marvin actually threatened to take them to court, but in the end he settled for twenty thousand. I was not looking forward to having to testify about this kind of thing in open court. On the other hand, the insurer's chiseling struck me as on a par with the ethics of the people I had helped to arrest.

Nadborne qualified for the witness-protection program of the Justice Department. He and his family were transported to another city and supposed to be given a new identity plus a living allowance until he could establish himself. Marvin's original choice for a new life was Miami, Florida. While he was down there, I became involved in another case on which I enlisted his help.

In September 1966, two priceless seventeenth-century paintings were stolen from a shipment of artwork traveling from Chicago to New York City. They were Rubens's *Judgment of Seleucus* and *Portrait of Juliana DeVries* by Gerard TerBorch.

They were apparently too hot for anyone to sell and stored away for future redemption. One of the wiseguys pinched in a securities swindle wanted to square a rap. He told an agent that he would be willing to introduce an undercover middleman to people with access to the paintings. I was chosen for the role.

My guide took me to an espresso joint in Brooklyn. But when we walked into the place, there must have been thirty guys sitting around, all giving me the eye. I walked out of there as quickly as possible and flew into a tantrum at the go-between, telling him I wasn't about to meet anyone in a place full of people, some of whom could easily be informers. What I was really worried about was that among those thirty individuals there might be a couple whom I had rousted at one time or another. I retired to my car, an opulent rental, and left him to go back with an explanation to the interested parties at the espresso bar.

I was almost asleep in the car when two men ambled over to talk. They spoke with the usual circumlocution, never quite saying what the offering was, but they did ask who the buyer was.

"I've got a Jewish fat cat in Miami; he's crazy for art." That drew a favorable reaction. I said my buyer would come up in a few days and would stay at the Summit Hotel. We used the Summit because one of the executives there was a former agent and the hotel offered us full cooperation as well as anonymity.

The Bureau agreed to have Marvin play my Miami art nut. In due course, Nadborne checked into the Summit. The first sitdown was a dinner in the Gaucho Room of the hotel. There were three of them; one of them looked like he just stepped off the boat. It was a big, expensive dinner; these were not heavyweights in the mob, and food like this didn't come their way too often. They described the paintings, and Marvin expressed his interest. They asked for $150,000. Marvin scoffed. "Why don'tcha turn them in to the feds? They'll give you three hundred grand." Finally Marvin agreed to pay $100,000 in small old bills not sequentially numbered.

"We'll call you in a day," said the leader of the group.

Nadborne really was a first-rate thespian. "I don't go for this call-me-the-next-day shit!" he roared. "I think you guys are just giving me a lot of guinea bullshit. Either you are ready to deal or the hell with you. I'll use my money somewhere else."

The performance spooked them into making a commitment for the following day in Marvin's hotel room. The plan was for an art expert of Marvin's choosing to go with one of these guys to examine the paintings. He would telephone us, and if he authenticated the art, we'd exchange the money for the paintings.

Joe Chapman, an agent I'd known in the early days, had studied enough art to serve as the Bureau's resident expert on paintings. But he had become so immersed in this field that he resigned from the Bureau to pursue a career as an art expert. Our resident art expert was now Robert Mason. Although lacking Chapman's panache, he was steady and reliable. Mason was nervous about the operation and, considering how it went, I don't blame him.

The scenario required that we have our money available for inspection in Marvin's room before the art expert and the sellers left to see the paintings. Unfortunately, the insurance company that was liable for the paintings had not gotten together the $100,000 in cash by the appointed time. For two hours we stalled, until I could go down and pick up a black bag with the cash.

When it was unveiled for inspection, $20,000 in crisp new bills was rejected. I scooped up the offensively fresh money and told Marvin. "You heard the man—get it changed." In the lobby Marvin conferred with one of our agents, who telephoned a nearby bank, explained the problem, and got them to agree to replace the money.

When a sweaty Marvin returned to the hotel room with the old, nonsequential bills, the three guys patiently counted it all. Unfortunately, the teller at the bank had shorted Marvin $300. They wouldn't settle for $99,700, so Marvin and I dug into our own pockets to come up with the $300.

At this point they insisted on searching Bob Mason, who was, fortunately, prepared for that eventuality. He carried an expensive attaché case with listings of auctions and various art showings about town. In fact he even had phony identification with printed business cards purporting him to be an art appraiser. He also carried a transmitter neatly taped to his crotch. They asked that he remove his jacket, which they searched, but either from modesty or embarrassment, they never asked that he remove his pants. One more hurdle over with.

Satisfied about Bob Mason, one of the opposition took him to look at the paintings. What followed was near total disaster. Although the Summit was awash with agents, inside and outside, Mason and one thug left the building without anyone observing them. They unwittingly eluded the awaiting surveillance teams stationed nearby. For all the expertise, we fumbled a simple tail job. Our well-laid plans called for Mason, after he was satisfied with the authenticity of the paintings, to say in a loud clear voice that the paintings looked bona fide. The transmitter neatly held in his crotch would broadcast the message to the tailing agents, who then would swoop down on the paintings, Mason, and the sellers. All of that was impossible now. (Later we learned that Mason had been taken to Staten Island and shown the paintings, which had been kept in a car trunk. After he was satisfied and had made small identifying marks on the rear of the frames, he began to repeat in increasingly louder tones, "Yep, they look bona fide." Nothing happened. Becoming bored with Mason's one-liner, the opposition drove Mason to the Staten Island ferry to make his own way back to the Summit.)

The Bureau people in the lobby of the hotel realized that our carefully engineered trap had stripped its gears. I learned about the trouble when I slipped out of the hotel room, ostensibly for a drink, and conferred with the Bureau Supervisors. I proposed an immediate alternative. After Mason's call telling me he was satisfied with the paintings, I would insist that he return to the hotel and repeat his assurances in person, to be certain he wasn't being coerced. Then we'd return with the vendors to the paintings and exchange cash for the art. I volunteered to carry the $100,000. We could arrest them and recover the stuff at the same time.

Absolutely not, said Frank Hitt, the same SAC who did his best to gum up on the Gambino kidnapping. His interpretation of Bureau policy dictated that show money was never exposed to any risk of loss—and thus embarrassment to the Bureau. Better to lose the whole case than be exposed to possible criticism. Shallow thinking; even the insurance company would risk a measly $100,000 to recover these irreplaceable masterpieces.

I argued, cajoled, swore, hinted that I would defy orders. "If Villano leaves the hotel with the money," Hitt told my supervisor, "I'll have him and you canned for disobeying orders, even if you break the case and lose not a dime of the money."

It was a lost cause. I went back to the hotel room to wait with Marvin and our visitors. After Mason called in from the Staten Island ferry, somewhat mystified by the absence of the cavalry to gallop to a charge as soon as he said the magic words, we drew from him the location of the paintings. I then delayed the consummation of the deal, insisting that our art expert show up in the flesh so I could be sure he hadn't been forced into verifying the art.

While we sat there waiting, allegedly for Mason to come back to the Summit, a message to the cops on Staten Island to hit the car described by him. Unfortunately, the communication to the cops was garbled. They discovered the wrong car. The Staten Island branch of the thieves disappeared, along with the paintings.

Back at the hotel room there was a thunderous knocking at our door. Agents burst in, putting everyone under arrest and confiscating the satchel of currency.

As the agents cuffed Marvin he wailed, "That's my money, my hundred thousand. I'm losing a hundred grand."

Seemingly out on bail, Marvin conferred at the local jail with the two guys arrested in the hotel room. "The feds told me they'll keep you here for twenty years. But they say that if you'll give up the paintings, we can all get off the hook and I can get my money back." The hoods told Marvin to speak to their attorney.

When Marvin tendered the proposal to the lawyer, he asserted that the insurance company would put up $100,000 for the return of the two items. Again Nadborne stressed that this was the only way he could get his hundred grand back and the lawyer's clients could get out of the pen.

But it was no deal. Word was that the paintings actually were in the hands of Gambino men and the people in charge felt there were too many risks attached to them. The talk was that they would be torched. A pity, and all due to SAC who glued himself to the manual.

Nobody was sorrier than Marvin about the collapse of the

caper. He had been promised a fee of $25,000 from the insurer and, as I later discovered, the company would even have been willing to pay the full $100,000 price.

Marvin Nadborne decided to move to the Northwest, where he continued to work for various law-enforcement agencies; at last count he had notched sixty-five individuals, who were indicted as a result of his undercover roles. Before he left for his new location, he contributed the name of Ronnie Morgan,* a supplier of hot cars.

Ray Tallia, a very good agent with whom I often worked, joined me for a visit to Morgan. We had discovered that other people had already caught up with Ronnie. He was under indictment in New York City for grand larceny, auto, so it wasn't hard for Ray and me to convince Morgan to cooperate. We promised to put in helpful words with the local DA if Ronnie went along with us. Morgan was the kind of guy who had spent most of his adult years trading in various commodities that he didn't own. He was always looking for an edge, and he saw a bargain in our offer.

A few days later, Ronnie telephoned to say that an acquaintance of his, Mike Sarajian,* had approached him about the sale of bearer bonds. From the description of the pieces it sounded as if it was loot from a two-million-dollar theft from Manufacturer's Hanover Trust. According to Ronnie, Sarajian indicated that he had a connection with Pete the Greek Diapoulos, the unsuccessful bodyguard for Joe Gallo. We were familiar with Pete the Greek's past, but Sarajian was a mystery man. He had no record, and all Ronnie could tell us was that Sarajian worked as a salesman in the garment district of the city.

We set up a meet at a place called Deli City, in the heart of Times Square. Ronnie introduced me to Sarajian and split. I played Tony Damiano again, the swinging fellow from East Harlem. For the part I selected a casual leather outfit, the type of thing that the younger hustlers preferred. Sarajian himself was around thirty, wearing the old-style flash of the rag trade, and he was nervous. I saw immediately that he was a neophyte in the business, unsure of how to proceed and easy to manipulate.

At this first encounter we wanted some good identification of Sarajian. For this purpose, Ray Tallia had staked himself out in a van across the street from Deli City. Inside the van, through a one-way glass, he focused a camera on the sidewalk in front of the restaurant. After Sarajian and I had chatted for a few minutes, I suddenly said, "Hey, let's get out of here. I don't like the looks of that guy in the booth over there. He could be a fed."

Impressed by my caution, Sarajian allowed me to steer him outside. He was so accommodating that I maneuvered him to face the panel truck for a nice clear shot by Ray. It was like having him pose for a portrait. Meanwhile, we continued our discussion about the paper. Sarajian wanted to know if I could handle fifty thousand dollars worth. He would take eight points for his end. "No problem," I said. But a hitch developed. Sarajian refused to relinquish custody of the paper until the last moment before he got his money. I was not about to hand over any cash and take the risk that he might never show again. "Look," I said. "I don't eat paper and instantly shit money. If that's the way you want it, we'll have to get together again and see my banker. Ronnie will let you know when I'm ready."

We stalled for a couple of days; it doesn't pay to be too eager on deals of this nature. And we did have some arrangements to make. The insurance company liable for the Manufacturer's Hanover Trust loss agreed to front us with four thousand dollars, which covered Sarajian's eight points. A bank on Joralemon Street in downtown Brooklyn consented to serve as a plant for us.

When everything was set, I rendezvoused with Sarajian and Ronnie at a Rexall drugstore in Times Square. In his Caddie, Ronnie Morgan drove us to the Brooklyn bank. On the way I tantalized Sarajian with possible deals. I talked about gold coins, traveler's checks, and even hot diamonds. Anyone a step beyond an idiot should have known that there are no "hot diamonds." Unless they are part of a jewelry setting, diamonds are untraceable; they don't carry serial numbers or marks of identification.

When we entered the bank, Sarajian finally pulled an envelope out of his jacket. As he had promised, it contained fifty thousand dollars in securities. We would have buried him right there had he not claimed access to a lot more loot. The insurance company was willing to play along for a four-thousand-dollar investment in hopes of recovering bigger and better things. And we hoped to perhaps rope in Sarajian's alleged friend, Pete the Greek.

"You guys wait here on the bench," I instructed. "I'll cash in the stuff through my friend." I pointed toward the open area in the back of the bank where the officers of the institution sat. Sarajian and Morgan could see me conferring with a bank official, but they were too far off to hear anything. The banker was actually Ken Spielfogel, another FBI agent. He put on an act, made a telephone call, scribbled on some papers, and then disappeared behind the money cages for a few minutes.

Sarajian panicked. He grabbed me, upset about his securities leaving his sight. I pacified him. "Calm down. He just went to get the cash." And in a couple of minutes Spielfogel reappeared and handed me a bulky envelope. Inside was the insurance company's four thousand dollars plus a lot of paper cut up in the size of bills.

I stuffed the envelope in the pocket of my jacket and left the bank with Ronnie and Sarajian. Outside, while they entered the car, I opened the envelope and removed the four thousand dollars. I didn't give the others a chance to see what remained in the envelope. Inside the car, I handed Sarajian his four grand.

He couldn't get over the fact that the envelope I retained was much thicker than his package of bills. "What did you really get? How much did he give you?" Sarajian pestered me.

Finally, like a very well satisfied guy who is delighted to boast about a big score, I answered, "I got seventy-five points, $37,500."

Sarajian almost launched himself through the Caddie's roof. "You got that much and I only come away with four grand?"

"Don't feel so bad," I consoled him. "I have to give ten grand to my banker, and my boss gets five for his share."

Hardly mollified, Sarajian switched the conversation around to his desire to buy a zippy new car and how he couldn't afford it. That sparked Ronnie into action. "How would you like a brand-new 300 SL Mercedes?"

"That'd be great," said Sarajian. "But how much?"

"A dealer sells the car for around twelve. I'll deliver it to you for only five. You give me twenty-five now and another twenty-five on receipt of the car."

Sarajian became cautious. "Can I register the car?"

"I'll make delivery of the Mercedes in front of 240 Centre Street [then New York City police headquarters]. You can invite the car squad to come out and inspect it. It's absolutely cool, stolen in Europe and shipped over here."

That sold Sarajian. He forked over the twenty-five hundred

dollars, plus another five hundred as Ronnie's cut for introducing Sarajian to me. My problem was to remove Ronnie from any further involvement in the operation. The next time out we would all be busted; my identity would be covered, but we'd never be able to continue to use Ronnie as an informant. So when we arrived back in New York, I managed to get a few minutes alone with Sarajian before he returned to his garment-center job.

"You paid Ronnie five hundred dollars," I remarked. "Did you know that he got five thousand from me for steering you to me? This is ridiculous. Now that we know one another, let's cut the middleman out. When you have some stuff, call me at this number." I gave him the private line I had in the FBI offices. Sarajian was as cost conscious as any businessman. He was delighted at the prospect of a reduction in overhead.

A day later he called to say that he had another package. I stalled and let him start breaking my phone with his anxiety calls. I figured that a few days of this treatment would get him to come forward with the maximum amount he could obtain. When I finally relented and told him to meet me at the Rexall with the largest-size package available, he showed up with a big manila envelope.

Sarajian and I took a taxi to Joralemon Street. On the way there we bargained. He had naturally turned greedy. "The price is twelve points."

"What is this, a goddamn shakedown? Just because I broke down and told you about the seventy-five points!" It was a proper tantrum and eventually I conceded him two extra points, since I didn't have to share with Ronnie.

He handed over the envelope to me in the cab, and the contents added up to more than $100,000 in securities. I gave him back the envelope to hold until we entered the bank—I wanted him to be in possession when we were busted. As soon as we paid off the taxi and before we entered the bank, Ray Tallia and a bunch of other agents grabbed us. At the request of the bank, we had agreed to make the bust outside in the street rather than in the offices, where the scene might be disturbing to legitimate customers.

Both of us were handcuffed and taken to the Bureau offices. I mumbled to Sarajian to keep his mouth shut if he wanted to stay healthy. As we jointly went through fingerprinting and routine interviews, an agent interrupted: "You, Damiano. They want to talk to you about a double homicide in Wyoming." I was led off to be questioned. As soon as I had gone, Sarajian rolled over, partially. He admitted to the agents that he had passed the stolen securities and that he had more stuff in his New Jersey home. Sean McWeeney took Sarajian there and located another $150,000 in paper. However, Sarajian would not give up Pete the Greek.

After Sarajian was bailed out, I suddenly received a call from Ronnie. "Jesus, Tony. Sarajian's gone to the Gallo people to tell them about his troubles. Now they've sent him back to me to find out your full name and address. Mike also wants his Mercedes. He's putting a lot of heat on me."

I was prepared for this eventuality. "You tell Sarajian that I came looking for you with blood in my eyes. That I want to know all about Sarajian's background and where he lives because I heard he's going to testify against us."

Ronnie followed the script. He told Sarajian, "Hey, you're asking for Tony's address when you ought to be watching your own step. He's heard that you're cooperating. He wants to know your address. Tony's a real tough guy. Be careful." That spooked Sarajian enough to drop out of sight until he copped a plea when he went to trial.

Ronnie of course kept the three thousand dollars given to him by Sarajian. I figured the total recovery was worth far more than that to the insurance company. However, Ronnie wasn't satisfied with modest deals. He tried to be too smart on our second venture.

Ray Tallia and I arranged for Ronnie to open up a garage in Brooklyn. We got the Bureau to invest two thousand dollars in the place, figuring that it would be ideal bait for hijackers. Either Ronnie got scared or else he figured he'd do better by playing footsie with the other side. He gave us zero with the garage. So, when it came time for his turn at bat on the car-theft charges, we refused to be anything more than silent spectators.

The more I worked on organized crime cases, the more difficult it became for me to sustain moral belief in the standards of the so-called respectable people. They bought thousands of hot cars, for instance, fully aware that there was no way that a ten-thousand-dollar automobile could legitimately sell for two thousand dollars. The car business became so profitable in the sixties that the wiseguys developed finely specialized tools to increase efficiency. Detroit representatives furnished genuine vehicle identification numbers. The car-theft rings had plants that made fascias for dashboards; the old one could be ripped out and replaced with something that covered a new identification number. Other sub-contractors in the hot-car business supplied stolen legitimate registrations and an official stamp from the New York State Motor Vehicle Bureau to authenticate registrations. They used names picked out of a telephone book; that made it easy to file papers covering sale and registration.

Cars were taken off the streets to fill job lots or custom orders. If a customer wanted a black Porsche Targa, employees would ride around town until they observed one. The license number and location would be recorded. At an opportune time the thieves would return and double-park alongside the target vehicle. From the passenger side, a mechanic using a knockaway tool would remove the lock cylinder in a matter of seconds. While his companion circled the block, the operator of the knockaway would try his master keys on the lock. When he found the proper one, the other car would be double-parked again while he replaced the lock cylinder in the Porsche. Using the master key, the thief then opened the Porsche and inserted his key into the ignition; the car was stolen in perhaps two minutes, roughly the time it took to circle the block. If the thief was stopped en route to the drop, he had his previously filed counterfeit registration to prove ownership.

Major customers for cars included most prospering European countries as well as officials of the Middle East. Exports of this nature made the hot-car business even less complicated, since the need to file papers with the state motor vehicle bureau was largely eliminated. A $10,000 car wholesaled for between $1,500 and $2,000; the cost to the boss of the ring amounted to perhaps $500 a car.

I received first-hand experience with the ethical values and the lawful behavior of the respectables in the late spring of 1971. An informant tipped us that the mob had an extortion plot going against Mobil Oil Company. Our people duly talked to Mobil, who stoutly denied any such shakedown. However, the informant insisted that Mobil had already paid out a big chunk of money and was being dunned for further amounts. We made a second, less gentle approach to Mobil. Unless the corporation agreed to cooperate, we would subpoena their books and thereby set off a noisome public investigation of company practices. That brought the reluctant admission that Mobil was indeed under siege.

In 1969, the drivers of fuel-oil trucks struck. The walkout by the union cost Mobil plenty, and the executives had resolved not to be caught in the same bind again. Feelers went out to parties that might be willing to strikebreak. The Sular Company offered its services and Mobil set up a section known as MOCO, Mobil Oil Continued Operation, to draft contingency plans. Sular just happened to be run by a number of soldiers in the Joe Colombo Family: Lazzaro A. San Giovanni, Carmine Franzese, and Modesto "Duke" Santoro. As a token of good faith, Mobil made four two thousand dollar payments to San Giovanni in the months before the actual strike.

On the first day of May, 1971, the Teamsters Union struck Mobil and the combined forces of Sular and MOCO were activated. Mobil agreed to pay $100 to Sular for each driver and helper it employed and $120 a load for each delivery made. The trucks would be Mobil's, rented to Sular for a whopping $1 a month.

The local Teamsters, however, failed to be cowed by the brass-knuckled fist behind Mobil's new talent. They prevented the trucks from making their rounds. Sular's executives came back to Mobil to report that an additional cost of the operation would be a car with five "helpers" to follow each truck and make sure no one interfered with the deliveries. For this added feature, Mobil would be obligated for another $200,000. MOCO, conscious of its responsibility to get fuel oil delivered, and with an equal sense of responsibility to the stockholders, agreed to the proposition.

The whole operation had hardly gotten under way when the union knuckled under and a settlement was reached with the Teamsters on May 6. A difference of opinion over how much Mobil owed Sular ensued. An initial payment of $27,000 had been made. But Sular felt cheated. In fact, Duke Santoro had telephoned an executive to say that if $100,000 in cash was not placed in the lobby of the Mobil building on May 7, where it would be retrieved by unidentified parties, the families of Mobil would be hit. Mobil followed orders, to the extent that a bag of $72,000 in five-, ten-, and twenty-dollar bills was deposited in the lobby of Mobil headquarters on Forty-second Street in New York. Three company executives, Robert Schoenthaler, Mitchel Anthony Burns, and Harmon Hoffman, observed an individual retrieve the payoff from the appointed location and leave the premises.

Now the representatives of Sular wanted an additional $400,000 as recompense for the services rendered in the six days of the strike. Our first proposal to Mobil was that they set up a negotiating session with Sular and we would bug the room. Once San Giovanni and cohorts made some incriminating remarks, we would arrest them for extortion. Mobil would be thus freed from jeopardy. Absolutely not, said Mobil's top brass. We are not about to sit down at a table and discuss business with hoodlums. Having made use of their services when it was thought necessary, the folks at Mobil now wanted to keep their distance from their hired thugs.

We suggested that an agent could sit in at the negotiations, direct the discussion, and provide security. Mobil now accepted the proposal. Because I had a degree in accountancy and it was believed that I would therefore be able to steer my way through any pseudo business language, I was chosen as the undercover man.

At the first meeting, I was introduced as James Kalitsis, Mobil's chief auditor. The head spokesman for Sular at this first session was Larry San Giovanni. He was accompanied by Carmine Franzese and John Lusterino, whom I recognized from photographs as "Johnny Tarzan," a muscle man for the Colombos.

"Let's make no bones about it," San Giovanni began. "We broke the strike for you and we want four hundred thousand dollars." As the company's voice, I succeeded in being as obnoxious as possible. "Where the hell do you come off asking for another four hundred thousand? Based on what you delivered, that amounts to a cost of a dollar forty per gallon of oil delivered. We operate on a profit margin of less than a cent a gallon and you want a dollar forty per gallon for your fee!"

Johnny Tarzan made a couple of remarks at this point, in the course of which he mispronounced the name of the company. I lit into him. "For Chrissakes, you ignoramus, the name of the company is Mobil; Mo*bile* is the name of a city in Alabama. How can anyone so stupid claim to have a responsible position with a company?"

"Don't get excited; don't lose your temper," this gorilla responded.

My purpose had been to stir a reaction, but San Giovanni had his troops well disciplined. I tried several more times to irritate Johnny Tarzan, but he remained a paragon of patient courtesy, even apologizing for any mistakes he might be making in grammar or locution.

"Who is this Duke something or other who telephones people here and threatens them?" I demanded.

San Giovanni took it smoothly. "I employ all sorts of people. They need this money and I can't control them. I'm in the middle on this."

Finally I said that as the chief auditor I couldn't possibly approve any further payments without some reasonable evidence of value given. I asked for a list of names of all the people hired by Sular, their Social Security numbers, the hours worked, the information necessary for withholding-tax forms.

San Giovanni agreed to come back prepared for a second meeting and we adjourned. On the next go-around, Johnny Tarzan was absent. In his place was a prominent attorney from Garden City, Long Island. He had a sheaf of papers in front of him and a pocket calculator. He recited a bunch of figures designed to demonstrate the value of Sular's efforts.

I still hoped to provoke an overt threat that would sew up extortion and I again came on nasty, disputing every statement and finally yelling that any contract with Sular was unauthorized. The lawyer became indigant but doggedly proceeded to recite the amounts of money obligated by Mobil to his clients. "There's all the elements of a fraud here, and you're perpetuating it," I shouted at him. "It's actionable in a court of law." That insulted him but San Giovanni still didn't take the bait. The meeting broke up with plans for a third try.

Our victim's spine was as stiff as a column of water. They moaned about the potential for a large lawsuit because of my slanderous statements. The head of Mobil's security, a former FBI agent but now a true company man, confided that if he could arrange a settlement for $200,000 the front office would consider him a hero.

We braced Mobil to give us another shot at Sular. The attorney from the second meeting was conspicuously absent. Our guests this time were San Giovanni, Johnny Tarzan, and, to my dismay, a hustler whom I knew as Bobby Bad Heart. As soon as he walked into the conference room he saw me and squeaked, "This guy's a Feebie—he busted me a couple of months ago!"

I grabbed Bobby Bad Heart and shoved him out of the room. I threw him against a wall, kicked him in the ass. "You've got a big fucking mouth. You ought to learn to keep it shut to protect your own ass." But there was no way we could continue the charade of negotiations.

We felt that we had enough for a prosecution, however, particularly with statements on tape that had been made to us by Mobil officials. Both the U.S. attorney and the Brooklyn district attorney initially agreed with us and indictments were drawn against San Giovanni, Franzese, and Santoro.

Naturally, Mobil now refused to push the case; there had been stories in the newspapers, and the union had even paid for an ad telling about the company's resorting to criminals as strikebreakers. Mobil had enough clout to get a pass from the Brooklyn DA on the grounds that the company had informed the FBI of the extortion threat, a flat-out lie. The DA also excused Mobil because there was no indication that the company habitually engaged in this kind of behavior, which is like excusing a murderer because he has only killed once.

The Department of Justice under John Mitchell, an avowed defender of law and order, likewise dropped the extortion case.

6

The Great Colombo Raid

IN 1970, DURING THE PERIOD of my greatest success in penetrating and understanding LCN, Joseph Colombo, head of one of
New York's five crime families, embarked on his campaign
against the FBI. Because of the Colombo-sponsored protests
against the Bureau by his front, the Italian American Civil Rights
League—sparked by the FBI arrest of Colombo's son, Joseph Jr.,
for melting silver coins, a charge on which a jury found him not
guilty—we had to file affidavits in court that defended our activities. My name appeared in a number of the documents that
justified warrants. Colombo people were aware of an Anthony
Villano who swore that the Bureau had probable cause for its
suspicions of various crimes, but they did not know what I looked
like because I had assumed a low profile, refraining from arrests,
interviews, and open surveillances of the Colombo clan.

After I testified before the U.S. commissioner, one of Colombo's
henchmen, a three-hundred-pound rain barrel I recognized as one
Caesar Vitali, waddled over to me in the corridor and gave me
what he hoped was a sinister Sicilian "drop dead" look. I stared
back and said, "Mark me well, Caesar." Apparently Vitali had no
appreciation of Shakespeare. He got all flustered, upset only because he had failed to put me down.

Joe Colombo's attack on the Bureau as anti-Italian earned him
points with some Americans of Italian background, but I can't say
that it diminished our desire to put him away. Therefore, when
Nick Billeti confided to me that he knew the location of a numbers drop for the Colombo gambling operation, we mobilized a
good-size task force to gather the evidence. It was a major piece
of work, stretching over perhaps six months. More significant for
me personally, the case contained the seeds for my battle with
the Bureau nearly three years later.

On Bath Avenue in the residential Bensonhurst section of Brooklyn was a leather shop. The father-and-son proprietors, known as Petey and Joey Leather, ostensibly repaired anything that required leather craftsmanship.

I explored the area and picked out a four-story apartment building as the closest safe vantage point for observation. With a woman from the Bureau masquerading as my wife, I rented a three-room apartment that had windows overlooking Bath Avenue. Aside from the rent and the security, I also had to slip fifty bucks to the landlady, who was suspicious of me and my broad. Inside the apartment I constructed a box to resemble an air-conditioning unit and stuck it out one of the windows. The box contained a ground-glass optical-quality mirror hooked up to a very expensive telescope that the Bureau had sent from Washington, D.C. Attached to the end of the telescope eyepiece was a fancy camera that would photograph whoever went in and out of the leather shop. The whole apparatus didn't work worth spit.

The Bureau sent us an optics expert bearing special lenses. Nothing. Since long-term, on-the-spot surveillance was an absolute must, we finally reverted to the more conventional technique of a specially rigged innocuous-looking truck. Con Edison and the New York Telephone Company always cooperated fully with us. They lent us their vans, uniforms, and equipment without question. On occasion we even set up barricades to add credence to our pose as working stiffs.

Our truck was parked by an agent a block or so from the leather shop. The driver put on a show of locking the van and then walked away. Inside the truck a pair of agents peered through the rear windows or special peepholes drilled in the sides and snapped photographs of people entering and leaving the leather shop. They also recorded license plate numbers of cars parked around the store.

Enough was seen to justify planting a bug. After getting the court order, and having installed our bug and a tap on the telephone, we were able to lease a line from the telephone company that carried the conversations to the comfort and sanctity of our office in Manhattan. The surveillance continued, however, in order to help identify the voices.

In the course of piling up evidence I sent my informant Herbie into the place to get money down on a number. A day later he called me and asked, "Did you hear me in the leather shop?"

"No, I was on the street. What happened?"

"I hit the number."

"That's great. Did you have a buck on it?"

"A buck—I had twenty on it and I made ten thousand. Any time you want me to place a bet anywhere, just call."

Herbie's triumph was one tiny bit of evidence; we wanted much more than just a couple of number takers and a drop. We kept listening. Petey and Joey sounded like a couple of characters out of Damon Runyon. Along with numbers they accepted bets on horses and other sports. I always thought that bookmakers drove around in Cadillacs, but to listen to Petey and Joey you would think that they were only a couple of bucks away from food stamps. "That fucking Colombo," one of them griped. "He takes all the profit; his girl friend lives like a queen." My experience is that organized crime is like any other industry. The bosses and the top executives make out well; the workers, the soldiers and loosely connected guys, scratch for enough to survive.

Petey and Joey Leather enjoyed certain perquisites from their association with Colombo. No small-timers could afford to be the banker in the numbers racket. On July 4 there would be hundreds of bets on 776. When the *Daily News* ran a shot of a train wreck with the engine number, 184, clearly visible in the picture, everybody hunched on that number. A hit on a massive hunch, or Herbie's twenty bucks, could wipe out someone without substantial backing. If you placed your action with Joe Colombo, the split was fifty-fifty on the profits. When your operation lost ten thousand dollars in a week because of some freak streak, Colombo advanced the money for your half of the loss, five thousand dollars. He red-lined the operation until you worked off the advance. Colombo had from ten to fifteen affiliates similar to the leather shop. He was like the Federal Depositors Insurance of any bank.

Eventually, the Leather family discovered our bug. They knew one of the agents from previous experience, a guy named Bernie Welsh, who was something of a wit and had an uncanny ability to annoy people, even individuals that he arrested. It became routine for Petey Leather to joke, "Hey, Joey. You better clear out now. I'm expecting Bernie Welsh to come by for his payoff." I wouldn't have snickered every time I heard that if I'd known what was coming out of this case.

The watch on the leather shop produced some big dividends. We observed that around one o'clock in the afternoon, either Petey, Joey, or a trusted henchman would visit a nearby gas station, which was in an area of many small stores that displayed their wares on the sidewalk in good weather. The density of the foot population made it easy for the runner to lose himself in the crowd; it also made it simpler for us to melt into the human traffic. We set up a watch of the filling station. On the adjacent street sat a wrecked Peugeot. The runners casually deposited their work envelopes behind its front seat, and about fifteen minutes later, a guy we nicknamed "the Mole" just as casually rummaged in the abandoned vehicle and then drove off with the envelopes. We tailed him to a small apartment building on East Twenty-third Street, but we couldn't figure out exactly where inside he dropped the stuff.

Jim Nelson, one of the agents on the case and a good ballsy guy with imagination, staked himself out on one of the landings with a girl from the office. They pretended to smooch, oblivious to all around them in their passion. When the Mole entered the building, he saw Nelson and the girl. Nelson peeked long enough to see the Mole unlock one of the mailboxes in the lobby and deposit the envelopes, just like any good mailman. Unfortunately, Jim couldn't determine which of the dozen or so boxes it was.

We tried again, shifting our Con Ed truck to within a block or so of the apartment house visited by the Mole. Just before he was due, an agent swiftly dusted the mailboxes with an ultraviolet-sensitive powder. After the Mole had completed his business, we rushed to the lobby with our ultraviolet light. Another frustrating zero; the Mole apparently did not use the boxes as protection unless he felt there were enough distractions around him—like Jim Nelson and the girl.

So we had to invent one. I put on work clothes, slapped a Con Ed hard hat on my head, and entered the building. I sprinkled the mailboxes with the powder and then went to the roof and disconnected the TV antennas. Having created a problem, and carrying an impressive electric testing device, I started to bang on doors and ask tenants if they were having trouble with their TV reception. My absurd story was that we had received a complaint of electric shock when some individuals switched on their sets. I made a helluva racket with my door banging and loud voice, and the Mole dutifully used the mailbox. As soon as he left, we examined the mailboxes and found out which apartment was part of the operation.

The name of the woman who lived there meant nothing to us, but Herbie knew all about her. She had a son who was a New York City cop. She was an active member of the Italian American Civil Rights League and supported herself largely by selling swag.

By this time we had also put a watch on a trim red brick two-family house on Cropsey Avenue, not too far away. On the first floor lived Phyllis Schettini, Joe Colombo's girl friend. Phyllis and her sister Rose, who lived across the street, and a sister-in-law, Teresa Schettini, who lived upstairs with Phyllis's younger brother, took care of Joe Colombo's accounts. Our aim now was to document the transfer of business from the leather shop to the Peugeot to the apartment house, and finally to the home of Phyllis Schettini. The evidence would consist of our observations, films, and tapes of telephone calls and from bugs.

As part of the chain, we prepared to follow the work to the house of Colombo's lady friend, particularly because that was the one point where his physical involvement could be demonstrated. For openers we hoped to record on film the Mole leaving his goodies in the mailbox. The stratagem for this endeavor was a Trojan horse. In the basement of our office I hammered together a packing crate the size of a desk, drilled three holes for camera lenses and to allow air inside for the occupant. One side of the crate served as a hatch, and it was equipped with handles for easier transport. The sides of the box bore a Con Ed stencil with a shipping order that described the contents as a 220-volt transformer. The higher voltage was selected instead of the customary 110 because we feared that anything that seemed like it might be useful would be stolen. Jim Nelson volunteered for the role of the Greeks.

Dick Tamaro, a big husky agent, was with me as I drove the Con Ed truck with the Trojan horse to the apartment house. We timed our arrival to precede Mole's by twenty minutes. Tamaro and I opened up the back doors of the van and used a skid with wheels to hump the crate to a place in the lobby where it had a good view of the mailboxes. It was a perfect day and there was lots of sunlight in the lobby—ideal for picture taking.

Dick and I returned to our truck and I parked it a few blocks away. About ten minutes into the vigil, Jim Nelson suddenly called us on his walkie-talkie. "Get me outta here! Get me outta here, quick."

We tear-assed back to the lobby. About ten residents stood around the box, including an old man in his underwear. A twelve-year-old girl kept screaming, "There's a body in the box! There's a body in the box!"

"We've found dead cats in these crates occasionally," I said. "But we just dropped this thing off ten minutes ago and if there's a stiff in it, it's been transformed." It wasn't much of a joke. The kid just kept right on yapping, "I saw a body, Daddy, in the box—"

We hauled away the crate with Nelson in it, making the excuse that the transformer had only been temporarily deposited there until it could be properly installed. Back inside the van, Nelson explained. "Everything was fine—I had a perfect sight line to the mailboxes. And then this girl comes along. She starts to play with the box and sing 'Con-sol-id-da-ted Ed-ih-son,' having a great time. Then she goes to peek in one of the holes. I saw her coming, so I plugged the hole with my thumb. I figured she'd try the next hole in the line and I blocked that one, but then she went to the third one. I didn't move, but she started to scream. That's when I asked for you to get me the hell out of there."

We lost out on film of the Mole making his deliveries, but through the bug in the leather shop and our surveillances, the whole network of Colombo operations began to spread out for us. We saw Joe Colombo visit Phyllis Schettini's house regularly, and we got a line on another route in Coney Island: first a bakery, then a small factory, and finally a cigar store, where the work was picked up.

We did that surveillance courtesy of Con Edison also. Jim Nelson and I, wearing the power company hard hats, parked the van in the vicinity and approached a grocery store that was one of Colombo's outlets. I walked into the place and said, "There's been a complaint about a gas leak. Have you smelled any around here?"

Sure enough, one of the neighborhood characters says, "Yeah, come to think of it, I'm glad you guys are here. I *have* smelled gas." That put us in a helluva hole. We couldn't fix a real leak, and if we had to send for a genuine repair crew our cover would be blown. In fact the whole thing was a transparent sham: In that part of the city the company responsible is Brooklyn Union Gas, and there we were in our Con Edison getups! Finally, we sniffed around and announced that the problem was only "sewer gas."

Meanwhile, we used the occasion to try to get friendly, have a sandwich in the place. I tried to place a bet, but the clerk wouldn't accept it, although he suggested I come back later, when someone might be able to accommodate me.

With all of the business going on at Phyllis's place, the next step was to tap into her phone. The practice of the telephone company is to draw all the lines—or "pairs," as they are called—from a neighborhood into a box in one building. The pairs for Phyllis's area were located in an apartment building four blocks from the Schettini house. Across the street was an office of the Italian American Civil Rights League. We flashed New York City detective badges at the super in the building and said we were on a major drug case against one Julian Sorel (I had a habit of picking aliases from literature). The super gave us access to the panel with the pairs and offered to warn us if the telephone company came prowling around.

The box contained about two thousand pairs; our problem was to determine which one belonged to the house where Joe Colombo combined business with pleasure. An electronics technician called Phyllis's number and kept her on the line with some story about a long-overdue department-store bill. While he was explaining the purpose of the call, the technician stroked the studs of the pairs with pliers. That shorted out the reception and the expert could hear the telltale click on the line when he hit the pairs belonging to Phyllis.

Having isolated which pair hooked up to the Schettini telephone, we now created genuine trouble for her. We screwed up her line so well that in exasperation she finally put in a call to the telephone company for service. I intercepted and gave her the business that things were very hectic and it might be two weeks before we could get a man to her place. She pleaded, I relented: Well, maybe a day or so.

The next day an agent wearing telephone-company clothes visited Phyllis Schettini's house. He examined her telephone and as part of the act went out to the nearby telephone pole. Soon he was back. "It's in the phone itself," said our agent.

"Can you give me a new one?" innocently asked Phyllis.

"I might have one in the truck," he generously offered. The one he had ready was a duplicate of the original except it contained a bug, for which we had obtained a legal court order. Phyllis was so grateful for the prompt, courteous service, she tipped our man two bucks and gave him a beer!

From intelligence gathered up to then, we picked up on the operation run by Al Salamone in lower Manhattan. We settled down to compile evidence. During daylight hours and into the evening our Con Ed van sat only a short distance from the Schettini residence. The agents inside observed the traffic into the house and jotted down license plate numbers.

On a day in April of 1971, two relatively new agents were on duty in the van. Rocco Miraglia, a lieutenant in good standing with the Colombo Family, drove past the Schettini house. (Miraglia had a public image of toughie, but I had heard he was nothing more than a puddle of oatmeal when things got tight. When we knocked down the phony loan business of the Colombo operation, I called Miraglia, pretending to be a friend of a friend who had recommended him as a helpful guy. That particular conversation was being recorded by us, and I used the name Luca Brasi, straight out of *The Godfather*. Miraglia bought it all the way.)

Miraglia drove by the van and went around the block twice to dry-clean himself. He apparently became somewhat suspicious of the truck, so he parked next to it. It was dark when he peered inside the truck and I doubt that he could've seen anything; nevertheless, the new agents panicked, started up the van, and drove off. Miraglia probably had the shit scared out of him. He ran back to his car and began to follow the van. Our people drove like crazy in an effort to shake Miraglia, finally losing him on the Belt Parkway.

A short time later we heard Joe Colombo on the bug in Phyllis's place saying something about the FBI being on to him and "we got to take all this shit and move it out." They started to pack boxes.

We had no choice but to get our warrants immediately and hit every drop in Colombo's system. In the case of Al Salamone it was premature. We just did not have time to collect enough evidence on his part of the business; we didn't even have time to notify his case agent Tommy Miglio.

Phyllis and her sister-in-law, Teresa, had already cleared out. We broke down the door and entered the house on Cropsey Avenue. We recovered some adding machines and betting slips. We finally located the fugitive women at Greenwood Lake, New Jersey.

Our case against Joe Colombo and about twenty-five of his associates, including the Schettini clan, looked excellent. For me, it was one of the slightly sweeter triumphs in a period of success piled on success. J. Edgar Hoover wrote me another one of his mash notes; a two-hundred-dollar incentive award was included. I filed away my recollections of the operation for the Colombo trial—unaware, of course, that the bullet fired into Colombo's brain at the 1971 Columbus Day rally would preclude it. And unaware, too, that the arrest of Al Salamone was to be the trigger to a series of events that led to my confrontation with the Bureau over Fred Juliano's story.

7

The Investigation: I

AFTER FRED JULIANO related to me what he heard about a possible payoff to the cop Lombardo and Tommy Miglio he asked me exactly what I planned to do. I answered that I was currently working on a very big case that involved the theft of cashier's checks from First National City Bank. Early that evening I expected to be introduced to some of the prominent figures in the scheme. As soon as that session ended, I intended to fly to Washington. Dick Baker, the former New York special agent in charge, now held an important job in the Bureau there. He had been impressed with my work on a number of cases, and I felt he was the kind of guy I could trust to run a proper investigation to find out whether Miglio was on the take. Juliano seemed satisfied—he was not looking forward to declaring himself in the case.

The people from the First National City Bank scheme whom I was supposed to see that evening never showed up. After nine o'clock I figured they would never make it. My supervisor, Sean McWeeney, and myself then adjourned to a bar for beer and sandwiches. The pressure of the information I had received about a possible payoff and the trust I felt for McWeeney induced me to confide in him to a limited degree. "Sean, I've got a source," I lied, to cover Fred Juliano. "He told me we have a crooked agent. Another agent thinks he may have got a kind of confession."

Stunned silence. Finally Sean asked me the tough question: "What are you going to do about it?" I related my plan to travel to Washington on my own and speak to Dick Baker.

"You do that," he said, "and you'll probably destroy yourself as an agent. You'll be going over the heads of your own SAC and John Malone. They'll never forgive you for that." Because of the things I had been able to accomplish, I had been given a lot of freedom, so I was somewhat of an innocent when it came to office politics. But I did realize the point here. To bypass my superiors would be foolhardy. "You should start with Alan Howard,"* advised Sean.

Howard had recently come to the New York office. He was about fifty, blue-eyed and affable—a real backslapper. An inveterate check grabber at lunches or in bars, he ruined the image of a big spender by boasting how much his neckties cost. That was all I knew about him. Later, an assistant U.S. attorney was to tell me that in his opinion Howard was the dumbest agent he'd ever met. But at the moment, McWeeney's suggestion seemed like a good one, and I felt better having a guy like him for an ally, even though he knew only the sketchiest details.

From the bar McWeeney telephoned Howard at his home and told him I had a problem that needed urgent, confidential handling. We were immediately invited to his apartment.

Late that February night, Howard's wife served the three of us drinks and left us alone to talk. Sean said, "Tell him the story, Tony." I did, only substituting Herbie, another talker I knew, for Juliano as my source of information.

Howard became very excited as I finished up. "Goddamn, I always felt there was something funny about Miglio. I'm not psychic, but I knew the guy wasn't right." The truth is that Howard was then so new to New York I doubt he even knew who Miglio was. Nevertheless, Howard now took over the direction of strategy. "Number one, we can't tell John Malone. He'll talk to the Bureau [meaning Washington] and he'll get the wrong person involved."

Sean prompted me. "Tell him there's somebody else who can confirm the story." I added what Juliano had told me, leaving out Fred's name.

The director of strategy now seemed to go a little wild. "Here's how we'll handle it," said Howard. "I'll bring in a hit man I know from Chicago. After he kills Miglio, we'll dump his body in the East River and the hit man will leave town."

"Wait a minute," I said. "I'm sure he's guilty, but we can't set ourselves up as jury, judge, and executioners."

"I've handled tough personnel matters before," blustered Howard. "Alan Howard knows how to do things. I'll put my fucking thirty-eight in his ear and we'll make him confess. Alan

Howard knows how to handle bad guys." Howard may not have been serious about hitting Miglio but because of previous experiences I tended to take him at face value.

An outsider may be shocked at an FBI agent's contemplating murder as a solution to a problem. But while it is certain you won't find homicide recommended as an option in the *Special Agents Manual,* this was not the first time I had heard of it. I once knew a hard-working, sincere agent in the Newark office who befriended a woman close to a middle-level mafioso named Artie "the Animal" Caruso.* At fourteen, the woman had been raped by Caruso, and over the years he had continued to force his affections, which included beatings as well as sexual demands.

One day, eyes blackened, her body welted and bruised, she came weeping to the agent about the Animal's loving attention. Outraged, the agent came to me, since Caruso was a New York resident and one of my investigative subjects, and asked if I would help him kill the Animal; it would simply look like a rubout by some unhappy hoodlum. I wouldn't go that far, but I did offer to assist the agent in beating the shit out of Caruso. The project never came off; the agent was transferred shortly after we spoke.

A second invitation to become an official hit man came shortly after the former loan shark and loan-out hit man named Harold "Kayo" Konigsberg had "rolled over" (turned informant) and given the Bureau the location of a Mafia graveyard in Oceanside, New Jersey. Since the site had once been a Prohibition still, the technique was to plant the bodies in the old mash pits. Kayo claimed that he had put a few there himself and expected that, with some careful digging, we could uncover at least a dozen corpses. According to Kayo, a depositor arriving at the cemetery checked in with the resident caretaker, who gave the instructions on where to put the corpse. The caretaker obviously possessed valuable information: He knew who came to visit the place, what was brought, and where it was put. But he would not crack under the heaviest pressure. It was highly frustrating.

One of the agents coordinating the case took me out for a cup of coffee one morning. I knew him only casually, but he was reputed to be a gung-ho type. He began the conversation with some remarks about how he'd heard I was a dedicated guy who

could be trusted. And then he said he was forming a hit squad—
"strictly voluntary, kept very small; each man will be hand
picked."

I picked myself off the floor and inquired, "What are your
intentions?"

"Our first target," said the coordinator, "is that little fuck of a
caretaker. We'll clip him first."

I offered an alternative. "Why don't we try sodium Pentothal
on the guy? We can grab him, shoot him with the juice, and get
what we want without anything so drastic as a hit, and maybe
even get some valuable information."

The agent bought it, after I volunteered to approach a close
personal friend, a doctor who, I assured him, could be trusted. My
friend was very straight, a man with the necessary reverence for
the work of the Bureau—I hoped.

I told the doctor exactly the kind of therapy we had in mind
and asked if he would be willing to participate. He advised me
that sodium Pentothal is a highly dangerous drug that should be
used only under controlled circumstances—in a hospital where
an antidote and life-support systems would be available in an
emergency.

But was he willing to help us out? "Sure," replied my friend,
"as soon as you show me the guy's written consent."

I related all this to the coordinator and then added, "I think I'll
take a pass on the truth serum and the new squad. It's a little too
clandestine, too drastic a solution, for me." A few days later,
because of a personal hardship, the agent suddenly received a
transfer far enough from New York to let me breathe easier.

Although these experiences did permit me to hear Howard's
proposal calmly enough, they had not immunized me to the point
where I could accept it. It seemed to me that he was overreacting;
after all, it was to be a hit on another agent simply to avoid
possible embarrassment for the Bureau. And his constant reference to himself in the third person made me uneasy, because it
suggested that he wasn't prepared to accept responsibility for a
solution devised by that third person, himself.

I offered an alternative. "Miglio is afraid of me. He lives out on
the Island. I'll call him, like at three A.M., make him meet me
somewhere. Put a body tape recorder on me. I'll confront him

with what I've learned, tell him that if he'll just quietly turn in his badge and credentials, I won't report him."

Howard instantly agreed. "That's a great idea!" He was really hot to trot.

But as we sat there I had second and third thoughts. "It's been a long day. I'm just not in any shape to pull off something like this tonight. Tomorrow is Friday, payday. If I know Miglio, he'll go out for a couple of drinks. When he's relaxed and in his first sleep, I'll call him. I'll be at a psychological advantage. And meanwhile, at the office tomorrow, we can go through the files and maybe dig out some corroborative material."

Howard still wanted to play with the idea of a hit on Miglio after he'd broken down and admitted his guilt. We were able to turn him off that idea after having several more drinks and listening to several more stories of how he had solved past personnel problems involving Peeping Tomism, Coke-machine thievery, and other mortal sins committed by clerical employees at the Bureau. At approximately one o'clock the discussion came to an end.

Before we left the apartment, Howard said, "I want a solemn promise that neither of you will say anything to anybody else about this. If Malone gets wind of it, he'll take over and blow the show." We pledged ourselves to secrecy. "One more thing, Tony. Who is the agent who can confirm this?"

"I gave my promise I would not reveal his name."

"I'll find out my own way. Alan Howard knows how to handle things like this. I'm going to fire him. He should have come to me."

"Don't get excited. He did the right thing—he knew I would handle it. He just didn't want to get embroiled in a personnel matter."

"When did he tell you?"

"A couple of days ago."

"I'll fire the son of a bitch."

There wasn't any point in further talk about it. I told Sean that I would see him around noon when we rendezvoused with the other agents working on the First National City case. Sean decided he was too tired to drive all the way out to his home. He would sleep on the nurse's couch at the office.

At seven-thirty in the morning, Sean woke me with a telephone call. "Holy shit, the bomb went off" is the way he put it. The man who had demanded that we keep the matter a secret, Alan Howard, was already in the executive suites of the Bureau telling anybody who would listen that there was talk of an agent on the take in our office. "You better get over here quick," counseled McWeeney. "And you better produce that agent who can support your story."

As soon as I hung up, I telephoned Fred Juliano. He was very unhappy about the turn of events. There was no way for him to avoid becoming part of the investigation and, like me, he was open to disciplinary action for a failure to immediately report any suggestion of misconduct by another agent.

When I arrived at our offices, I learned that Sean McWeeney had collapsed and passed out from fatigue. I was forced to face a battery of SACs by myself. Malone was out of town, but he had already been notified of big trouble and was on his way back. So I told the SACs the story. The only piece of fiction I added was how I came to hear about the alleged bribe. I said I got it all from Herbie, an informant whom I had used in the past. I did explain that Fred Juliano had had a conversation with Tommy Miglio that seemed to back up my informant. But I could not afford to give every detail to the investigators because that would have inevitably disclosed the true identity of my informant. And anyway, I believed they would discover all of the details when they looked at the case thoroughly.

The SACs listened but made no comment. I was released in time to pursue a lead that would put me in touch with Paddy Cocco, a conduit for stolen securities and the man I had hoped to see the previous night.

The meeting with Cocco went well. As soon as I was clear, I telephoned the office to report in. I was told my presence there was imperative. When I arrived at our floor I realized that the place was quaking. There were small groups of people conferring, the little knots of gossipers that always sprouted when anything momentous occurred. I spotted a very pale Fred Juliano.

I went to the executive floor, where I was shown an accurate transcription of my statement to the SACs. It was in the form of an affidavit, and I raised my right hand and swore to it.

By noon, John Malone had returned to direct the investigation.

He was a tall, good-looking man who didn't smoke or drink. During the first five minutes of conversation, Malone would be most impressive. But the strong image he initially projected would slowly collapse like a leaky balloon. He loved to attend dinners, where he could display his handsome figure, mouth some platitudes, and generally add to the prestige of the Bureau. As a hatchet man for Hoover, Malone's job was to inspect Bureau offices and ladle out discipline. He took pains to assist the Princes of the Church in any way he could, even if the matter did not fall under FBI jurisdiction. Malone was a daily communicant and apparently a deeply religious man.

One of his strong points was that he never ducked responsibility. But when it came to tactics and actually taking effective command, John Malone was a bumbler.

One night while I was at the office late, word came that there was a plane at La Guardia with an armed man holding the crew captive. Per regulations, I notified the head of the office; Malone told me to pick him up. When we arrived, Malone went through his PR bit, shaking hands with all the representatives of every group involved—the airport security cops, the New York City police, the Port Authority officials, and even the man from the Airline Pilots Association.

The ALPA rep feared for the life of the crew, and he was half wrecked with worry. He was willing to give the hijacker anything he demanded. But the Bureau favored the get-tough technique in order to discourage further planenappers.

The hijacker wanted fuel for the plane. The ALPA rep wanted to give it to him.

"If we do that we're just caving in again," I said.

"No fuel," said Malone.

"Damn right, boss," I encouraged him.

The hijacker asked to see his wife and kid. "Why not?" someone suggested. "We've got nothing to lose."

"Somebody arrange for his family to come," ordered Malone.

"Why don't we park a truck in front of the plane, which will make it impossible to move?" was my next idea. I knew that these planes could not back up under their own power.

The ALPA rep complained. "You will be jeopardizing the crew if you do that—the guy's nuts, he could do anything."

I then prompted Malone to ask where the crew faced greater jeopardy, in the air or on the ground. Malone parroted me.

The incident demonstrated Malone's character and his weakness. He never shirked his responsibility for command; he simply lacked the capacity to take charge. If there was nobody to prop him up, he had no idea of how to proceed. As a result he was one of the Bureau's prime examples of the back-office principle "Ignorance is no bar to advancement." At the shop, Malone's nickname was "Cement Head." The hijacker, incidentally, gave up after a couple of hours of talk.

On assuming direction of the Miglio investigation, Malone's first decision was to confront the suspect with the accusation. I was astonished. A cardinal rule of the Bureau was to avoid confrontation until after a thorough investigation of possible evidence. Only some guilt-ridden suspect like a father killer ever confesses when the cops flat out ask him if he did it. Even though, the night before, I'd proposed strapping on a body recorder and confronting Miglio, it was different; I would've been coming on as a fellow agent, an unofficial inquisitor. But for the SACs to ask an agent about charges against him would only allow him to first deny everything, then concoct a cover story and make damn sure to bury any possible evidence.

Malone later told me that he had "called down to Pat Gray [acting FBI chief since the death of Hoover in 1972] and he said, 'Shake the tree' and let the bad fruit fall—bury any poisoned ones."

Gray was already in trouble. The Senate had begun to hold hearings to confirm his appointment as permanent director. Gray's testimony indicated that, under White House orders, he had contributed to the cover-up of the Watergate break-in. So, with Congress beginning to take potshots at him, Gray wanted to restrict the target area. Malone indicated to me that Gray's instructions to Malone seemed clear enough: Don't do the customary thorough, clandestine investigation; just get rid of anything obvious.

One more brilliant piece of strategy: the SACs, Tommy Miglio, Fred Juliano, and me in a kind of group encounter. Bob Sweeney took me aside. "Make sure you have your hand on your gun in that meeting," he said. "Be very careful." Granted, Miglio had an explosive personality, but the danger factor had never crossed my mind. In fact, the reason I became an FBI agent was that danger excited me. I was full of bravado; I was really quite stupid on that score.

So I waited for the showdown. For some inexplicable reason, nobody was able to reach Miglio for about five hours. When he finally called in, a supervisor spent a number of minutes on the phone with him, speaking in Italian—hardly the usual way to conduct sensitive FBI business.

I did manage a few minutes of circumspect talk with Fred Juliano while we waited. I encouraged him to tell the truth and not waver under pressure to avoid embarrassment of the Bureau.

When Miglio finally arrived at the office, I motioned a "let's go" to Fred Juliano, but Bob Sweeney stopped me. "The confrontation is to be between Fred and Tommy. You didn't hear anything directly, Tony. All you had was hearsay." The brass had apparently agreed that the pivotal question was the confirmation of the words that had passed between Juliano and Miglio. I felt that that wasn't a good way to proceed. If there was to be a confrontation over the accusation, I wanted to be in on the initial head to head and try to use my knowledge to test his story. I wanted to interrogate him the way any investigator goes after a possible suspect, hit him with information before he had an opportunity to create a scenario that protected him.

"Malone doesn't want you there," said Sweeney firmly. "Fred, you wait, too," he added. "We'll call you when we need you." That meant that the "investigators" would be questioning only through my affidavit and whatever Juliano had told them. If Miglio really were on the take, it would be a pushover for him. He had all the acting skills that go with being a natural mimic. And he was anything but stupid, unlike some of those who were to question him.

So Fred and I waited, mostly silent, on the fifteenth floor while Miglio was interrogated. Juliano said, "I don't like this. How come they're handling the case like this? Why don't they handle it like all the other horror stories—put a tail on him, bug him, scratch into his finances?"

On the same floor was the FBI switchboard and also the "sutech" division, the technical surveillance workshop and monitoring area—the section where the experts put together devices for bugs and phone taps. While Fred and I lounged around, one of the kids on the switchboard hollered to a messenger, "Get Sutech to stand by!"

Fred and I looked at one another. "It doesn't figure," he said. "First they tip him off and *then* they tap his phone. It doesn't make any sense."

Finally, they summoned Juliano and he too disappeared into the meeting for what was to seem like an interminable amount of time. During the proceedings Alan Howard called on the interoffice phone. "Holy shit, Tony, this guy won't crack." Howard reported that Miglio had explained the payment from Pete Lombardo as the receipts from an investment club. Miglio said he had thrown $1,500 into the pot and his family accounted for another $4,700.

"That doesn't add up, Alan. Your figures come to a total of sixty-two hundred, but the word was that Miglio said he got ten thousand."

Howard agreed that this was a major discrepancy in Miglio's account. Juliano had told the investigators that he also had heard the figure of ten thousand dollars as the amount collected by Miglio. However, Howard reported that Juliano could not recall whether Miglio had used the word "score" or "deal." "Score," of course, carries a strong connotation of illegality.

"Don't you think we ought to dig into Miglio's finances? If he's in bed with Salamone, we ought to look at his assets before he gets a chance to cook the books," I suggested to Howard.

"The trouble is, Malone just isn't too strong," complained Howard, "and the truth is, I feel my ass is hanging out on this already."

It seemed that the Bureau was unprepared for a formal, thorough look at the case. If Miglio came up innocent after a genuine investigation, that would have been fine with me. I could then stop worrying about the health of my sources. But if he were guilty I wanted him out fast. The Bureau's primary requirement appeared to be to avoid any hint that its nest might be fouled.

When the session between Juliano and Miglio broke up, I went to Malone's office. It was a delicate situation; I didn't want to appear to be calling him incompetent. "I wish, Mr. Malone, that I could have been there to push a little. But tell me honestly, what's your gut feeling about this?"

"I'd prefer to think that it never happened," he answered like any well-schooled bureaucrat. "I want to believe Tommy, but the more he talked, the less I believed him."

I asked what the plans were for the future. "We'll keep it as an in-house investigation, a personnel matter."

I pleaded. "Let me try to dig around. I think I might be able to do something with him." Since Malone was very impressed with the informants I'd developed inside organized crime, it seemed to me that he might be willing to give me a free hand now.

But he foresaw the worst kind of trouble if he let me off the reservation. "We don't want to let this get outside of the family. It's a Bureau problem."

The Bureau acts as the investigative arm of the Department of Justice. The decision to prosecute is not the prerogative of the Bureau; evidence gathered pertaining to a possible federal violation is furnished by the Bureau to the local U.S. attorney, who makes the decision on whether to proceed. While I knew Malone would not appreciate my reminding him of the Bureau's obligation, I had to goad him.

"It's not just a federal violation; if there's been a payoff it's also a local offense. Remember, Lombardo has already been canned by the cops for corruption."

As usual, Malone was afflicted with the wobbles; the last guy to get to him had the best shot. And in this instance I was the last and had converted him at least slightly. "Come in tomorrow, Tony, and we'll go over this some more."

When I showed up the next morning, a Saturday, some of the SACs were there, along with Malone and SAC Howard. We went through case files and Tommy Miglio's desk, looking for anything that might corroborate what I'd been told. We came up empty. I approached Alan Howard. "Turn me loose on this thing for seventy-two hours; I guarantee I'll find evidence good enough for a prosecutor to use in court or else show Miglio's innocent."

"Absolutely not," ordered Howard. "You cannot lead the investigation."

One of the SACs remarked, "Personally, I don't think this thing will ever be resolved." By late evening, when we all left, I was beginning to have a terrible fear that maybe the SAC was right— and that it would be because the Bureau preferred it that way.

The next day, instead of giving the thing a rest, I went out to Queens to see Fred Juliano. "You heard something pretty stiff against Miglio," I said, "but when they asked you about it, you backed off."

"Tony," he pleaded, "if you only could have been in that room during the confrontation and saw Miglio. He sat there pale as a fucking ghost and he had this blood vessel on his forehead that seemed to be popping. I could see him having a heart attack; the disgrace for his family would be awful. In fact, when I left the building, Miglio was waiting outside for me and he invited me for a drink. I told him we'd better not be seen together."

Fred wanted to see the right things done but, if it came to that, he didn't want to be the one to pull the switch!

A little over a week after the bomb went off, Tommy Miglio came into the office to report that he had received a telephone call the night before from his old friend, ex-Sergeant Pete Lombardo. The call had been of a purely innocent nature, but Miglio went on record that he had heard from one of the alleged members of the conspiracy. I don't know how many Brownie points that earned for him from people at the Bureau, but it meant nothing to me. I figured that, one way or the other, he could have heard about the request for Sutech to stand by on that first day at the office. He knew how the Bureau worked, and he realized that his phone might be tapped.

On February 19, 1973, two of our supervisors, Bob Sweeney and John McGinley, confronted Pete Lombardo. Facing prosecution for corruption and suspended by the New York City Police Department, Lombardo was working as assistant manager of a pub in lower Manhattan. He attributed his present circumstances to charges of an organized shakedown of peddlers in his precinct. Lombardo described to the supervisors his relationship with Miglio as that of a "close acquaintance." He said he had known him since both of them had been patrolmen in New York. After Tommy Miglio became an agent and returned to New York, the two bumped into one another at the offices of their stockbroker.

The reunion at the brokerage firm led to an agreement that they advise one another about attractive investments. Lombardo remarked that the precinct where he had been assigned was "stock crazy"; the men were driven wild by the smell of money from the Wall Street area and many had contacts in the financial district. Lombardo cited one legendary figure who supposedly cleared a million dollars through investments with insiders.

As part of his service to fellow officers, Lombardo had organized an investment club in which the members pooled funds to profit on the stock tips thus obtained. Around twenty-five men joined up, with an initial contribution of two thousand dollars apiece. Lombardo had offered a spot to his close acquaintance, Tommy Miglio, but the agent at first avoided any involvement. Pete Lombardo understood that Miglio's reluctance came from a lack of money rather than principle! However, a few months after the investment club opened for business, Miglio, with two friends and his brother, bought into the organization. Miglio put up fifteen hundred dollars; the others kicked in another twenty-five hundred.

Although the club was set up with a capitalization of about fifty thousand dollars, Lombardo claimed that by the time Tommy Miglio joined up, the shares had appreciated perhaps twenty percent. However, the outfit kept no books. Nor, for that matter, asserted Lombardo, did it issue receipts for the sums put up by the investors—a rather peculiar way to operate a business devoted to high finance. Late in 1971 a vote by the members authorized a five-hundred-dollar payment to each participant, including Tommy Miglio. Lombardo pointed out that the agent should not have received even that much, since his initial investment in the club was less than that of the original players.

Pete Lombardo created a second club as a potential source of revenue, to which only five people belonged—the former police sergeant himself, a retired police officer and two members of his family, and Tommy Miglio. Each invested five thousand dollars, which was supposed to establish a restaurant featuring pasta, with no item on the menu to exceed ninety-nine cents. Eventually, this second club hoped to open a string of such places. But after renting some office space, the backers discovered they lacked enough money to open even one eatery. The remains of the capital were planted in the stock market.

As far as I could determine from the report filed by Sweeney and McGinley, the highest figure that could possibly be attributed to Tommy Miglio's investments with Pete Lombardo was nine thousand dollars; less a one-thousand-dollar dividend, that left a net investment of eight thousand dollars. It still didn't add up to ten thousand dollars if that was what Miglio told Juliano he'd received from Lombardo. An even stranger figure is the sixty-two hundred dollars he spoke of when first interviewed by Howard and company. And, from Lombardo's description, both investment clubs were losers; it was unlikely that they could have kicked back anything.

During the interrogation Lombardo was pressed about the links with Al Salamone. The cop admitted he was more than vaguely aware of Salamone; in fact, in the past, Lombardo said, he had arrested some of Salamone's runners. Lombardo also remarked that Salamone had run a policy bank (numbers) in one of the city precincts but that although he might even have been in courtrooms on cases involving the gambler, he did not remember ever meeting him. And when Tommy Miglio approached his old friend from the cops and asked for some help in tracking Salamone, Lombardo was reluctant to make the effort. He said he had actually supplied no information about Salamone to Miglio.

When he was asked the real money question, Pete Lombardo flat out denied any kind of payoff from the gambler. He insisted he hadn't even seen Al Salamone in four or five years, and he swore on his children that he had never been connected with any scheme to bribe Tommy Miglio. Likewise, he also swore that he was innocent of all the charges brought against him by the New York Police Department and the other agencies seeking to prosecute him.

Lombardo explained that the recent telephone call to Tommy Miglio was due to his feeling that his old friend might be avoiding him because of word about his dismissal from the police force. He figured he ought to call Miglio and advise him on the status of the original investment club.

A few days after the Lombardo interview, Alan Howard visited Al Salamone at his apartment in New York City. Salamone denied everything, said he did not even know Pete Lombardo. Tommy Miglio, Salamone said, had made contact with him following his arrest in April of 1971 on the gambling charge. Miglio had told Salamone he was in serious trouble but that he, Miglio, could be of assistance. Salamone said that he had interpreted this to mean that Miglio, like all agents, only wanted to make him an informant. Salamone stated that if he was called before a grand jury he would vigorously contest any suggestion that he ever paid off an FBI agent; after all, he said, it was well known that agents could not be reached. With that endorsement of the incorruptibility of the Bureau, the interrogation ended.

The interviews with Al Salamone and Pete Lombardo produced only denials of any conspiracy to bribe an FBI agent. It seemed to me that the investigation failed to dig deep enough to either clear Miglio or find the evidence to prosecute him. There was no challenge of inconsistencies in the accounts. For example, Lombardo said that Miglio had come to him and asked for Salamone's address. But why had he done that when the address was in our own files? How much money had Lombardo actually paid to Miglio? And where were the cancelled checks? Why hadn't the agents snooped around the bar where the payoff supposedly occurred?

The whole thing was terribly frustrating to me, and my anxiety was not alleviated by the atmosphere in the office. The constant meetings between the SACs and supervisors, to which I was not invited, added further to my own uneasiness. One day, after the usual closed meeting, one of the attending supervisors approached me and said, "What a lot of shit. I just told them the only thing that should be investigated at this point is the investigation." I was not surprised after that to see that he too seemed to be left out.

Another disquieting tidbit came from Fred Juliano. He had had some second thoughts about his vacillating performance before the SACs. He told me that he'd telephoned Bob Sweeney at home one night and said, "I don't think they understand the situation there. There's a problem with Tommy Miglio."

Sweeney interrupted. "Are you calling through the switchboard?"

"No, direct," said Juliano. "There's a lot more to this than you know. Miglio's story is all bullshit." Sweeney shut him off.

Sweeney's reluctance to listen didn't surprise me. He had confided to me that he had criticized Miglio to Malone. Instead of being grateful for information on the accused's personality, Malone scorched Sweeney for his earlier failure to tell him that the office had an ineffective agent like Miglio.

I put my brain on the rack, looking for ways to find evidence. I turned to my strongest resources, the informants. A number of them either knew nothing or didn't care to tell. But there were others with particles of information. One of them was the swag dealer and jewel fence with connections in the Genovese and Gambino crime families, Paul Ginder.* I paid Ginder a visit at his shop in the city. He comes on as a wholesale jeweler.

Paul was very cordial. We waltzed around a while, and then I began. "Paul, it looks like the FBI is going to become involved in the field of narcotics." (This ploy had a basis in fact; at the time there were many indications that the Bureau was going to absorb the Bureau of Narcotics and Dangerous Drugs.) "I've gotten some rumbles about a bad FBI agent, a guy already reached by the wiseguys. That could be dangerous for all of us."

Paul looked down at the floor. I pushed a little harder. "Paul, I hate to put you on the spot, but if we get into junk we'll never succeed with dirty hands."

"Please don't ask me," he pleaded. "I have a very good idea of what you're talking about, but the wiseguys are involved and you're going to get me killed if you make me talk about it."

I told him that ordinarily I would respect his problems, but this matter was of the utmost importance; it was my ass on the line. Ginder still wouldn't give me a name, but he was willing to play a kind of Twenty Questions.

"He's in his forties; he's an Italian." That description could almost fit me. "He's a former cop."

I was bursting.

"Is it Tommy Miglio?"

"You got it; that's him."

"Miglio came to my booth one day," Ginder continued. "I was out and he left his name with my girl. When I come in she gives me the slip. Sounds like a wiseguy name but it don't mean nothing to me, so I forget it. A few days later he comes back and introduces himself. The way he talked, it sounded like a shakedown to me. After he left, I telephoned a wiseguy I know. I explained about the visit from Miglio. The wiseguy laughs and says, 'Don't worry about him, he's okay.' "

But Paul absolutely refused to hand me the name of the wiseguy. "Cut my tongue out and I still won't tell you" was his way of letting me know that there were limits to his cooperation.

Now I had to convince Paul to feed what he knew to John Malone. Actually, Paul Ginder had met Malone at one of the resorts in the Catskills. Malone was there doing his missionary work for the Bureau. Paul was there taking some sun. Malone probably would not remember Paul, but the swag man recalled their few minutes together and, like most people who had spent only a limited time with the head of our New York office, he was much impressed. I pumped up Malone even more, telling Paul that he was a prince of a fellow, a true gentleman, and a guy who would remember a favor.

Having thus primed Ginder, I made immediate contact with Malone at his private number in the office. "Boss, I have something very hot. I have corroboration. The man was invaluable to us in a big organized crime case. He's very reliable."

Malone bought the package and we agreed to drive up to Paul Ginder's home in an exclusive suburban area north of New York City. I was afraid that Malone might come on as the starchy FBI chief and Paul would freeze up, so I suggested that he dress informally. It was a shock to see Malone in a turtleneck and sports jacket, but the pose worked beautifully. Malone flattered Paul Ginder with statements about how interested we were in what he had to say, how important it was, and how much we appreciated his cooperation. For a guy like Ginder, who never knows when somebody is going to put the arm on him, there are never too many friends in high places.

Thanks to Malone's smooth approach, Ginder gave a much more complete account of his chats with Tommy Miglio. Rebuffed on his first visit, Miglio had come to see the swag man again, accompanied this time by another agent. Miglio announced, "Paul, I know the time, the date, the place, the hour you're going to get killed. If you do the right thing, we'll protect you."

Ginder was very sure of himself with the wiseguys. He told Miglio he was full of shit. Miglio poured abuse on Ginder but he sloughed it off, and the agents left. "It was the craziest thing," Ginder remarked. "This other agent just sits there and doesn't say one fucking word. Tommy does all the talking. But by the second visit I know what he is—remember I was told."

The real question was what had Tommy meant by "the right thing," a familiar euphemism in police jargon for a bribe. On the other hand, it could have been a request for Ginder to become an informant. Paul Ginder didn't believe it for a moment. "Miglio is in business. He's got an intermediary—I won't give you his name, but he's a wiseguy. He deals in big numbers—five thousand dollars, eight thousand dollars. He even uses a code name, Al S."

I was astounded, and Malone was very excited: "If you won't give us the name, will you acknowledge the correct one? Is it Al Salamone?"

Ginder wouldn't budge, but he did go far enough to say, "You're not barking up the wrong tree."

Malone was so grateful that he said, "Take Tony's home telephone number. If any agent approaches you, get Tony and he'll notify me. The matter will be taken care of immediately."

The second approach to Paul Ginder could have been Miglio's cover-up. The return visit could have been used to legitimize the earlier one; the silent agent would be a dupe.

Back at the office, Miglio was asked about his dealings with Paul Ginder. He alibied that an informant of his had mentioned that Ginder was a good prospect as a source of information. I knew the informant; he was the kind who would tell you: "You get me off the hook with the district attorney and I'll say anything you want me to say in court." He was a sneaky, creepy shylock on the outskirts of the Genovese Family.

There was always a problem with some informants. They tried to guess what agents would like to hear. Or they puffed up their importance and their sense of security with you by feeding you wild stories, rumors, anything that might boost their stock. I trusted Paul not to do this, but you never could be 100 percent sure that what you were told was gospel.

Malone seemed to be very much influenced by his conversation with Paul Ginder. "Tony," he said, "that was one of the finest informants I've ever seen. You have such a good relationship with him; you ought to develop him much further."

The advice was a mark of Malone's naiveté. "He's not that kind of a guy," I explained. "He won't be a regular stool pigeon; it would rub against his grain. He'll only help you if he's sure there's no skin off his ass."

Malone's excitement raged on; he appeared to have scented blood. And that was the factor in my favor. I think, for all his weaknesses, John Malone did want to know the truth, if only to protect himself. Apparently he was not very happy with the result of Howard's interrogation of Al Salamone, because when I proposed a second try at questioning him, Malone readily agreed. In his own inimitable style, he decided that he would have a crack at the gambler himself, but that he would take me along for any assistance I could offer. Acting on our instructions, our agent in the area where Salamone kept a country house arranged the meeting for March of 1973.

As we drove there that late Saturday afternoon, Malone spoke of his desire to "clean house." For the first time since that night at Alan Howard's apartment I began to think virtue was going to have its day.

For a man who now lived on his Social Security and whose biggest weekly salary check had been about $250 as a salesman, Salamone sure knew how to stretch a buck. He owned about four hundred choice acres. I'd have been happy to live in his garage, and the house was a natural-wood and fieldstone mansion. The road leading up to it was a better piece of work than the state highway. It was built on top of a dam he'd had made to create a lake from a stream near his house.

When we arrived, Malone announced, "Tony, you wait in the car. I'll talk to him godfather to godfather."

"But if you don't get anything," I pleaded, "will you let me talk to him?" Malone agreed to the stipulation and walked off, while I sat there discouraged by this latest revelation about his thinking. Godfather to godfather—for Christ's sake! This wasn't Marlon Brando sitting down with Efrem Zimbalist, Jr. Hell, this was the head of the largest office of the Federal Bureau of Investigation interrogating a convicted felon, a bona fide member of the criminal conspiracy we were supposed to be fighting against.

The light was just about gone when Malone hailed me from the veranda of the house. As soon as I stepped onto the porch, he told me Salamone would not change his story a jot. Just as he had informed Sweeney and Howard, he knew nothing of any payoffs to a cop and an FBI agent.

Malone escorted me into the house, where Salamone, recumbent in his pajamas, received us. He was slim, without an old man's pot stomach, and very soft-spoken. I started out easy, sincere, reinforcing the image of the FBI projected by John Malone. I reminded him of the sacrifice Malone, an assistant director, had made by journeying all the way from New York City just to see him. I asked Salamone about his numbers operations and payoffs to the police, but nicely.

"Sure, I was involved in gambling for years," he answered. "I had to pay off the cops then. But I never paid off anyone in the FBI and I've been retired for a long time. Anything you hear about me being involved in gambling now is all lies. I'm clean— you can ask me about anything."

"You've probably got a drop in this bedroom," I told Salamone. "I bet I could find it in five minutes."

Salamone grinned. "You know, he probably could," he said to Malone. All of this cordiality was not getting us any closer to finding the truth. I tried another tack, tough, accusatory.

"We know you've been paying off cops and now you've reached an agent. This isn't a hunch—we've got two separate sources who confirm it. We're not out to crucify Tommy Miglio or even prosecute him. We think maybe he's sick and needs treatment."

Salamone denied any knowledge of the affair. "You got a problem with Tommy, don't ask me to help you."

"What about Tommy? He's got a wife and kids. You're messing up their lives, too." Salamone wouldn't budge for beans. I was warming up and deliberately dropped my cool. "You're a liar, a cocksucker, a corrupter of cops and now of an agent."

"Any time an FBI agent comes to my house he is a welcome guest," huffed Salamone. "But, Malone, from now on when they come to my door and behave like this, I call my lawyer."

"You motherfucker, if you see me at your door, you better call a priest," I shouted. Meanwhile, Malone tried to quiet me down by saying that we were guests, and then Salamone's wife came in and Malone got into a conversation with her. I took the opportunity to grab Salamone by the arm and drag the poor bastard off to a corner where I could blast him some more. I dropped a few choice phrases in Sicilian on him to give him the impression that I was a guy he could talk to. But he was too tough. He knew how to seek out a person's interests, turn the conversation to something other than the real business at hand. His grandfatherly, gentle behavior was the antithesis of evil, but inside he was thoroughly evil, rotting, a Dorian Gray with the picture concealed inside him. Finally Malone, fearing we'd overstayed our welcome, which is an understatement, got us out of there.

Back in the car Malone said, "That was wonderful. He's a lying bastard, the son of a bitch. I wish I could have talked to him the way you did, but I am an assistant director and have to act that way." He was in fact awed enough by my performance to spring for dinner at a fancy restaurant, something extremely rare for Malone, who had a waiting list of so-called winebuyers—his expense-account spenders. He even invited me to have a drink, but I was riding too high at the moment. I felt that I had him convinced of the need for a thorough, real investigation, so I passed up the cocktail offer.

With Malone at the wheel en route to the city, I drafted the interview report and read it to him. He approved it, and it was subsequently transcribed into the record. The record indicated that Malone had asked Salamone if he knew Al S. The gambler acted surprised at first, then denied ever having heard of him. Malone also asked Salamone if he would mind submitting to a lie detector test. He said he had no confidence in such gadgets, but volunteered to swear to the truth in church on anything holy to him. That might have impressed a daily communicant like Malone, but I thought it was nonsense to even include it in an official report. Salamone was characterized as "making every effort to appear cooperative; however, it was obvious that at every opportunity he tried to change the subject and speak about inconsequential matters."

Meanwhile, Alan Howard and Sweeney had interrogated Herbie, the stand-in source to whom I had attributed the tip on the payoff. I had already primed him with the right answers, so he was ready. Herbie lived on the lower East Side of Manhattan, one of the reasons I had chosen him as the beard for Fred Juliano. Herbie was also on his own quite knowledgeable about Salamone's gambling operations, having once been a runner for Salamone, and he supplied Howard and Sweeney with details of the business. He explained to them that one day he had bumped into Salamone and whined about a heavy rap facing him. Salamone supposedly commiserated, and then told him maybe he had a friend who could help.

At the end of their report, Howard and Sweeney said it was New York's conviction that, because of the contradictions in all the stories, everyone involved should undergo a lie detector test. Investigators for the Bureau had asked Tommy Miglio about his

interviews with Paul Ginder. Miglio asserted that he had seen
Ginder only one time, and that was with Agent Charlie Garvey as
his associate. That directly contradicted Ginder's statements to
me and John Malone; Miglio also said he knew nothing of any
Al S. I asked Charlie Garvey about their visit to Ginder, but, while
he saw no purpose in the meeting, he also did not hear anything
incriminating.

My immediate problem, however, was the polygraph that I was
facing. For all the Bureau's belief in the machines, I knew that
they were extremely limited in their ability to perceive the truth.
The polygraph's effectiveness supposedly depends upon the per-
ceptible changes in heartbeat and other body functions when an
individual veers from the truth. A series of control questions
establish what those changes are when the subject is truthful and
when he or she is lying. An expert in the field who works for the
FBI once told me that the polygraph is almost useless when
turned on someone like an FBI agent, "who has to lie from his
first day on the street." This is true. Agents spend half their
careers lying to people they interview, trying to cozen them into
confessing or giving up information.

I never "flaked" anyone—planted evidence on a suspect—nor
did I ever lie in testimony in court. But as an agent I had to break
almost every rule in the book in order to do my job. The Bureau
never wanted to know about such transgressions, so, in the reports we filed, they were either not mentioned or else covered by
lies. We also spent a good part of our time distorting the truth in
administrative accounts our supervisors received. The system,
with all of its cumbersome record keeping, forces a premium to
be put on fakery. For example, an agent is supposed daily to file
Number Three cards, which summarize what he expects to do
during that day. Theoretically, that enables the Bureau to know
where he is and how he can be reached. But nobody could be sure
how the day would be spent, so the cards were at best mere
approximations. Each agent has maybe twenty cases assigned to
him; every forty-five days he files a report on each case, listing
the days of investigation and what was accomplished. If the
inspectors want to stick an agent, they need only pull the Three
cards for a given period and match them against the case reports.

Smart guys protected themselves by rewriting their Three cards to harmonize with the data in the case reports.

Anyone who has spent ten or twenty years of his life creating these fictions does not have predictable reactions. Therefore, FBI agents, like the pathological liars of organized crime, make poor subjects for a polygraph machine. We all knew that the lie detector can be fooled by drugs; a stiff dose of tranquilizers, for instance, confuses the record.

Not only did I have very little faith in the polygraph as a dowsing rod for truth, I was also aware that I was going to have to lie. I could not give up Fred Juliano and that meant I would have to repeat the account of his beard, Herbie.

On March 13, 1973, I sat for the polygraph. I had taken some pills for a cold, but I was still very nervous. One question was "Did Herbie tell you Salamone paid money to an agent to have his case fixed?" When I answered yes, the polygraph indicated a reaction. To cover myself, I subsequently said that Herbie might have been playing cute with me and not been entirely truthful about his source of information.

The examiner said he'd like to run me through the machine one more time. I could see no profit for me in this, and so I begged off. The next day I was asked to take a second test and again refused. There was no way I could convince people that the substance of what I had said was factual but that the source was otherwise. "We can't make you take one, but it doesn't look good," Alan Howard advised me. "Think some more about it."

The following day two Bureau supervisors interviewed me at the Westbury Hotel about my reluctance to undergo another polygraph session. In the course of the discussion they staggered me with a wholly unexpected attack. An anonymous letter had been received at the Bureau and it contained a series of allegations about me. Far from being the accuser, I was now the defendant.

I was handed a copy of the letter. Although the contents was almost pathetic, it was obviously a very professional piece of work. The author had used a child's typewriter. A neat trick—you buy one for ten bucks, use it for the anonymous message, and then throw it away. It's untraceable, and everybody in the Bureau knew all about how we could track down typewriters—remember the ancient Woodstock supposedly used by Alger Hiss to write notes to Whittaker Chambers?

The letter accused me of having sold narcotics, of having been involved in hijackings committed by one of my member sources —an informant inside organized crime—and of shylocking. It also claimed that I had a stockbroker who handled my illicitly obtained funds and my secret bank accounts, and that I had fixed a junk case for a guy in Connecticut and then arranged for him to bring the stuff to New York for sale. But the boldest accusation of all was that I had tried to put out a contract on Tommy Miglio because he was aware of my supposed extracurricular activities, but that Pete DeFeo, my alleged intermediary, nixed the deal and instead suggested a bribery scandal to destroy Miglio's credibility.

Nothing in the letter was true. The most significant thing about it was that it could only have been written by someone in the FBI offices, someone familiar with at least the gossip about my activities. I had already checked with one of my sources, an LCN soldier, about whether anyone ever talked of hitting Miglio. "Hell no," said the button man, although he himself said he would certainly consider whacking out any agent who put him in possible jeopardy by giving his name to the wiseguys. As for Pete DeFeo, I knew he was a well-connected guy but I had never met him.

Now I not only volunteered for, I demanded another polygraph test on the contents of the letter. The Bureau insisted on an all-or-nothing deal—my testimony about the alleged bribe as well as the anonymous letter. I wasn't happy about it, but I finally agreed. The official report of the polygraph examination states: "Based on the charts obtained, it appears that Villano was truthful in his answers to questions concerning information he received from the source." I also passed the test when I denied each and every allegation contained in the letter.

It was a victory without any results, however. Tommy Miglio had passed the polygraph, too, and he'd taken only one.

With nothing produced on the polygraphs, the Bureau seemed uninterested in searching any further. Once, after being interrogated, Fred Juliano passed me in the hall. I heard just one word: "Whitewash."

The New York office, like much of the Bureau, is thick with Irish Catholics. One of the more discouraging tidbits passed to me by a friend who attended the endless office-brass meetings, from which I continued to be excluded, reflected the psyche-happy thinking that ethnic overbalance occasionally produced. The discussion had got around to whether there had been a payoff from Salamone. "You have to realize who is involved," someone said. "Miglio, Villano, Juliano—all Italians. They think differently— kind of Byzantine thought processes. They have these vendettas, and everyone knows there's been bad blood between Villano and Miglio. . . ."

What had started out, I thought, as a simple but sensational charge had turned into a kind of free-fire-zone situation, with me occupying the most exposed position. At this point I wasn't aware that we hadn't yet heard from some of the biggest guns, that I myself could come up with a few pretty good-sized bombs before it was over. I was simply living from day to day, hoping to survive until the enemy, the inertia, the reluctance of the Bureau to seek answers, was beaten.

I did not usually discuss my work at home, partly out of the habit of prudence developed by all brick agents. But in this instance, with a gumbo-thick muddle beginning to smother the entire affair, I explained to my wife what was happening. She had once worked as a clerk in the Bureau, and so was thoroughly familiar with the way things worked there. When I finished my recitation of the facts, she said, "You should have known better. Why did you expect anything different?"

It was a question I should have asked myself earlier. I'd had twenty-three years with the FBI—what should I have expected the reaction to be to a charge of corruption? Should I have done things differently? Had I been naive? How did I ever get myself into this situation . . . ?

8

The Investigation: II

As 1973 BEGAN, I was working full-time on a case that involved the theft of six cashier's checks worth sixteen million dollars from First National City Bank. Another agent had been tipped that the individuals associated with the remains of the Gallo gang were looking to negotiate the checks. The Bureau's strategy was to pass me off as a wiseguy who had connections with people who handled paper. I made contact on the second try, the day after I had come into the office to tell the SACs the story given to me by Fred Juliano.

The site was one of those Brooklyn "social clubs" so esteemed by the cognoscenti for their privacy. The clubs are in unused stores or office back rooms and are open only to LCN members and friends. As private institutions, they are not under the scrutiny of cops or the State Liquor Authority.

The informant—I called him El Gato*—was a very dignified old guy. He reminded me of a big fat cat until he opened his toothless mouth and destroyed the image. El Gato was quite nervous about the whole thing. In fact, he was damn near scared to death. He had heard that Paddy Cocco carried a pistol. And nobody was going to holler for the cops if a fracas broke out in a social club. When Cocco showed, El Gato introduced me—"This is Tony Damiano"—and then split instantly.

After a little feeling-out talk, I told Cocco I had some securities to unload. The securities, I explained, had a face value of maybe forty thousand dollars (they were in reality worthless) and had been stolen by a "flat rat" (apartment burglar). Cocco replied that he would have to show the paper to his principal, who was well versed in this field. Cocco then suggested I return in a few days and meet him at a nearby bar or, if he wasn't there, at his apartment, which was in the same building. To further open

Cocco's nose, I told him I had access to limitless quantities of fugazy (counterfeit currency) of excellent quality. Cocco immediately summoned his brother to talk. He was an expert on fugazy, or almost an expert—he'd spent five years in a federal penitentiary on a counterfeit charge. They seemed interested in what I had to sell, and I was likewise anxious for their property, which neither of us mentioned. I left, confident he was hooked.

Four days later, while my head was still spinning with the Juliano-Miglio mess, Herb Ulsberg (another government witness we later relocated) and I drove out to a Brooklyn bar in a red Cadillac convertible. Cocco met us and guided the way to a residence nearby, where a man he introduced as "Joe" joined the conference.

Paddy Cocco described Joe and himself as partners in the First National City Bank cashier's checks. They proposed to sell $2.5 million to us for only twenty-five points, roughly $640,000. The rest went to their boss. Ulsberg and I could pocket close to $2 million, less our expenses. We were assured that the checks had come out of a warehouse, had never been missed, and bore a perfectly forged signature. We were also assured the bank's computer would unhesitatingly accept them. Further discussion revealed that Cocco and friends had already managed to put through one check this size by means of a dummy corporation in Canada. The funds were then transferred to a Swiss account and were now awaiting transfer to U.S. accounts. If Ulsberg and I were able to negotiate a check, several more would be available for us. We demanded a look at the merchandise before putting up any dough.

A third meeting occurred at Paxton's Restaurant in New York. Cocco came with a different man, a tall, black-haired young guy with a beard. Cocco called him Mario. After a couple of drinks at the bar we adjourned to a secluded table. I noted that the two of them wore heavy leather jackets. I played cute. "It's hot as hell in here. Why don't you guys take off your jackets?"

"No, I'm sorry, but we'll have to keep them on," apologized Paddy. "We're both packing." El Gato hadn't been wrong. Paddy apologized that his boss was unable to attend because of the press of other business. Ulsberg expressed his disappointment because that meant we would not be able to determine the viability of the checks.

Cocco displayed a photostat of one of the checks, but that was not only worthless in determining how genuine their merchandise was, it was also useless to me as evidence. Besides, we still wanted to nab Paddy's so-far invisible boss. We filled out the time by diddling over how much cash on delivery would be proper. Ulsberg and Paddy settled on twenty-five thousand dollars in an escrow account in the names of Ulsberg and the boss. Ulsberg then spun out a masterpiece of financial double-talk about how he would work the checks through some corporate accounts under his control and then into Bahamian, Swiss, and eventually Florida banks. Paddy was visibly impressed with Ulsberg's fiscal bullshit. We settled on another session a week later at Paxton's. We were assured that the boss as well as the checks would be present.

We were in Paxton's on February 27 and so was Cocco—with a free-lance private investigator named Bruce Romanoff, who had, unknown to us then, been a close associate of the late Gallo brothers. Also in Paxton's, within earshot, were four agents from the Bureau.

The conversation at our table centered on horse racing, girls, money, and swinging restaurants. I had carefully worked the conversation around to the last topic in order to talk about Pembles Discotheque. "That's one helluva spot for girls," I said. "I went there regularly—that's where I met Joey Gallo. He was some kind of guy." It registered perfectly. Bruce Romanoff became slightly depressed, and Cocco explained to me that Bruce had been very close to Joe and still took his death badly.

We turned to the subject at hand. Cocco invited me to the bar while Bruce and Ulsberg went over the details on the cashier's checks. After about fifteen minutes, Cocco walked back to the table to inquire how it looked. Everything was apparently splendid; Romanoff had flashed to Ulsberg three photostatic copies of checks worth over nine million dollars. I asked about the financial details. Ulsberg reported, "They want between twenty-five and fifty thousand in the escrow account."

"Jesus Christ, I'm going to have to go to the shylocks in East Harlem for this kind of cash. Let's keep it at a minimum. They'll take my lungs." Finally they accepted the bottom figure.

"One more thing," Ulsberg announced. "I have to see the originals of the checks." Romanoff handed Cocco the keys to his

Cadillac and instructed him to bring the briefcase from the trunk. Paddy returned a few minutes later with the case. He and I adjourned again to the bar to leave the others to examine the stuff. While Paddy and I sat at the bar, Ulsberg studied the three checks. "They look bona fide," he said, a trifle loudly. That was the magic word, the signal to the assembled agents. They grabbed Ulsberg and Romanoff at the table, Cocco and me at the bar. The whole thing was done so efficiently that we were hustled out of Paxton's in just over two minutes flat. The management of the restaurant wrote a note to the office thanking the agents for the absence of commotion connected with the arrests.

At our office, Romanoff rolled over quickly. A seventeen-year-old girl who worked at the bank admitted to having lifted the six checks, which she then turned over to a pair of brothers in the Gallo organization. From there, the stuff funneled to Romanoff and Paddy Cocco.

It was a good piece of work, but I was in no position to enjoy it. The investigation of the corruption charges, which I had launched, threatened to roll over me. The polygraphs had added up to nothing, which by my calculations made me a loser in the Bureau. I had suggested in good faith that there might be some dirty linen in the Bureau. Instead of running the kind of investigation that would establish guilt or innocence, the Bureau at best had bungled the matter and at worst had, in the language of Watergate, stonewalled it. And it seemed obvious to me that my head was on the block for even raising the possibility of corruption, or anything that might embarrass the organization.

The only way out seemed to be for me to run my own investigation. The place to start was the cop who had confided in Fred Juliano and who said he'd been a go-between for Salamone and Pete Lombardo. Juliano stubbornly refused to give me the cop's name because he said he had promised not to get the cop involved. If I had known that he was related to the owner of the bar where the meeting occurred, I might have been able to identify him through the New York State Liquor Authority. But, unaware of this fact, I staked out the bar, an old frame building dating back to the turn of the century. From the entrance to the place you can see the graceful sweep of the Brooklyn Bridge. In the morning, the dark shadow of the FDR Drive falls on the building.

The smell of fish is constant, and even in the dead of summer people make bonfires of crates and refuse in the street.

The place itself is the epitome of the workingman's saloon. At the heavy oak bar you could still buy a small glass of tap beer for a quarter in 1971. A lunch counter satisfied hunger, and the one-hundred-year-old clock on the bile-green wall is a remembrance of times past even as it marks the passage toward the future.

Because of the nature of the fresh fish business, the area buzzes with life while the rest of the city is still waking up. Places like the bar open before the sun rises, and their customers have nearly vanished by midday. For a daily hour or so over a ten-day period I had hung around the place before reporting in to work at the Bureau, looking for somebody that I might recognize or even a license plate or insignia that I could use as a lead to the cop's identity. But I struck out.

I went to work on Juliano. I knew that Fred wouldn't simply give him up. I casually asked him if the cop was in plainclothes (a vice squad cop) and, just as absently, Juliano replied, "Naw, he's in Burglary." That was enough as a starter. I figured that since Fred was a former Staten Island boy, there was a good likelihood that the cop, like Fred, also came from there.

As soon as Juliano and I parted company, I made a pretext phone call to New York City police headquarters. I found out that there was only one burglary unit on Staten Island, composed of eight detectives. That narrowed the hunt considerably.

Next I asked Nick Billeti what he knew about Salamone's connections with the cops. "Shit, he had them all on the pad," said Billeti. "He reaches the precinct, the division, the borough, and even the deputy commissioner's office. Ain't you heard, Tony? Gambling is a victimless crime; it's clean money." Billeti said that a cop nicknamed Bill Dingo* was carrier of bribe money for Salamone in a downtown precinct. In addition, Salamone had such limitless faith in his bag man Dingo that he even commissioned him to build a drop in Salamone's apartment.

I called the New York Police Department's burglary unit on Staten Island. "I've got some carpentry work to be done at my house," I told the sergeant on duty, "and somebody in our garage said one of your guys, Bill something or other—a guy with an Italian name—is a helluva carpenter."

"The only Bill we got who is Italian is Bolla,* but I never heard about his carpentry," answered the sergeant. In spite of this I was certain that Bolla was my man. I obtained his number from the sergeant and called him. Again I played the role of the customer in search of a moonlighting cop who was good with a hammer and nails. Bolla, however, protested that I had the wrong name. He swore that he had never driven a straight nail in his life. But he did give me a yes on what I considered the thirty-two-dollar question: Did he work occasionally as a bartender at the bar?

There wasn't any way I could move Bolla beyond that fact. He totally denied the entire tale about an arrangement for a meeting between Pete Lombardo and Salamone and any story about a payoff. "Sure, I may have made a phone call for somebody at one time or another, but that's all I know, period."

I went back to sources in the underworld. Sean McWeeney agreed to approach Allie Boy Persico on my behalf. There was a perfect excuse: Gino Asturi had recently told me that Carmine's kid, Larry the Pillpopper, had just recovered from an overdose. Sean got a message through to Allie Boy that he wanted to discuss the nephew's situation.

The meet was set up for Prospect Park in Brooklyn on a drizzly, bleak afternoon. I drove Sean there in a Bureau car. After we waited a few minutes, the standard-issue, big black car arrived. The bodyguard sat in his vehicle while I waited in ours. Sean and Allie Boy took a stroll through the park. McWeeney later related their conversation. He began with some commiserating words. "Sorry about your nephew. Can we intercede in any way? We're particularly interested because of the possibility that the Bureau will be getting into drug control."

Persico thanked McWeeney for his interest but saw no way for the Bureau to aid the nephew. Then, as casually as possible, Sean remarked, "Since we are going into narcotics, we're worried that we may have a bad apple in the barrel, an agent selling us out. That would be horrendous; it could be bad for everyone. Have you any idea of a leak?"

Allie Boy answered, "If I did know, I couldn't tell you. I appreciate how you've acted, but please don't ask me about this sort of thing."

To me it sounded as if Allie Boy might know something; he

would have said a flat no otherwise. But in terms of what the Bureau brass wanted as corroboration—a smoking gun—the conversation was worthless. And, of course, it was circumstantial; I wouldn't want Tommy Miglio to be convicted on that type of featherweight evidence.

Another tantalizing gossamer of support floated into the case from a series of wiretaps against Joe Gentile, aka Joe Lane, a Brooklyn gambler highly trusted but never made. Gentile was talking to Ernie Lapanzina, a soldier directly under Joe Colombo. Going through the transcripts, Dick Genova, in charge of the case, saw some garbled conversation to the effect of Lapanzina telling Gentile about a "dear friend," the customary reference to a made guy. This particular dear friend had a problem. Someone had given him twenty-five thousand dollars but the IRS had heard of the transaction and forced him to pay the taxes.

Said Lapanzina: "They're out to get him; he's a target and he says he knows it—you know they mentioned that they had nine or ten guys on the list." The word "target" was an in-house expression used by agents, one not likely to have come into the vocabulary of mugs like Lapanzina or Salamone unless it had first come from some blabbermouth agent.

Later in the tapes, Ernie continued: "His name is Salamone." After a few references to the danger of a grand jury subpoena, Ernie advised: "Well, that's the only place that guy can help us. He hears anything, he's going to let us know." It indicated that Al Salamone had a source in law enforcement.

That was all that we could extract from the tapes, which were barely audible, at best, in some places. The name Salamone, however, was unmistakably there, along with indications that the mob would count on someone to give intelligence on the tactics of the FBI.

When I waved this at the assembled powers in the New York office, they were unimpressed. They saw no reason to investigate further or even to give any information to the U.S. attorney's office for its decision on whether to proceed.

I had followed any lead I could find; I had dredged up every piece of information that my sources could supply, and I had pushed the people in New York to the limits of my capacity. Despite the presence of what I considered enough circumstantial evidence to warrant further and deeper study, the New York

Office investigation under SAC Alan Howard was being considered closed, the charges unfounded.

On April 13, 1973, I received a personal letter about the case from Acting Director Patrick Gray, who had just finished testifying before the Senate Watergate Committee, admitting that he had destroyed potential evidence taken from the safe of John Dean. It was a letter of censure for having failed to act more promptly and for not properly interrogating my sources in order to get "more precise data." If Gray had looked into the matter more thoroughly and not been enmeshed in his appearances before the Watergate Committee, he would have been aware that my delay was only a disguise to protect a source. His notion that I failed to properly interrogate my source is a mark of his ignorance about how agents work, a prime example of why it was a colossal mistake to take a former submarine commander and put him in charge of what is supposed to be the most sophisticated law-enforcement agency in the world—unless, of course, the administration really wanted a dummy whose chief asset was an ability to blindly take orders.

And Gray was the fellow who had recently awarded me four of my incentive awards and whose most recent two letters to me had been love notes with compliments on handling "important responsibilities with unwavering loyalty and devotion to the FBI," and on the high quality of my work as a "fine reflection on you and on your organization as well." These compliments not only weren't good enough for a free ride on the subway, they weren't worth enough for him to even ask for a personal conference with me.

At the same time, I received another piece of mail, dated April 13. It was a form letter transferring me to the Philadelphia office of the Bureau. The acting director had completed his resolution of the case by sending similar notes to Tommy Miglio and Fred Juliano, shifting them to other assignments. It was the classic way of burying an incident and those connected with it.

I was handed these letters after being invited into the office of Alan Howard, the man I felt was responsible for this betrayal. In the face of his oozing good-fellowship—how happy my family and I would be in Philadelphia and how much the Bureau there was looking forward to seeing me—I retreated to Shakespeare:

"There are those who from their sins rise and others from their virtues fall." Howard just looked confused. I walked out.

I decided to request an opportunity to speak with Gray directly. I typed it out and sent it through proper channels, but he never got around to answering me. He had asked the Administration to withdraw his name from confirmation as director as a result of the testimony he offered the Watergate Committee. Instead of a reply from him I got one from William Ruckelshaus, who was kind of an acting acting director of the Bureau. He wrote that the matter in question had been "thoroughly reviewed" and he saw no reason to change "the action taken." He threw me a meatless bone: If I still insisted on any further discussion I could contact a second-ranking personnel officer at FBI headquarters, which was less than telling me to see the chaplain.

I made my plans to work out of Philadelphia, but a series of random events upset everything. In the course of investigations, the agents on organized crime squads worked closely with the Organized Crime Strike Forces of the Justice Department. One of the best was that of Denis Dillon, a former New York City cop and an assistant U.S. attorney. He was the chief of the strike force in the eastern district of New York, which covered Brooklyn, Queens, and all of Long Island. Just about the time I exchanged correspondence with Patrick Gray, a close personal friend of Dillon's was having a drink at a joint called Wednesday's, not far from FBI New York headquarters. Two individuals, obviously agents, sat nearby. Dillon's astonished friend heard one of them mention gossip about an attempt to bribe an agent. The friend immediately passed the word to Dillon. He might have forgotten the indiscreet talk except that a few nights later, an agent on the squad (in violation of the accepted practices of the Bureau) threw me a farewell party. Dillon was invited, and he asked me why I was being shipped out to the boondocks. We met later that week and, on a park bench, I poured out some of the details to him.

While Dillon was still mulling over my account—trying, perhaps, to be sure that I hadn't flipped out—Fred Juliano dropped by Denis's office to say farewell. "I'm being transferred," explained Juliano, "and I want you to know the truth."

With Juliano's story to partly back up mine, Dillon questioned John Malone, the assistant director of the New York office.

Malone downgraded the whole business, said it was an in-house investigation and that there was nothing to substantiate the allegations. Dillon wasn't put off. He asked to see the investigatory reports.

Instead, Malone arranged for Alan Howard to brief Dillon on the case. After listening to Howard's summary, Dillon criticized the way things had been handled. He wanted to know why the Bureau had not wired Fred Juliano in an attempt to see if Miglio could be induced to admit his complicity in a bribe. Dillon reprimanded Howard and the Bureau for the decision to classify the affair as an in-house matter when an LCN member was a principal. At the very least, the allegations should have been presented to a prosecutor to allow him to make the determination of whether there was enough evidence to warrant grand jury proceedings. Dillon also pointed out that the allegation of a bribe concerned him personally, since it occurred in a case being handled in his office and then still pending.

Dillon demanded access to all of the pertinent material. He was not dissuaded when Alan Howard reverted to an old explanation: "Look, Denis, you've got to realize who was involved. Miglio, Juliano, Villano—they're all Italians. They've got Byzantine thought processes." Later, Dillon remarked to me that until that moment it had never occurred to him that the hierarchy of the Bureau was dominated by WASPS and Irish Roman Catholics.

While Dillon waited for his reports from the Bureau, I prepared for my move to Philadelphia, cleaning up the details of my cases in New York and my responsibilities to some of my informants. I had begun to turn a wiseguy, Sam Lucca,* and I introduced him to another agent in New York. This potential source was shot and killed about six months later after he was put in a bind and forced to testify in a heroin case against a connected guy. Possibly, if I had remained in New York, I could have protected him against the pressure that made him go public, and go dead.

On the way to one of my final acts as part of the New York office, a meeting with an informant in Brooklyn, a car smashed into mine on the Brooklyn Bridge roadway. I went to a hospital, but they found no concussion or broken bones, I was outfitted with a cervical collar, a heat pad, and pain killers, and I tried to mend at home. When I felt strong enough to report to Philly, and against my doctor's desires, I received an instant reminder of my pariah status. The supervisor of the organized crime squad there was an old friend. He had heard about my problems in New York and commiserated with me, but he was delighted I was in Philadelphia. He believed I could give his unit some help. But then orders came through that I was under no circumstances to work on organized crime. Instead, I was posted to the unit concerned with discrimination in housing.

Another indication of my standing surfaced when the acting director refused to acknowledge, let alone approve, an incentive award for me on the Paddy Cocco case, even though my supervisor had written a glowing report of my undercover actions.

I made another stab at cutting through the bureaucratic blubber in search of the Director's conscience. I wrote a strong letter to Clarence Kelley (a former agent who had been confirmed by Congress as head of the FBI) in which I alluded to bizarre events which took place in the New York office. But he, too, wanted to hear no allegations of evil. He refused to talk to me, fobbed me off on the personnel office. This was the man who publicly proclaimed his open-door policy. I think things might have been different if Hoover had still been alive. For all of his narrowness, he took enormous pride in the incorruptibility of the Bureau. People forget that he initially made his reputation by cleaning out political hacks and guys on the take.

In spite of the reverses, I resolved not to let them put me away. I would do my job and eventually bring some daylight to the case. At that point, I learned that an old friend had been newly named as an assistant director in the administrative division in Washington, D.C. I immediately called him and asked if he would see me, suggesting I take leave and travel to Washington at my own expense. He said he could spare me a couple of hours one week hence. The day before our appointment I was summoned to the Philadelphia boss's office and informed that Assistant Director Eugene Walsh wouldn't be able to see me the next day but would get in touch in the future. That was probably the "unkindest cut of all."

Two days after I reported to Philadelphia, the injury from the car accident flared anew. My back simply gave out. I couldn't tie my shoes and every waking moment was agony, no matter what posture I took. I returned to New York to see still another special-

ist. His diagnosis was not encouraging. I flatly rejected considera-
tion of surgery; there was no guarantee it would restore me. But I
couldn't handle an agent's job. Discouraged, in pain, I surrendered. I filed my papers for retirement on a disability pension.

While my lifetime with the Bureau was coming to an end,
Denis Dillon had been digging deeper into the mine of clues,
bouncing off the Bureau's bedrock resistance. All that Howard
had turned over to Dillon were summaries of the various investigations on the matter. There was an inordinate and singular
delay in producing the complete reports. Dillon protested the
lack of cooperation. James Mulroy, one of the supervisors
charged with the investigation, told Dillon that what I should
have done was write an anonymous letter. The Bureau apparently preferred this technique to having an agent stand up and
denounce another man face to face. Of course you don't have to
answer an anonymous letter.

The reason for the obstructionism came into sharper focus
when Dillon received word from his superiors at the Justice
Department in Washington that Clarence Kelley demanded the
investigation be called off. Kelley said the FBI had investigated
thoroughly and could find no violations of law! In addition, he
huffed and puffed about the effect upon morale. He was certainly
not considering my morale.

Dillon's answer to Henry Petersen, who was at the time chief
of the Criminal Division in the Justice Department and Dillon's
boss, was convincing enough for Petersen to politely rebuff
Kelley. Dillon and company continued to look into the matter.

Among those whom Dillon personally interviewed was the now
retired detective, Bill Bolla. Bolla was much more talkative when
confronted by Dillon. He replayed the entire scene at the bar,
complete with the names of Pete Lombardo, Al Salamone, and
Tommy Miglio. Bolla had been close enough to Lombardo to have
invested five thousand dollars in the company set up to sell ninety-
nine-cent meals. At Dillon's request, Bolla agreed to trade on this
relationship by getting in touch with Pete Lombardo to see if he
might be more forthcoming with information. It seems Lombardo
was about to be indicted by New York State Special Prosecutor
Maurice Nadjari. Now Dillon was breathing down his back.
Bolla reported he could not induce Lombardo to give up anything or anybody. Lombardo's attorney, who also happened to be

Al Salamone's lawyer, suggested to Dillon that perhaps if Lombardo beefs all around town were dropped, he might be in a better position to talk. But Dillon was not about to make such a deal with the likes of a Pete Lombardo.

What he did do, however, was very skillfully put together enough elements from the investigations of Salamone, the Miglio case, and other similar affairs to parade witnesses before a grand jury, where Bolla repeated his story. Shortly after Bolla gave his testimony, Al Salamone contacted him at a place where Bolla regularly hung out, around the Fulton Fish Market. As Bolla later reported to a strike force agent, Salamone interrogated him. "Has anyone been around questioning you on the phone call [the one to Lombardo to meet Salamone at the bar]?" Bolla lied to Salamone and said no. Bolla said no again when Salamone asked about the ex-detective's appearance before the grand jury. It was strange that Salamone would know enough to ask such questions when certainly Bolla wasn't publicizing his cooperation.

When Al Salamone himself went before the grand jury, he, of course, denied the meeting with Pete Lombardo, and any payoff to an FBI agent. In fact he swore that he never said he bribed cops. The denials earned him four counts of perjury and he was arrested, under Dillon's direction, shortly after he left the grand jury room. However, Bolla refused to testify and a jury acquitted Salamone.

Two of the perjury charges against Salamone failed to convince the jury because of a lack of precision in the questions that the agents put to him in their interrogation. Bill Bolla refused to testify against the old man on other discrepancies in Salamone's story before the grand jury.

It seems to me that this aspect of the case was also mishandled. When Salamone appeared before the grand jury, he said that he had never met Tommy Miglio until after we arrested him on the gambling charge. But Miglio had insisted to John McGinley and others at the Bureau that he had been working to turn the old man before the arrest. In fact that was why Miglio was sore about not having been notified before we busted Salamone. If the Bureau had picked up on this discrepancy, Miglio should have been the witness to nail Salamone for perjury.

About the same time all of this was going on, Fred Juliano swore to a new affidavit in response to requests from Denis

Dillon. Juliano recalled that in late 1972 or early 1973, he had bumped into Bolla in a precinct squad room and Bolla had remarked, "I hear you got an agent who made a good score downtown." Juliano said he asked Bolla for more information and the detective implied that the agent had been involved in a hijacking matter. The discussion was interrupted by the appearance of other officers in the squad room. Juliano excused his failure to follow up as due to a feeling that jealousy between New York cops and FBI agents often led to malicious gossip.

However, continued Juliano in his affidavit, in April of 1973 (which was after the Bureau consigned me to Philadelphia and interred the case), Bolla saw Juliano at his Queens home and detailed the events at the waterfront bar, specifically mentioning that Salamone had asked him to get hold of Pete Lombardo and that Lombardo subsequently explained there was a fifteen-thousand-dollar deal to fix a gambling case against Salamone. To the best of Bolla's recollection, he was told that Tommy Miglio was part of the conspiracy.

Juliano's statement contained a fascinating addition to what Bolla had told the government of his contact with Al Salamone. When Bolla visited Fred, he described his meeting with Salamone at the Fulton Fish Market. During the conversation, Salamone said to Bolla that "they" might ask Tommy Miglio to retire from the Bureau to take the heat off. The pronoun's missing antecedent could have been Salamone's colleagues in the LCN.

On the other hand, Fred testified that Tommy Miglio had never admitted to him that he accepted a bribe for dropping a gambling charge against Salamone. Fred did climb partway out on a limb with his opinion that the entire investigation had been mishandled and said he was willing to be wired up to see if his former pal Miglio would incriminate himself.

An agent still with the Bureau tipped me one day that a convict, Peter Sauers, in local custody claimed to have been told of an FBI agent who was on the take. The bad agent's first name was Tom. The convict said that another hood, Joseph Nagy, who was involved in the discussion had since been murdered. Another active agent told me that he had come across some vague inferences of corruption. A friendly agent in California mentioned an agent there who was involved with OC guys in gambling. His boss, the SAC, hushed it up, but when the California strike force found out about it, I heard talk of prosecuting the SAC for obstruction of justice. The SAC was busted and transferred, as was the agent. Stories appeared in the Florida papers that the local SAC was being investigated by the strike force for some major gratuities he had allegedly accepted, like getting a kid through college on a union pension fund. The SAC was transferred. Recently another agent followed the advice of Supervisor James Mulroy, but instead of writing anonymously to the Bureau, he directed letters to Attorney General Levi and Senator Frank Church, accusing the SAC of innumerable acts of misconduct. The SAC quietly retired a week later; he was a close personal friend of Director Clarence Kelley.

All these rumbles caused inspectors from the Bureau to get in touch with me and rehash the story. Basically I felt that they were not so much concerned with uncovering any more evidence as they were with learning whether I intended to embarrass the Bureau.

That was as far as it ever went. Denis Dillon left the strike force to successfully campaign for District Attorney of Nassau County on Long Island. No one else around seemed interested in pursuing the case. The matter was buried. A clerk at the New York FBI offices tipped me that some of the files concerning the matter had been ordered destroyed. The corpse putrefied but as far as the Bureau was concerned, the stink was successfully hidden.

One law enforcement official says he has some doubts about whether or not Miglio did accept a bribe. The case against him rests largely upon some circumstantial evidence and hearsay by witnesses who like Bill Bolla won't testify or like Fred Juliano and even myself who changed our stories. Juliano signed contradictory affidavits, because he was afraid that the Bureau might come down hard on him for concealing what he was told by Bolla and Miglio. I created the cover story of Herbie to protect Juliano. In both of our cases, a smart defense attorney could attack our credibility to a jury. And under these circumstances it's hard to say what a jury would decide if the available evidence was presented.

What actually happened remains a mystery. But it is clear to me that the reason why the case was not resolved was the obfuscation of the Bureau brass who were far more concerned about its pristine image to the public than of the responsibilities to handle allegations about agents the same way the book directs agents to treat charges about the other 220 million Americans.

Epilogue

SINCE I RETIRED FROM THE BUREAU, I've had some time to think about the so-called war on crime and those who, like myself, engaged in the battles. I guess I was always a cop at heart. When I read Victor Hugo's *Les Misérables*, the character who fascinated me most was Javert, the policeman. Certainly one of the things that attracted me to the career of an agent was the opportunity to match wits in situations that seemed to count for something and where there was a sizable risk factor. There was an excitement in the job that never flagged, even at the dismal end. I can understand a guy like Willie Sutton, who said he only came alive when he was robbing banks. And I felt I was accomplishing something in my work against organized crime.

Like most agents, I had a life away from my work. In that respect I turned what I thought was my shrewd intelligence toward the stockmarket for a while. The Bureau didn't care for its agents speculating, but that was one more rule I sidestepped. In the course of my work, I had met a broker who was highly knowledgeable on new issues. Within a couple of years, he and I parlayed my modest investment into a stake worth a modest fortune. Then he seemed to run out of information and I lost my apparent smarts. We wound up back at zero.

That kind of defeat doesn't haunt me. Nor do I have any regrets about losing a bundle in a Honduras gold-mine property after I retired from the Bureau. It was a long shot; I had measured the risks, and the action itself brought me considerable pleasure. Even when I play backgammon there's got to be something at stake—my mind against his or hers with a prize for success, some cost for failure.

That doesn't mean that as an agent I thought of the other people as just simple opponents. Although several of the OC informants almost became friends of mine, I recognized that I was dealing with criminals, a largely depraved bunch of guys with vicious appetites who were totally dedicated to ripping off anyone, including their colleagues. But generally I resisted becoming emotionally committed. It's like a doctor who deals daily with disease. After a while the enemy becomes so familiar that you accept its presence. You don't get angry at its latest destructive act, because you recognize that it is the nature of the beast; you only try to figure out a new way to handle it. That may sound cold, but when a cop or an agent turns his job into a crusade, he becomes tempted to justify his sins by his goal.

Because I approached the job this way, I put in far more hours than even the most loyal supporter of Hoover could have demanded. My comings and goings, the kind of people I hung out with, and the time involved hardly helped my marriage. My wife and I had been drifting apart for a number of years. With my retirement, our relationship came to an end.

The fact is, for twenty-three years I was married to the Bureau, and I think I gave that spouse its money's worth. Not that it was a wholly harmonious union. I picked up a couple of letters of censure. But I was never an individual to accept the simple rules of the book, and as an agent I learned that to be really effective I would have to use my initiative in ways unsanctioned by any manual. Some of the rules that I broke the Bureau knew about, but tried to ignore. Consider the black-bag jobs. I have mixed emotions about the Bureau's policy on them. Everyone was after us to do something about organized crime. I remember that Attorney General Robert Kennedy came to New York and gave us a pep talk on fighting it. His language suggested that he wasn't interested in any excuses, like failure to obtain evidence and convictions because we were staying scrupulously inside the limits of behavior for law-enforcement agents.

The records of organized crime, the discussions between wiseguys, the deals with public officials don't get neatly transcribed by secretaries and accountants for ready inspection by the law-enforcement agencies that subpoena check stubs and bookkeeper's ledgers. The courts do not automatically dish out writs that permit the Bureau or any other organization to install bugs or taps, and anyway, the criminals are increasingly circumspect in the way they talk if there is any possibility of electronic eavesdropping.

Informants can tell you what's happening, but their testimony in court is very chancy. Good defense lawyers can convince a jury that the chief prosecution witness stands to benefit from a conviction by earning his freedom through testifying.

The 1976 revelations about the Bureau's black-bag jobs against supposed radical groups stressed that J. Edgar Hoover's official policy banned burglaries after 1966. Perhaps that was true for the Bureau's internal security squads, but if the ban included agents dealing with criminals, they kept that a secret from me.

All of them came about after discussion about the particular case with my supervisor and other agents on the same chase. For instance, when I traced Jackie Gucci to that high rise in Manhattan, I was anxious to find out what he and his friends were doing in the apartment. In a conference I said, "Why don't we go into the place?" The boss in this instance demurred; he felt the possibility of our being caught there was too great.

Sometimes we wanted a look at a place such as Jackie's apartment in order to discover evidence, which we would later attribute to a confidential informant. But it was also standard at the Bureau that a bug job required a detailed survey of the premises. In other words, we could not seek a writ to install the bug until we had been inside a place and determined whether the best spot for it was under the dining-room table, in a bedroom, or even the toilet, since some guys seemed to think that they escaped our ears if they talked in the bathroom.

Now that the illegal break-ins have become public knowledge, there's talk of prosecuting the agents who took part in them. The Bureau insists that its top officials never authorized or knew about the black-bag work. I find that very hard to believe, even when higher-ups whom I respect claim they were ignorant. As I said, an agent did not casually break into a place by himself. All of us were wise enough in the *modus operandi* of the Bureau— cover your ass—to avoid the kind of initiative that would leave an agent out on a skinny limb. A black-bag job not only was okayed in a conference with a supervisor; it was also carefully planned and involved a number of agents.

The prime time for black-bag jobs was 5 A.M. Bars were closed by then; the chances of being noticed by straggling pedestrians were slim at that hour. We always detailed agents to watch the homes of store owners to make certain that the suspects did not surprise us by coming to work early. Obviously, the operations required both detailed planning and approval from superiors. If nothing else, we had to be able to justify our daily Three cards. How far up the line a supervisor passed the word I don't know. But, considering the general attitude of the Bureaucracy, I'd be astonished if very many supervisors ever failed to make sure that somebody above them shared some responsibility.

Outside of a surprise appearance by residents or owners of an establishment, the biggest worry on a black-bag job was the local cops. I know of several instances where New York policemen did come upon break-ins. In one incident, the agents managed to convince the cop that they were on a national security matter. Another time, the agents slugged the cop before he could discover their identities, and they escaped.

I can justify what was done to organized crime more readily than I can the actions taken against so-called subversive groups. There were other ways the Bureau could have dealt with political militants. It was feasible to infiltrate these organizations and collect evidence without pulling a black-bag job. It's really not possible to penetrate organized crime the same way. The Mafia is much more choosy about its membership. To be accepted, one usually had to be Sicilian with a traceable pedigree. You needed a background that went beyond being able to mouth off a few tough speeches or get busted for sassing the cops in a demonstration. Even notches on a gun weren't sufficient credentials to get one automatically admitted to the inner circles. In his own dim way Hoover seemed to recognize this. While he was all for infiltrating political-action groups, he shied away from undercover work in crime. He realized that the agents would have to commit crimes to establish themselves and they would also be exposed to the temptations of corruption.

Actually, organized crime, which keeps its membership lists in its hat—unlike political groups, who file away neat Xerox copies of members' names—closed its books to new colleagues in 1957. In the spring of 1976, almost twenty years later, OC accepted its first new "dear fellows."

I can even understand the behavior of some of the brick agents who used very dirty tricks against individuals and groups considered to be "radical." There was constant pressure from above on these agents, just as those of us assigned to pursue organized crime felt squeezed. The Bureau is like any modern institution, whether the Army in Vietnam, an ad agency on Madison Avenue, or a manufacturer's sales department. The individuals in charge, the ones who control your career and your future, keep demanding tangible evidence of progress—body counts, clients contacted, sales charts. In the Bureau, agents supplied body counts, names identified as belonging to an organization—political or criminal—even if they faked some entries or kited the figures. For clients contacted, read "actions taken," whether pointless surveillances, nasty harassments, or roustings designed only to remind people you were still around. For the sales charts, there were the investigations completed; some of those amounted to significant prosecutions, some did not.

A lawyer remarked to a friend of mine that the FBI got away with all of its ugly acts against political groups because they were unpopular outfits without financial or legal clout to protest. He insisted that if the Bureau had done these things to organized crime, which had both money and top legal talent, the Bureau's activities would have been immediately exposed. He was quite wrong.

Joe Colombo wanted to turn the heat away from his operations and make it appear only that we had a thing about people whose last names ended in vowels. He never was stupid enough to protest some action that was directed against one of his drops. Perhaps when a case came before a judge, a defense lawyer might try to get the evidence thrown out on the grounds that there had been an illegal search. But that would be a nice dry argument for the benefit of a judge and not something that would identify places where criminal acts occurred. The truth is that everyone else in OC viewed Colombo's campaign against the FBI as about as sensible as General Custer making rude noises to attract the attention of the Indians.

I think I can make a better case for some of the illegal moves against organized crime than can be offered by operations such as Cointelpro or by other internal security units. The Bureau seemed to react against political groups on the basis of their rhetoric or its own narrow interpretations of statements of purpose by individuals whose view of the United States didn't fit in with that coming out of Hoover's office. The targets in these actions often had not actually committed any crimes, but in the minds of 400-percent Americans they seemed to be contemplating a breach of the established order. They were not in most cases a clear and present danger, and they hadn't broken any laws.

With organized crime the situation was different. We knew, through information, that these people had robbed, hijacked, extorted, and murdered—that in fact their whole way of life was outside the law. They weren't just talking about criminal acts, they were committing them. We were frustrated, because we didn't have the evidence to convict. So we black-bagged it, bugged them, and tried to stir up trouble within their ranks.

Like some of the agents in Internal Security, we turned an occasional dirty trick against LCN people. We regularly leaked stories to a reporter on the New York *Daily News* that were calculated to cause bad feeling. I once placed an item that suggested that Carmine Persico had broken down and was feeding us stuff—wildly improbable, but it might have made life difficult for him. I would telephone a made guy's house and tell his wife, "This is Tony. If he doesn't pay me what he owes, I'm going to break both his legs." A call like that had no specific tactical value; it was only an attempt to create a climate of insecurity that might make an individual susceptible to sweet talk. I personally drew the line at writing anonymous letters to wives informing them about their husband's mistresses, but it was done.

I've heard apologists for the Bureau and for other organizations that have done illegal acts say, "You have to remember the context of the times." If the speaker is talking about political extremists, he then cites the exploding pipe bombs and the violent demonstrations. (These explanations are the kinds supplied by creators of order such as Adolf Hitler or the Watergaters.) If the apologist is defending the methods employed against crime, he points out that the hoods were getting away with murder and they seem to have local police and politicians in their hip pockets.

But when law enforcement stoops to immorality or, worse, downright criminality, you get the most malignant form of corruption: those sworn to uphold the law develop the habit of breaking it. As a consequence, the police agency tends to hide its ways of doing things. It becomes increasingly isolated and removed from the outside world, and begins to believe that even fair criticism of it and legitimate investigations into it and its employees must be resisted—as, for instance, my experience when I tried to get the Bureau to investigate the allegations about Tommy Miglio.

Legal wiretaps, to say nothing of illegal ones, and black-bag jobs erode civil liberties. But I don't see any alternatives to controlling organized crime, considering the nature of the beast. So we made a choice. We sacrificed the rights of the dons to protect the interests of society. Whether we were right or wrong is something to be decided by the voters, or maybe the philosophers and historians. But what continually sickened me was the sanctimonious response of Bureau brass when it became public knowledge that we were in the black-bag game. How could Clarence Kelley, a former agent, big-city police chief, and finally head of the FBI, ever say that break-ins were only done in national security cases! He had to know better. A guy with guts would have stood up and admitted that we went black bag because we felt we had to do it—that the public wanted something done about organized crime. The problem is that the men at the top have created a phony picture of what a special agent is like. The attempt to preserve that false image has bred the corruptive deliberate blindness of which I was a victim.

One of the unhealthy facts about our acquisitive American dream society is that it has become a natural milieu for thieves, hustlers, organized crime—everything from pickpocketing to murder to protect the profit. We are obliged to maintain a system that counteracts that of the criminal advantage-takers, but the question is where do the tactics of the law-enforcement agencies become inseparable from those of the criminals?

The top echelons of the Bureau have come to resemble those of the Colombos, the Genoveses, the Gambinos of organized crime. In both worlds a high priority is placed on honor and respectability. The chiefs and the dons do not want to be out in the street with the people who work for them or acknowledge what is done in their names—for different reasons, of course. The dons want to avoid prosecution; the chiefs wish to forestall criticism from those who are ever watching—the legislators, the press people, the social scientists. When I was young I had thought ignorance, stupidity, corruption were qualities that afflicted only the lower ranks of the pecking order. Now I see much of the infection has spread from the top down, rather than the other way.

I don't claim to have any answers. I still think about a talk I had with my son when I explained why I was leaving the Bureau. "I'm forty-five," I said, "and all of my idols have turned out to have feet of clay."

"That's the difference between us," he said. "By the time I was seventeen I had no idols."